MARCH 2021

U.S. Military Forces in FY 2021

The Last Year of Growth?

AUTHOR
Mark F. Cancian

A Report of the CSIS International Security Program

CSIS | CENTER FOR STRATEGIC & INTERNATIONAL STUDIES

ROWMAN &
LITTLEFIELD
Lanham • Boulder • New York • London

About CSIS

The Center for Strategic and International Studies (CSIS) is a bipartisan, nonprofit policy research organization dedicated to advancing practical ideas to address the world's greatest challenges.

Thomas J. Pritzker was named chairman of the CSIS Board of Trustees in 2015, succeeding former U.S. senator Sam Nunn (D-GA). Founded in 1962, CSIS is led by John J. Hamre, who has served as president and chief executive officer since 2000.

CSIS's purpose is to define the future of national security. We are guided by a distinct set of values—nonpartisanship, independent thought, innovative thinking, cross-disciplinary scholarship, integrity and professionalism, and talent development. CSIS's values work in concert toward the goal of making real-world impact.

CSIS scholars bring their policy expertise, judgment, and robust networks to their research, analysis, and recommendations. We organize conferences, publish, lecture, and make media appearances that aim to increase the knowledge, awareness, and salience of policy issues with relevant stakeholders and the interested public.

CSIS has impact when our research helps to inform the decisionmaking of key policymakers and the thinking of key influencers. We work toward a vision of a safer and more prosperous world.

CSIS does not take specific policy positions; accordingly, all views expressed herein should be understood to be solely those of the author(s).

© 2021 by the Center for Strategic and International Studies. All rights reserved.

ISBN: 978-1-5381-4035-2 (pb); 978-1-5381-4036-9 (ebook)

Center for Strategic & International Studies
1616 Rhode Island Avenue, NW
Washington, DC 20036
202-887-0200 | www.csis.org

Rowman & Littlefield
4501 Forbes Boulevard
Lanham, MD 20706
301-459-3366 | www.rowman.com

Acknowledgments

"Defense Outlook" is an annual series of studies on the linkages between strategy, budgets, forces, and acquisition. As part of the series, this paper examines how changes in the FY 2021 budget and in the national security environment are shaping the size and composition of the force, and what those changes mean in terms of cost, strategy, and risk. The series is part of a broader effort on Defense 360 (http://defense360.csis.org/) to collect in one location the analysis that CSIS has done on current security issues.

This report is funded by the International Security Program at CSIS. The author would like to thank Nidal Morrison and Adam Saxton for their research support throughout this study.

Finally, the author thanks the many reviewers, inside CSIS and outside, who read the draft and provided valuable comments. Their insights improved the report, but the content presented—including any errors—remain solely the responsibility of the author.

Contents

Foreword	VI
**1	The Budget and Strategy Overview: Four Challenges and a Wild Card**	1
**2	Army**	19
**3	Navy**	31
**4	Marine Corps**	62
**5	Air Force**	75
**6	Space, SOF, Civilians, and Contractors**	95
About the Author	116

Foreword

Building Military Forces for the 2020s

EXERCISING GLOBAL LEADERSHIP IN AN ERA OF REDUCED RESOURCES

The bulk of this report was written before the election and therefore contains projections for both Trump and Biden administrations. This foreword is written as the administration is about one month into its term and uses the insights of the individual chapters to project what a Biden administration might do regarding military forces. The public will get an initial view of these plans when the administration submits its FY 2022 budget in late April or early May. The full view will not be available until the administration publishes a new national security strategy and the national defense strategy, likely in January or February 2022. This foreword is an adaptation of a CSIS transition paper on military forces.

Under the Biden administration, trade-offs among readiness, force structure, and modernization will get more difficult as the Department of Defense (DOD) budget flattens out and likely falls. Forces are likely to get smaller—perhaps much smaller in some places—and that will engender significant pushback as the services attempt to maintain global commitments and cover wartime requirements. Force design will also change as the services adapt to meet the needs of great power competition.

The Biden Administration's Strategic Priorities

The Biden administration, despite its criticism of the Trump administration's national security policy, will likely retain many key elements of its strategy. In a 2020 *Foreign Affairs* article, then-candidate Joseph R. Biden noted that "China represents a special challenge" and that Russia seeks to undermine liberal democracy. He also cited "national security challenges from North Korea to Iran, from Syria to

Afghanistan to Venezuela."[1] This signals continuity with both the Obama administration's strategy and the Trump administration's *National Defense Strategy* (NDS) (although the new administration will be loath to admit that).[2]

To implement this strategy, President Biden has pledged, "the United States has the strongest military in the world, and as president, I will ensure it stays that way."[3] That pledge and the robust strategy are good news for force structure.

The bad news for force structure is twofold. The first is that the DOD budget will likely fall as the Biden administration focuses on domestic priorities and includes non-DOD initiatives—such as climate change and global health—in a broader conception of national security. (For a detailed discussion of the prospective Biden defense budget, see the CSIS transition paper "Defense Budget Priorities for the Biden Administration."[4]) Second, strategists will emphasize modernization—often termed "capability"—rather than force structure—"capacity."[5] Many strategists propose cutting the size of forces to invest in the high-end capabilities needed for a great power conflict.[6] The Democratic Party platform proposes retiring "legacy" platforms, as do many strategists.[7] There is disagreement, however, about the definition of "legacy." The military services typically interpret "legacy" as older weapons. They would retire these older weapons to buy newer versions. Strategists see "legacy" as old kinds of systems that do not meet the needs of new operational concepts. They would redesign military forces to incorporate new operational concepts and move from manned to unmanned aircraft. In the end, the military services are likely to win this argument since they control the money.

The Impact of the New Strategy and Reduced Budget on the Services

ARMY

Army force structure will likely be cut significantly as an offset for other initiatives.[8] The strategy's focus on China and the Western Pacific, which is mainly a naval and air theater, implies that Navy and Air Force capabilities will have priority. Although the Army has an important role to play—and has recently emphasized its activities in the Indo-Pacific region—that role is secondary.[9]

---

1   Joseph R. Biden, "Why America Must Lead Again," *Foreign Affairs*, March/April 2020, https://www.foreignaffairs.com/articles/united-states/2020-01-23/why-america-must-lead-again.

2   Department of Defense, *Summary of the 2018 National Defense Strategy of the United States of America* (Washington, DC: Department of Defense), https://dod.defense.gov/Portals/1/Documents/pubs/2018-National-Defense-Strategy-Summary.pdf.

3   Biden, "Why America Must Lead Again."

4   Seamus Daniels, "Defense Budget Priorities for the Biden Administration," CSIS, February 2, 2021, https://defense360.csis.org/defense-budget-priorities-for-the-biden-administration/.

5   Thomas G. Mahnken, "Reagan Institute and the Center for Strategic and Budgetary Assessments Warn Policy Makers About the Consequences of Defense Budget Cuts," Center for Strategic and Budgetary Assessments, January 14, 2021, https://csbaonline.org/about/news/reagan-institute-and-the-center-for-strategic-and-budgetary-assessments-warn-policy-makers-about-the-consequences-of-defense-budget-cuts.

6   Susanna Blume, "What Congress Should Do with the 2020 Defense Budget," Center for a New American Security, May 22, 2019, https://www.cnas.org/publications/commentary/what-congress-should-do-with-the-2020-defense-budget.

7   "The 2020 Democratic Platform," Democratic National Committee, https://democrats.org/where-we-stand/party-platform/.

8   See the "U.S. Military Forces in FY2021: Army" chapter in this report.

9   Sydney J. Freedberg Jr., "Facing Cuts, Army Chief Touts Pacific Role," Breaking Defense, January 19, 2021, https://breakingdefense.com/2021/01/facing-cuts-army-chief-touts-pacific-role/.

The Army does have a primary role in any conflict with Russia. However, bringing large forces to bear in likely areas of conflict such as the Baltics and Eastern Europe is difficult. This limits the size of the force needed. Further, many strategists argue that the Europeans—far wealthier than Russia and with much larger military forces—should take the lead in such conflicts. Thus, a future conflict with Russia might drive Army modernization and force design but not its force size.

The Obama administration planned to cut regular Army end strength to 450,000 personnel, though the actual level never quite got there. Some discussions had proposed cuts to 420,000 or even lower. The Biden administration may resurrect such plans. Currently, the regular Army is at 486,000 and has plans to grow into the 490,000s.[10]

If Army end strength is squeezed as hard as many people expect, then Army redesign and modernization will slow considerably.

AIR FORCE

The Air Force will likely cut its forces to pay for modernization.[11] It has done this traditionally, seeking cutting-edge technology at the expense of force size.[12] The current Air Force chief of staff, General Charles Brown, has explicitly stated his desire to do this.[13] Over the years, the Air Force has proposed cutting the A-10, KC-10, F-16, and B-1 inventories—in some cases radically—but Congress has generally frustrated those efforts.

Because the Air Force is not buying enough new aircraft to maintain its inventory over the long term, fleet size will shrink even without accelerated retirement of "legacy" systems. Plans for a next-generation air dominance aircraft indicate a continuing preference for manned over unmanned systems. Although strategists in the Biden administration may want to change this, they will likely be unable to in face of service opposition.

The Biden administration's focus on arms control and discomfort with some elements of nuclear modernization will affect several Air Force programs. Particularly vulnerable are the long-range standoff weapon, the B61 tail-kit program, and the Ground-Based Strategic Deterrent (the replacement for Minuteman ICBMs).

MARINE CORPS

The Marine Corps has embarked on an ambitious restructuring effort, called Force Design 2030, which will orient the Marine Corps toward maritime operations in the Western Pacific.[14] Because it aligns with strategists' focus on China, the Biden administration will likely support the concept. However,

---

10 "DMDC," Defense Manpower Data Center, https://dwp.dmdc.osd.mil/dwp/app/main.

11 See the chapter "U.S. Military Forces in FY 2021: Air Force."

12 Carl H. Builder, *The Masks of War: American Military Styles in Strategy and Analysis* (Baltimore, MD: The Johns Hopkins University Press, 1989), https://www.ndu.edu/Portals/59/Documents/AA_Documents/Officer%20Prep%20Courses/Lesson%201/The%20Masks%20of%20War%20-%20Service%20Cultures.pdf?ver=2019-05-22-125817-220.

13 Charles Q. Brown, Jr., *Accelerate Change or Lose* (Washington, DC: U.S. Air Force, August 2020), https://www.airforcemag.com/app/uploads/2020/08/CSAF-22-Strategic-Approach-Accelerate-Change-or-Lose-31-Aug-2020.pdf.

14 See the chapter "U.S. Military Forces in FY 2021: Marine Corps"; and Marine Corps, *Force Design 2030* (Washington, DC: DoD, March 2020), https://www.hqmc.marines.mil/Portals/142/Docs/CMC38%20Force%20Design%202030%20Report%20Phase%20I%20and%20II.pdf?ver=2020-03-26-121328-460.

the restructuring has been criticized for focusing too much on a maritime campaign in the Western Pacific, ignoring other global conflicts and relying on unproven operational concepts.

To pay for this restructuring, the Marine Corps intends to shrink end strength from 185,000 personnel to 172,000. If the DOD budget is cut, however, the force cuts might pay for the Marine Corps' share of the budget cuts and not be available for restructuring. That would require further cuts. However, Marine Corps peacetime end strength has been at 175,000 to 200,000 since the Korean War. Thus, rather than cut end strength further, the Marine Corps will likely be forced to stretch out its restructuring plans.

SPACE FORCE

Because it would take another act of Congress to disestablish it, there is no chance that the Space Force will be eliminated, despite the recommendations of some progressive groups.[15] However, the Space Force will remain small, at under 20,000 personnel.

The Space Force will continue to develop as other programs and personnel transfer into the new service.[16] The major decision in the next year will be how many Army, Navy, and Marine Corps space assets to incorporate. Currently, the Space Force consists only of transferred Air Force personnel and organizations.

The Biden administration might chart a new direction in space. Secretary of Defense Lloyd Austin has expressed reservations about the "pugilistic aspects" of space operations.[17] He also referred to space as a supporting effort, not as a lead warfighter.

SPECIAL OPERATIONS FORCES, GOVERNMENT CIVILIANS, AND CONTRACTORS

Special Operations Forces—now a separate service in all but name—will likely continue its gradual growth.[18] Although small by U.S. standards, it is nearly as large as the British army. One challenge will be maintaining quality as expansion continues. So far, that has not been a problem, though there have been ethical challenges.[19] The strategic challenge will be articulating how these forces—dedicated mostly to counterterrorism and regional stability operations—can contribute to great power conflicts.

Government civilians may face a hiring freeze as part of an effort to cut costs and reduce overhead. New administrations often impose such a policy until they conduct a management review. This will be a change from the Trump administration's increases in DOD civilian personnel. However, a Biden administration will likely cease attempts to cut benefits and will eliminate the Trump administration's institution of "Schedule F," which would remove civil service protections from many permanent personnel.

Contractors have become a permanent part of the federal workforce but remain controversial due to enduring questions about cost and what contractors should or should not do.

---

15 Victor Tangermann, "Progressive Groups Call For Elimination of Space Force," *Futurism*, November 18, 2020, https://futurism.com/progressive-groups-elimination-space-force.

16 See the chapter "U.S. Military Forces in FY 2021: Space, SOF, Civilians, and Contractors."

17 Theresa Hitchens, "Austin Signals Shift Back To Focus On Space Resilience," *Breaking Defense*, January 21, 2021, https://breakingdefense.com/2021/01/austin-signals-shift-back-to-focus-on-space-resilience/.

18 See the chapter "U.S. Military Forces in FY 2021: Space, SOF, Civilians, and Contractors."

19 Meghann Myers, "Spec ops in trouble: Mired in scandal and under Pentagon review, what will it take to clean house?" *Military Times*, March 13, 2019, https://www.militarytimes.com/news/your-army/2019/03/13/spec-ops-in-trouble-mired-in-scandal-and-under-pentagon-review-what-will-it-take-to-clean-house/.

Contractors might face some cuts because Democratic administrations favor government employees. The Obama administration had attempted "insourcing" but halted those efforts after two years, having failed to produce savings and received criticism for increasing the visible size of government. A Biden administration might try the same approach but will end up with the same result. In the long term, contractors will continue to be a significant element of infrastructure activities in the United States and operations overseas because of their generally lower cost, greater flexibility, and reduced visibility.

THE 350-SHIP (OR 500-SHIP) NAVY

The Navy is a special case both because it will likely receive high priority in a Biden strategy and because of the many recent proposals regarding its structure.[20] President Donald Trump had set a goal of 355 ships, but the Navy could not develop an affordable plan to meet this goal. DOD published a shipbuilding plan at the end of the Trump administration that called for 500 ships, manned and unmanned, but the plan required large increases in the shipbuilding budget.[21] Secretary Austin has stated his intention to review the Navy shipbuilding plan.[22]

The Biden administration will almost certainly cut the target fleet size, probably to something in the 320s, because of concerns about affordability. (Currently, the fleet size is about 300.) However, the major fleet elements will continue. The fleet will include unmanned surface and undersea systems because these have broad support as innovative technologies. It will build attack submarines, much favored by strategists because of their covert capabilities, at a consistent rate of two per year, but not reach the three per year rate that the DOD plan had called for, due to the high cost. The Navy will continue construction of destroyers at about the current rate of two per year and fund both the new frigate program and the new light amphibious warship. All three initiatives have bipartisan support. To save money, the plan will call for retiring older ships such as the CG-47-class cruisers and early versions of the littoral combat ships.

Two major uncertainties are aircraft carriers and unmanned aircraft. Former Secretary Mark Esper had implied a reduction in the number of large nuclear carriers in favor of smaller carriers.[23] The last shipbuilding plan showed no such change. Strategists have long argued to reduce the number of aircraft carriers because of their high cost and perceived vulnerability in great power conflicts. However, the imperatives of maintaining the industrial base and continuing day-to-day crisis response have pushed Congress to maintain higher carrier force levels.

The controversy about unmanned aircraft centers on function. The Navy is developing the MQ-25 for refueling missions, whereas many strategists want the aircraft developed for strike missions.[24]

---

20 See the chapter "U.S. Military Forces in FY 2021: Navy."

21 Office of the Chief of Naval Operations, *Report to Congress on the Annual Long-Range Plan for Construction of Naval Vessels* (Washington, DC: Department of Defense), https://media.defense.gov/2020/Dec/10/2002549918/-1/1/0/SHIPBUILDING%20PLAN%20DEC%2020_NAVY_OSD_OMB_FINAL.PDF/SHIPBUILDING%20PLAN%20DEC%2020_NAVY_OSD_OMB_FINAL.PDF.

22 Paul Mcleary, "Biden's Pentagon Ready To Take Hard New Look At Navy Plans," Breaking Defense, January 19, 2021, https://breakingdefense.com/2021/01/bidens-pentagon-preparing-to-take-hard-new-look-at-navy-plans/.

23 Mark F. Cancian and Adam Saxton, "Secretary Esper Previews the Future Navy," CSIS, *Critical Questions*, October 8, 2020, https://www.csis.org/analysis/secretary-esper-previews-future-navy.

24 Jan Tegler, "Grading the MQ-25," Aerospace America, May 2018, https://aerospaceamerica.aiaa.org/features/grading-the-mq-25/.

Likely Criticisms of the New Force Structure

On the left, progressives will want deeper budget cuts and, therefore, smaller forces. Libertarians will want more restraint in foreign policy objectives and smaller forces that are based primarily at home. Defense hawks will want higher budgets and larger forces, or at least fewer force cuts. Many strategists will want more rapid restructuring for great power competition.

From the service perspective, the key tension for force structure will be between the desire to cut size to invest in modernization and the need to maintain day-to-day deployments for crisis response, ongoing operations, and allied and partner engagement. If the forces get too small, then the operational tempo required to maintain these deployments will stress personnel. This would hurt sustainability of the all-volunteer force, particularly if the economy recovers and recruiting and retention get more challenging as a result of competition for labor. The Biden administration, like every administration before it, will pledge to support service members, so it will need to heed complaints about stress.

To get out of this dilemma, the Trump administration in its NDS proposed prioritizing deployments through a process called Dynamic Force Employment. However, the press of overseas events prevented any significant reduction in the level of deployments.

The Biden administration will be particularly conflicted here because of its often-stated desire to reassert U.S. global leadership. The United States cannot be a global leader if it pulls its forces back from global deployments.[25] Some strategists have argued that a "virtual" or intermittent presence from the United States can substitute for forward stationing or continuous rotations.[26] However, critics point out that virtual presence is actual absence.[27] Knowing that a carrier is in Norfolk does not have the same impact as seeing 90,000 tons sail into one's harbor.

How Should the Biden Administration Structure Military Forces?

The best course for Biden's DOD will be to pursue a strategy that implements a high-low mix, increases reliance on reserve forces, and promotes a gradual transition toward new kinds of technologies that can meet strategic needs at lower cost, though with some risk.

A high-low mix recognizes that there is not enough money to equip all forces with expensive, high-end systems and still retain enough size to meet global deployment commitments. Thus, the high end of the force should be equipped with new systems, such as stealth (though not in the numbers desired).

The low end of the mix would extend the life of older systems and upgrade their capabilities to have the numbers needed for global commitments and warfighting depth. The low-end systems would still overmatch most militaries of the world other than Russia and China. It could take on regional

---

25 Raphael S. Cohen, "Why Overseas Military Bases Continue to Make Sense for the United States," War on the Rocks, January 14, 2021, https://warontherocks.com/2021/01/why-overseas-military-bases-continue-to-make-sense-for-the-united-states/.

26 Sheila Widnall and Ronald Fogleman, "Global Presence," *Joint Forces Quarterly* (Spring 1995), https://apps.dtic.mil/sti/pdfs/ADA528819.pdf.

27 Paul Shinkman, "Army Chief Chafes at New Reliance on Technology," U.S. News, October 23, 2013, https://www.usnews.com/news/articles/2013/10/23/army-chief-chafes-at-new-reliance-on-technology.

adversaries such as North Korea or Iran or participate in follow-on operations in great power conflicts after initial attrition of the high-end forces.

Unmanned systems can constitute the low end in many warfighting situations but are unsuitable for most day-to-day deployments. Such systems cannot do the peacekeeping, presence, training of partners and allies, evacuations of U.S. citizens, or humanitarian relief missions that are expected of deployed forces.

More reliance on reserve forces provides a hedge against a conflict that is larger or longer than a smaller active force can sustain. The scale of great power conflict is often hard to imagine after the regional wars of the last half-century. Further, military planners typically envision short wars, but the reality is often much longer than these plans allow for. Reserve forces provide the depth needed. The risk is in timing since reserve units take longer to deploy than active-duty forces. Reserve forces are also less useful for day-to-day deployments.

Gradual transition to unmanned systems would put limited numbers of these new technologies into the field quickly, see how they work, and then have them replace existing platforms at a steady rate as those older platforms reach the end of their service lives. That means dialing back on the older systems as new systems show their value, rather than trying to make an abrupt shift.

The Navy's experience with aircraft carriers is a lesson in how not to make the shift. The Navy has sought to retire existing carriers early, even while continuing to build new carriers. This is extraordinarily expensive and has failed because Congress forces the Navy to operate existing carriers to their full service lives.[28] Instead, the Navy should move toward slower carrier construction—one every eight years rather than one every five years—and let the carrier fleet decline gradually. Slower construction would free up funds to invest in new technologies while not causing a major disruption of the shipbuilding industrial base and allow a hedge for the future should shipbuilding plans change.

---

28   Mark F. Cancian, "Penny Wise and Pound Foolish: The Navy's Carrier Construction Strategy," U.S. Naval Institute, *Proceedings*, March 2019, https://www.usni.org/magazines/proceedings/2019/march/penny-wise-and-pound-foolish-navys-carrier-construction-strategy.

1

The Budget and Strategy Overview

Four Challenges and a Wild Card

KEY TAKEAWAYS

- From FY 2017 to FY 2020, the administration increased the defense budget to fund its national defense strategy. However, that growth ended in FY 2021, requiring some trade-offs. The FY 2021 budget maintains the readiness gains of the last several years and expands force size modestly but squeezes modernization.

- Active component end strength is projected to increase from 1,346,000 in FY 2020 to 1,351,500 in FY 2021 and 1,361,000 by FY 2025. Congress has been supportive.

- In the long term, force structure faces four challenges and a wild card. The challenges include:

    1. The need to respond to heavy day-to-day demands for crisis response, allied engagement, gray zone competition, and ongoing regional conflicts. One observer called this "a bear trap of current commitments," and it works against reducing force size.

    2. The opening of a resources-strategy gap as budgets are flat or reduced, but the strategy does not change. This increases risk as actions may not be able to back words.

    3. The desire to move more aggressively toward a structure designed for great power conflict, increasing modernization, and trading off force structure if necessary. A major uncertainty is how the concept of "legacy" systems will be applied—does that means old systems or old types of systems?

    4. Disagreements about strategy, as many libertarians and progressives support a foreign policy of "restraint" that would have the United States less involved militarily with nations overseas. Such a strategy would make large segments of existing force structure unnecessary.

- The wild card is the long-term effect of the pandemic, and whether this would change the nature or size of the defense effort.
- The public will be the ultimate arbiter. Polling indicates public support for a U.S. role in the world but not increased spending.

What is force structure? The Department of Defense (DOD) defines force structure as "the number, size, and structure of units." Force structure is one of four elements of military capability, the others being readiness ("the ability of units and equipment to deliver the outputs for which they were designed"), modernization ("the technical sophistication of weapon systems and equipment"), and sustainment ("the ability to maintain the necessary level of military activity").[29]

The Trump Administration's Strategy

Analysis of force structure must begin with strategy, since that, at least in theory, drives all elements of military capability as well as national security policy and budgets.

The administration's *National Security Strategy* (NSS), issued in December 2017, and *National Defense Strategy* (NDS), published in January 2018, describe the national security environment the administration sees.[30] The NDS bluntly depicted a U.S. military that is losing its edge over potential competitors and urges "increased and sustained investment" for "long-term strategic competitions with China and Russia."

There is no need to reiterate the strategy at length here. The key points are as follows

- **Five threats:** China, Russia, North Korea, Iran, and global terrorism. These are the same threats that Secretary Ash Carter described at the end of the Obama administration, but the order has changed.[31] Whereas Carter had put Russia first, the Trump administration puts China first. Further, the administration's strategy places greater emphasis on China and Russia than the other three threats.
- **The importance of allies:** The NDS extolls their value, the long-standing relationships, and the need for these connections in the future. This contrasts with the president's often critical comments.
- **The need for management reform:** The NDS notes the importance of being good stewards of the public's money. This is particularly important during a defense buildup when DOD asks the taxpayers for an increased financial commitment.

A big change is the force sizing construct—the way the strategy calculates how many forces are needed and of what kind. A "1+" construct—"defeating aggression by a major power . . . [and] deterring aggression by [another] major power"—replaced the two major conflict construct, which had been a constant in various configurations since the end of the Cold War. This change reflects that conflict

---

29 Joint Staff, *DOD Dictionary of Military and Associated Terms* (Washington, DC: Department of Defense (DOD), updated June 2020), https://www.jcs.mil/Portals/36/Documents/Doctrine/pubs/dictionary.pdf.

30 White House, *A New National Security Strategy for a New Era* (NSS) (Washington, DC: December 2017), https://www.whitehouse.gov/articles/new-national-security-strategy-new-era/; and DOD, *A Summary of the 2018 National Defense Strategy: Sharpening the American Military's Competitive Edge* (NDS) (Washington, DC: January 2018), https://dod.defense.gov/Portals/1/Documents/pubs/2018-National-Defense-Strategy-Summary.pdf.

31 For example, Secretary of Defense Ash Carter, "U.S. National Security Challenges and Ongoing Military Operations," Senate Armed Services Committee, 114th Cong., 2nd sess., September 22, 2016, https://www.armed-services.senate.gov/imo/media/doc/Carter_09-22-16.pdf.

with a major power such as China or Russia would be more demanding than the typical regional conflicts of the past, such as with North Korea or Iraq. What it means for force planning, however, is unclear in the unclassified documents.

Overall, both the NSS and the NDS have a strong tone of U.S. primacy: "[t]he Department of Defense will . . . remain the preeminent military power in the world, ensure the balance of power remains in our favor, and advance an international order that is most conducive to our security and prosperity." The department will "prevail in conflict and preserve peace through strength."[32] There is no hint that the United States will accept a decline in status or even a multipolar world.

The Trump Administration's Budget

PUTTING ITS MONEY WHERE ITS MOUTH IS

As budgeteers like to say, "Plans without funding are hallucinations." To its credit, the Trump administration put resources against its strategy. Chart 1 shows DOD's budget history and the projection for FY 2021. Resources are substantially higher than the BCA cap and what the Obama administration had planned. These budget increases have allowed the services to rebuild readiness, institute a robust modernization program, and grow force structure a little.

Chart 1: DoD Base Budget History (then-year dollars)

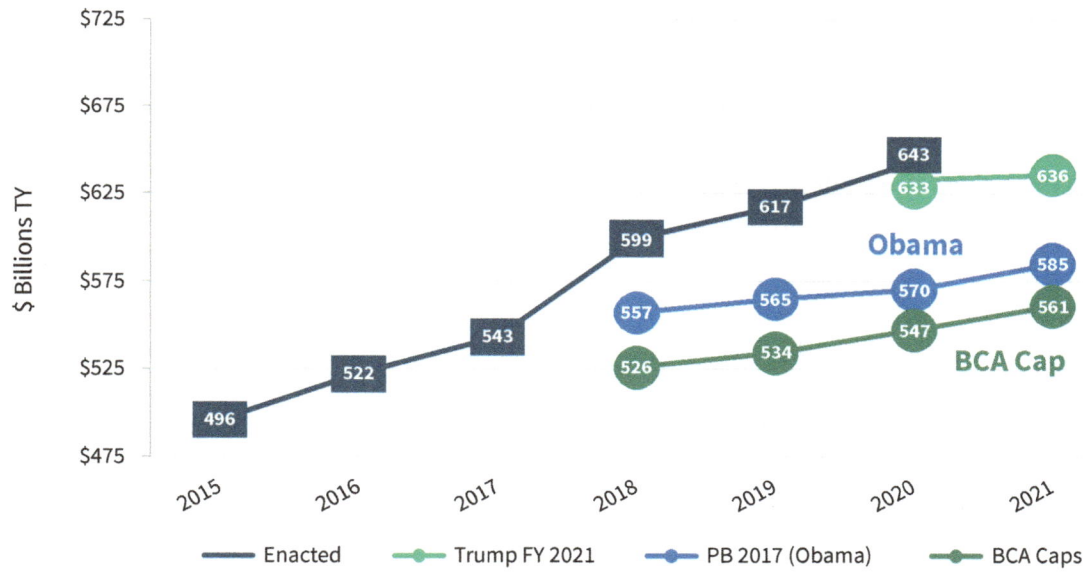

Note: Base budget only, excludes OCO. BCA cap calculated for DOD only. Here in throughout this report, DOD budget totals include discretionary funds only. The enacted amount for FY 2020 includes pandemic supplementals. The Trump FY 2021 projection was originally made from the budget without supplementals; hence it starts at a lower level in FY 2020.

Source: Office of the Under Secretary for Defense, National Defense Budget Estimates for FY 2017 (Washington, DC: Department of Defense, March 2016), https://comptroller.defense.gov/Portals/45/Documents/defbudget/fy2017/FY17_Green_Book.pdf; and Office of the Under Secretary for Defense, National Defense Budget Estimates for FY 2021 (Washington, DC: Department of Defense, April 2020), https://comptroller.defense.gov/Portals/45/Documents/defbudget/fy2021/FY21_Green_Book.pdf. Includes base budget only, excludes OCO.

---

32   DOD, NDS, 4–5.

Trade-offs in the FY 2021 Budget

In an ideal world, forces would be highly ready, thoroughly modernized, and large enough to meet the demands of both surge warfighting and day-to-day deployments. However, limits on resources require some trade-offs, and those are evident in the FY 2021 budget.

Active component end strength would increase slightly in the FY 2021 budget (by 5,500 servicemembers). Reserve component end strength stays essentially the same: 801,900 in FY 2020, increasing by only 100 in FY 2021, to 802,000. This stability in a budget that declines in real terms likely reflects several factors: residual plans to expand, the difficulty in cutting forces, and the continuing high demand for day-to-day force deployments.

Readiness stays generally constant as measured by the publicly available metrics such as flying hours, steaming days, and number of major exercises. (The one exception may be the decline of Air Force flying hours, though the number of exercises does not go down. This may reflect the decline in combat flying.) Although classified metrics (such as the Defense Readiness Reporting System, or DRRS) are not publicly available, service statements indicate that they remain at a relatively high level.[33] The department also asserts that it is on track with its Readiness Recovery Framework, although it has not released any details about what the metrics are or how they have changed.

Table 1: Service Readiness Metrics FY 2019–FY 2021

	FY 2019	FY 2020	FY 2021
Army rotations at combat training centers	41	42	40
Navy flying hours	1.030	1.037M	1.099M
Navy steaming days per quarter (deployed/non-deployed)	58/24	54/24	54/24
Navy integrated exercises—Basic	75	76	95
Navy integrated exercises—Integrated	70	70	93
Marine Corps large exercises—Ground	24	24	24
Marine Corps large exercises—Air	9+2 Det	9+2 Det	9+2 Det
Air Force flying hours	1.454M	1.325M	1.238M
Air Force full-spectrum exercises	25	24	25

This sustainment of readiness occurs despite a $4.5 billion reduction in operations and maintenance funding in the base budget (which covers a wide variety of activities, not just those related to force readiness). Although the FYDP projects continued decline in O&M funding, the changing treatment of war funding makes year-to-year comparisons difficult. However, O&M has typically grown in constant dollar terms, despite administrations repeatedly projecting declines.[34]

A major uncertainty for readiness is the long-term effect of the Covid-19 pandemic. In March and April 2020, the military services shut down most of their training and paused the induction of recruits into

---

33 DRRS, the Defense Readiness Reporting System, is the latest version of DOD's unit readiness reporting systems that cover personnel, equipment, training, ordnance, and supply. It incorporates the previous Status of Readiness and Training System (SORTS).

34 The Future Years Defense Program (FYDP) is DOD's internal program and financial database as approved by the secretary.

basic training. This created a situation that was not sustainable. Readiness and force size would soon deteriorate. However, the services soon restarted deployments and high-level training, though with continuing precautions. Whether the resulting level of activity is sufficient for long-term readiness remains to be seen. Reports indicate that the services may not have been able to execute all the planned training in 2020. The Army for example, had to give up three rotations at its combat training centers and might have similar restrictions next year. [35]

Modernization, measured by total procurement and RDT&E funding (base plus war funding but excluding pandemic supplementals), decreases by $4.8 billion in nominal terms in FY 2021 but by $9.8 billion in constant dollars. Over the five years of the defense program, procurement dips in constant dollars and then recovers to the FY 2020 level, but research, development, testing, and evaluation (RDT&E) funding declines substantially, from $106.7 billion in FY 2021 to $92.3 billion in FY 2025 (FY 2021 dollars).[36] Although this could represent the transition of developmental programs into procurement, it may not produce all of the advanced, and expensive, new systems that the strategy requires and in the numbers needed to fill the force structure.

The Trump Administration's FY 2021 Plan for Force Structure

Table 1 shows the evolution of force structure plans. The bottom line is that even an expanded budget does not allow large force structure increases. Force structure is a lower priority under the current national defense strategy, and the modest increases in the administration's plans reflect that reality.

The FYDP arrays cost data, manpower, and force structure over a five-year period. Because these plans are fiscally constrained to a level directed by the president, they represent an official statement about priorities. The current FYDP period is FY 2021–FY 2025.

35   Colin Clark, "Army Lost Three NTC Rotations to Covid; FORSCOM Curbs Pace for Next Year Also," Breaking Defense, October 13, 2020, https://breakingdefense.com/2020/10/army-lost-3-ntc-training-rotations-to-covid-forscom-curbs-pace-next-year-too/; For broader discussion of readiness, see Mark Cancian and Adam Saxton, "Mission First: US Military Must Train and Recruit during Pandemic," Breaking Defense, April 27, 2020, https://breakingdefense.com/2020/04/mission-first-us-military-must-train-recruit-during-pandemic/.

36   Office of the Under Secretary Of Defense (Comptroller), *National Defense Budget Estimates for FY 2021* (Washington, DC: DOD, April 2020), table 6-8, https://comptroller.defense.gov/Portals/45/Documents/defbudget/fy2021/FY21_Green_Book.pdf. Hereafter known as *FY 2021 Green Book* (named for the color of its customary cover). Calculations here and throughout this report use DOD deflators.

Table 2: Force Structure Targets

	BCA Caps LT Effects ("Sequestration")[a]	Obama FY 2017 FYDP Goal	Trump Campaign (9/2016)	FY 2021 Budget
Army end strength (regular/reserve)	421,000/ 498,000	450,000/ 530,000	540,000/ [563,000][b]	485,900/ 526,300
Army brigade combat teams (AC/RC)	53 (27/26)	58 (30/28)	68 (40/28)	58 (31/27)
Navy carriers	10	11	12	11
Navy ships	274	295	350	306
Air Force TacAir A/C (4th/5th generation)	1,015 (668/347)	1,101 (699/402)	1,310 (837/473)	1,194 (939/255)
USMC end strength	175,000	180,000	242,000 (!)[c]	184,100

Note: "End strength" is the number of military personnel in the service at the end of the fiscal year (September 30).

a "Sequestration" is the term often associated with cuts that would be required if the caps of the Budget Control Act of 2011 were imposed. However, the term is a misnomer. Sequestration applies to the mechanism by which the cuts would be made, not to their extent. Nevertheless, because the term has gained widespread currency, it is used here.

b Not specified in Trump's speech but taken from the Heritage Foundation study on which the speech was based: Dakota Wood ed., *2019 Index of U.S. Military Strength* (Washington, DC: Heritage Foundation, November 2018), https://www.heritage.org/sites/default/files/2018-09/2019_IndexOfUSMilitaryStrength_WEB.pdf.

c This was the implied size of the Marine Corps in the Heritage study that Trump cited. It is not clear that the study intended such a large increase.

- The left column shows the force structure that would have resulted if the caps set by the Budget Control Act of 2011 (BCA) had been imposed. Although the BCA caps are now expired, the "sequestration" force provides a useful benchmark because it received bipartisan criticism as inadequate for national security.[37]

- The second column shows the last plans of the Obama administration. While higher than the BCA level, these levels were still not adequate to implement the multi-theater strategy that the Obama administration had adopted at the end of its time in office.

- The third column shows what President Trump had laid out during the campaign. Based on work by the Heritage Foundation, described later, it shows a large force increase.

- The fourth column shows the forces for FY 2021 in the president's budget proposal.

The later chapters on individual services in this series will discuss the specifics of each of the services' forces.

---

37   Force levels from Department of Defense, *2014 Quadrennial Defense Review* (Washington, DC: March 2014), https://archive.defense.gov/pubs/2014_Quadrennial_Defense_Review.pdf.

Long-Term Force Structure Plans

Data on future force structure are sparse. Long-term plans for force structure and personnel have nearly disappeared from DOD's budget documents. There is no explanation for this disappearance. However, it likely arises from a misplaced concern that potential adversaries might benefit from the information.[38]

Nevertheless, the budget exhibits do contain some information about future end strength (Chart 2). Because these budget exhibits show end strength levels for FY 2021 and FY 2025 only, the intervening years were interpolated.[39]

Chart 2: DOD Active Component End Strength FY 2019–FY 2025

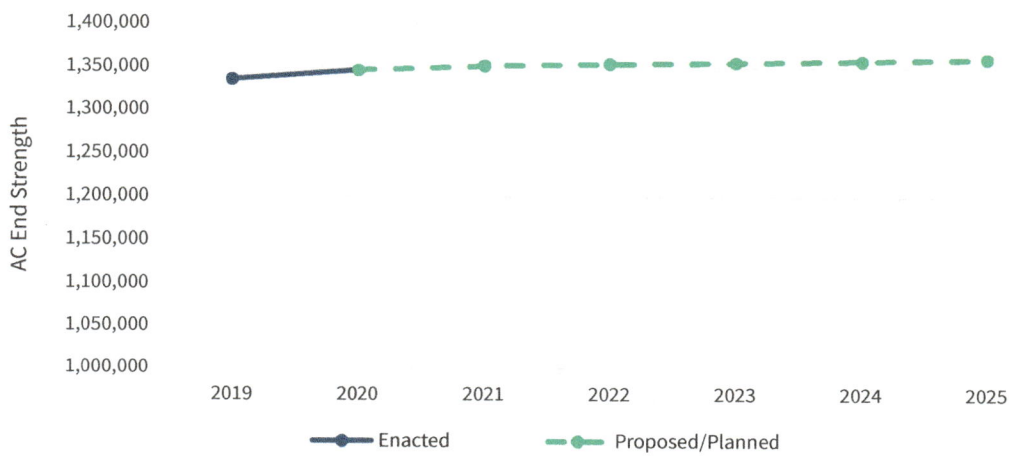

Note: FY 2020 level reflects expected end strength, which is slightly higher than the congressionally authorized strength. The services are given some latitude to deviate from congressional authorizations in response to developments through the year, such as recruiting results and budget execution.

---

38 This secrecy has become a major issue for the Pentagon press corps. See, for example, Jeff Schogol, "The Pentagon Is Terrified of Talking to Reporters Again," Task and Purpose, September 4, 2020, https://taskandpurpose.com/pentagon-run-down/pentagon-media-relations.

39 Technically, end strength is the number of personnel in the service at the end of the fiscal year, September 30. The number of personnel in the service varies through the year, so this number is used for year-to-year estimates. For budgeting purposes, the services often use average strength.

The projection shows a small increase between FY 2021 and FY 2025 of about 15,100 (1.1 percent). The Army and Navy increase while the Air Force and Marine Corps decrease.

Chart 3: DOD Reserve Component End Strength FY 2019–FY 2025

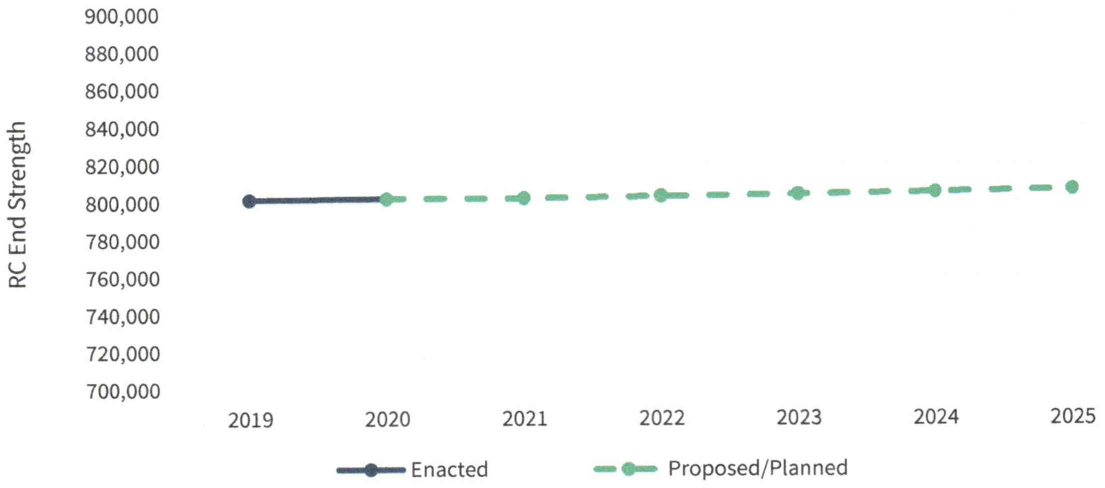

The reserve components show the same small increase that the active component forces show, growing by about 4,300 (0.5 percent). The Army and Air Force reserve components increase, the Marine Corps reserve stays steady, and the Navy reserve continues its long-term decline. This likely reflects that the Army and Air Force rely more on the reserve components and that their reserve components are politically more powerful. (The service chapters contain details about what is happening with their personnel.)

End strength is not force structure ("the number size and composition of units"); it lacks detail about how those personnel are organized and equipped and, hence, how the services intend to fight future conflicts. Nevertheless, end strength is all that is currently available.

Maintaining and slightly expanding end strength reflects a judgment by the services to protect force structure, even at the expense of modernization, despite what the strategy says.

Challenge #1: Retaining Capacity for Regional Conflicts, Crisis Response, and Allied Engagement.

In this view, the world is in a state of persistent conflict that demands a high level of U.S. global presence for regional conflicts, crisis response, and allied engagement.[40] The notion that great power conflict will occur mostly in the "gray area" further increases demand for military forces. As many experts point out, physical presence is needed to meet these demands and to exercise global

---

40 See, for one example among many: James Thomas, "Reshaping the U.S. Military," Testimony Before the Senate Armed Services Committee, 115th Cong., 1st sess., February 16, 2017, https://www.armed-services.senate.gov/hearings/17-02-16-reshaping-the-us-military.

leadership; virtual presence is actual absence.[41] Former secretary of defense Robert Gates called ignoring current conflicts and focusing on future conflicts "next war-itis."[42]

Continuing high demand for forces increases operational tempo. DOD has a global force management process to prioritize force requests and allocate forces to meet them so that they do not overly stress personnel. The tension is that combatant commanders have no restrictions on their requests for forces, and therefore a gap always exists between requests and the forces available.[43] Further, national leadership often directs deployments and commitments in response to global events despite intentions to reduce demands. For example, deployments to Europe have increased greatly since Russia seized the Crimea and the invasion of Ukraine. Thus, the services are caught in "a bear trap of current commitments."

To meet both wartime and day-to-day force demands, conservative think tanks have proposed larger force structures.

- Heritage's *Index of U.S. Military Strength* proposes a large expansion of U.S. active-duty components: 50 regular Army brigade combat teams, 400 battle force ships, 625 strike aircraft, 36 active-duty Marine Corps battalions, and 1,200 active-duty Air Force fighter/ground-attack aircraft. All the military services were rated as "marginal" and particularly deficient on capacity, that is, the size of the forces.[44]

- The American Enterprise Institute has similarly recommended a broad expansion of forces to cover a "three-theater" demand. It argued that "America's deteriorating international position requires an urgent reinvestment in and expansion of U.S. military forces." The recommended budget is 4 percent of GDP, about $180 billion above the Trump administration's planned FY 2021 budget.[45] In a supplemental report aimed at "repairing and rebuilding" the armed forces, Mackenzie Eaglen outlined a path whereby in 2025 the Army would have 519,000 active end strength, the Marine Corps 202,000, and the Air Force 350,000. In addition, an accelerated shipbuilding plan would bring the Navy's fleet up to 339 ships.[46]

The competing demands of a high-end conflict and day-to-day force deployments push the military services toward a high-low mix: a force that incorporates advanced, and often very expensive, technologies along with less expensive elements that can cover less demanding threats, such as regional

---

41 For example, Thomas Donnelly, "Peers, Near-Peers, and Partial Peers: Making Sense of America's Balance-of-Power Interests," Statement before the Senate Committee on Armed Services, 115th Cong., 1st sess., February 16, 2017, https://www.aei.org/research-products/speech/peers-near-peers-and-partial-peers/; Michael J. Mazarr, "Presence v. Warfighting: A Looming Dilemma in Defense Planning," War On The Rocks, April 26, 2016, https://warontherocks.com/2016/04/presence-vs-warfighting-a-looming-dilemma-in-defense-planning.

42 Associated Press, "Military Must Focus on Current Wars, Gates Says," NBC News, 2008, http://www.nbcnews.com/id/24600218/ns/us_news-military/t/military-must-focus-current-wars-gates-says/#.XURBD-hKhPY.

43 For an excellent description of how force demands are generated, forces are allocated, and services cycle units through deployments, see Edward J. Filiberti, Generating Military Capabilities (Carlisle, PA: U.S. Army War College Press, 2019).

44 Dakota Wood ed., *2020 Index of U.S. Military Strength* (Washington, DC: Heritage Foundation, October 2019), https://www.heritage.org/sites/default/files/2019-11/2020_IndexOfUSMilitaryStrength_WEB.pdf.

45 Calculated by taking 4 percent of the latest reported U.S. GDP according to OMB in "Historical Tables," table 1-2 and "FY 2020 Midsession Review," from https://www.whitehouse.gov/omb/budget/; 4 percent requirement from American Enterprise Institute, *To Rebuild America's Military* (Washington, DC: October 2015), http://www.aei.org/wp-content/uploads/2015/10/To-Rebuild-Americas-Military.pdf.

46 Mackenzie Eaglen, *Repair and Rebuild: Balancing New Military Spending for a Three-Theater Strategy* (Washington, DC: American Enterprise Institute, October 2017), 17, http://www.aei.org/wp-content/uploads/2017/11/Repair-and-Rebuild.pdf.

opponents and crisis response. The administration's program does not acknowledge such an approach. However, the services appear to have moved in that direction with regard to particular decisions, such as the Air Force's decision to retain the A-10 and procure some F-15EXs and the Navy's decision to continue the frigate program, continue procurement of F-18s, and investigate less expensive amphibious ships.

Seth Jones, director of CSIS's Transnational Threats Project, has argued that a focus on great power competition should not obscure the fact that the most likely demands on DOD will be to respond to global terrorism and actions in the gray area between peace and conflict. He notes: "It would be imprudent if the United States were to move too quickly away from countering terrorists while the threat is still high."[47] While the NDS does include terrorism as a threat, it also notes that "[i]nterstate strategic competition, not terrorism, is now the primary concern in U.S. national security."[48]

Challenge #2: A Strategy-Resources Gap

Strategy/resource gaps are a recurring theme in national security literature. The strategic desires of policy officials often outrun the resources that the budget process provides. The gap will particularly affect force structure because the national defense strategy prioritizes readiness and modernization, as will any likely successor. Force structure in all the services would likely be a bill payer.

A restricted budget future collides with the need for growth. General Dunford set off a debate when he was chairman of the Joint Chiefs by saying that the defense strategy requires 3–5 percent real growth per year. Dunford and other senior officials made that point many times, so it was not a casual observation. Many use that as a benchmark for resource requirements.[49]

Although General Dunford and others provided no analytic justification for the 3–5 percent requirement, other analyses have shown the need for real increases in the DOD budget just to stand still. Compensation for military and civilian personnel has historically had to increase faster than inflation to compete in the labor market. For military personnel compensation, that has been 1 percent real growth.[50] Further, spending in the operations and maintenance account, which includes a wide variety of activities from military operations to healthcare base operations to environmental restoration, has also increased in real terms, averaging 2.6 percent above inflation.[51] The Congressional Budget Office estimates that DOD's current plans will require an additional $77 billion over the FYDP period, FY 2021–FY 2025.[52]

---

47 Seth G. Jones, "America's Counterterrorism Gamble," CSIS, *CSIS Briefs*, July 2018, https://www.csis.org/analysis/americas-counterterrorism-gamble.

48 DOD, NDS, 1.

49 See, for example, "A Conversation with Chairman of the Joint Chiefs Of Staff Joseph Dunford," Brookings Institution, Washington, DC, May 29, 2019, https://www.brookings.edu/events/a-conversation-with-chairman-of-the-joint-chiefs-of-staff-general-dunford/; and Aaron Mehta, "DoD needs 3-5 percent annual growth through 2023, top officials say," Defense News, June 13, 2017, https://www.defensenews.com/pentagon/2017/06/13/dod-needs-3-5-percent-annual-growth-through-2023-top-officials-say/.

50 Calculated by comparing inflation for the military personnel account with DOD's overall inflation in FY 2021 Green Book, table 5-6.

51 Todd Harrison and Seamus P. Daniels, *Analysis of the FY 2021 Defense Budget* (Washington, DC: CSIS, August 2020), 7, http://defense360.csis.org/wp-content/uploads/2020/08/Analysis-of-the-FY-2021-Defense-Budget.pdf.

52 CBO's figures include acquisition cost growth as well as military personnel and O&M costs. Congressional Budget Office, *Long-Term Implications of the 2021 Future Years Defense Program* (Washington, DC: September 2020), https://www.cbo.gov/publication/56554.

Chart 4: DOD Budget Projections (Base plus OCO, FY 2021 dollars, billions)

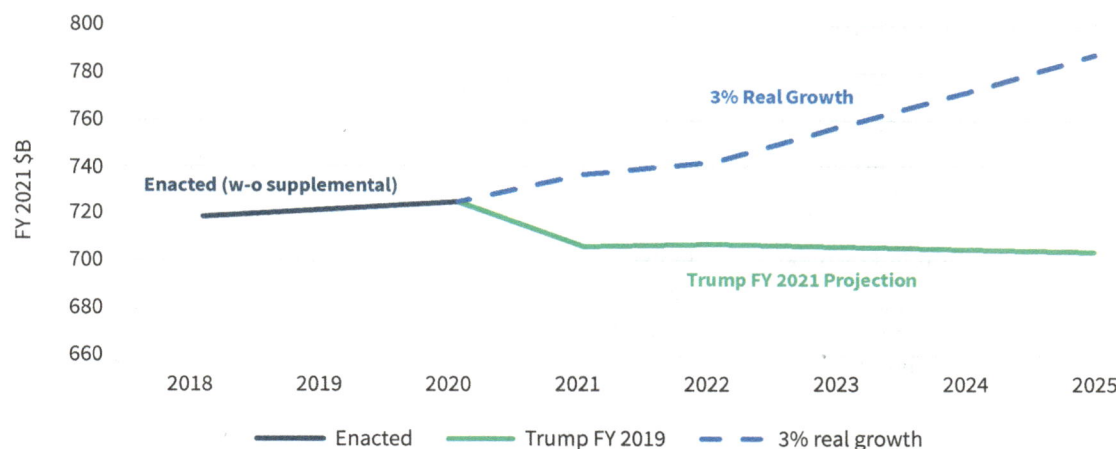

Rising budgets mitigated this concern over the last few years because the debate was whether budgets were rising fast enough. However, for the last two years, the Trump administration has projected flat future budget levels. Chart 3 shows the administration's budget projections and 3 percent budget growth line.[53]

The administration has long stated its intention to pay for these new initiatives through cuts in overhead and infrastructure. The NDS, for example, has management reform as one of its three major elements. Such efforts are needed. However, while it is easy to criticize excess overhead, the specifics get messy and hard to implement.[54] For example, the administration has been unable, and recently unwilling, to push for base closures, which is the most well-documented and widely supported mechanism for achieving overhead savings. The FY 2021 budget does identify $5.7 billion in savings, which is commendable, but Congress has rejected major elements, such as healthcare reforms. The much-anticipated audit identified no savings because that is not its function.[55]

The bottom line is that the gap between projected resources and the 3 percent "requirement" grows rapidly.

Criticisms of a strategy-resources gap. Even when the defense budget was rising, there was criticism that resources were inadequate. The National Defense Strategy Commission, a group created by Congress to consider the DOD's NDS and provide an independent perspective, harshly criticized what it saw as the lack of adequate resources and called the current situation "an emergency." It finds, "[t]he

---

53 To increase comparability, these projections include both the base and OCO but exclude supplementals for natural disasters such as hurricanes and the Covid-19 pandemic. The decline in FY 2021 represents the effects of the Bipartisan Budget Agreement of 2020. The Trump projections also assume some reduction wartime operations, which are subtracted from the 3 percent real growth requirement. "Bipartisan Budget Agreement for Fiscal Years FY 2020 and FY 2021," Senate Appropriations Committee, https://www.appropriations.senate.gov/imo/media/doc/Bipartisan%20Budget%20Agreement%20July%2022%202019.pdf.

54 See, for example, Mark Cancian, "Bad Idea: Easy Savings from DOD Management Reform," Breaking Defense, December 11, 2017, https://breakingdefense.com/2017/12/41070/. This piece and several others show how savings are possible but face strong opposition and require investment of political capital.

55 Mark Cancian, "Why Auditing the Pentagon Audit Isn't Turning up a Windfall of Waste," Forbes, November 19, 2018, https://www.forbes.com/sites/markcancian/2018/11/19/the-dod-audit-no-pot-of-gold-at-the-end-of-that-rainbow/#490a8f9f3230.

NDS is not adequately resourced," and "America is very near the point of strategic insolvency, where its 'means' are badly out of the alignment with its 'ends.'" It strongly endorsed Chairman Dunford's goal of 3–5 percent real budget growth.[56]

Conservative think tanks have picked up this theme. The Heritage Foundation affirmed the 3–5 percent annual growth standard.[57] Similarly, Rick Berger and Gary Schmitt of the American Enterprise Institute argued that "the proposed budget . . . falls short of the funding the military needs to carry out the strategy with confidence."[58]

A Biden administration might make this gap even wider. The Democratic platform proposed cuts to the defense budget, though the magnitude is unstated: "We can maintain a strong defense and protect our safety and security for less." The consensus among the national security community is that these cuts might total 5 percent. Signals about where cuts would come are modest, including some trimming of nuclear forces and elimination of "legacy" forces.[59] On the other hand, Biden policy documents so far, which are quite vague, reiterate many of the points of the Obama and Trump administrations about the need for global engagement, a strong military, and support for the troops. Biden has stated that he has no plans for "major" defense cuts.[60]

Challenge #3:
The Need to Shift More Aggressively to a Great Power Structure

The Trump administration's stated priorities (and possibly those of a Biden administration) are readiness, modernization, and force structure last.[61]

However, a continuing criticism is that the post-NDS budgets have not gone far enough in implementing the strategy; the budgets retain too many legacy forces and systems and do not move aggressively enough in funding and fielding the kinds of advanced technologies that the strategy requires. In general, such critics call for cutting forces to fund more modernization. As one example

---

56 National Defense Strategy Commission, *Providing for the Common Defense: The Assessment and Recommendations of the National Defense Strategy Commission* (Washington, DC: United States Institute of Peace, November 13, 2018), https://www.usip.org/publications/2018/11/providing-common-defense.

57 Frederico Bartels et al., "How Congress Can Improve the President's 2020 Defense Budget Request," Heritage Foundation, *Backgrounder* 3402, March 27, 2019, p. 1-2, https://www.heritage.org/sites/default/files/2019-03/BG3402.pdf.

58 Rick Berger and Gary Schmitt, "Budget Deal Is No-Win for the Military," *Wall Street Journal*, July 28, 2019, https://www.wsj.com/articles/budget-deal-is-no-win-for-the-military-11564337478.

59 Democratic Party, *2020 Democratic Party Platform*, 67, https://www.demconvention.com/wp-content/uploads/2020/08/2020-07-31-Democratic-Party-Platform-For-Distribution.pdf; Joseph R Biden, Jr., "Why America Must Lead Again: Rescuing US Foreign Policy after Trump," *Foreign Affairs*, March/April 2020, https://www.foreignaffairs.com/articles/united-states/2020-01-23/why-america-must-lead-again.

60 Steve Beynon, "Biden says US must maintain small force in Middle East, has no plans for major defense cuts," Stars & Stripes, September 10, 2020, https://www.stripes.com/news/us/biden-says-us-must-maintain-small-force-in-middle-east-has-no-plans-for-major-defense-cuts-1.644631#:~:text=Space%20Force-,Biden%20says%20US%20must%20maintain%20small%20force%20in%20Middle%20East,plans%20for%20major%20Defense%20cuts&text=He%20also%20said%20he%20does,such%20as%20China%20and%20Russia.

61 For likely priorities of a Biden administration, see Mark Cancian, "The Fuzzy Outlines of Biden's National Security Policies," Breaking Defense, August 26, 2020, https://breakingdefense.com/2020/08/the-fuzzy-outlines-of-bidens-national-security-policies/.

among many, Paul Scharre of the Center for New American Security writes, "[t]he United States is a military optimized for refighting the 1991 Persian Gulf war. Why? Because it's comfortable . . ..The United States hasn't adapted its forces to a rising China."[62]

The Democratic Party platform weighed in on this controversy. Like many critics of the defense program, it decried legacy platforms and forces:

> Rather than continuing to rely on legacy platforms that are increasingly exposed and vulnerable, Democrats support funding a more cost-effective, agile, flexible, and resilient force with modern transportation and logistics capabilities that can operate in more contested environments. Democrats will accelerate defense transformation.[63]

To illustrate what the impact on force structure might be if this approach were aggressively implemented, CSIS used its Force Cost Calculator. This tool calculates a defense budget based on a wide variety of inputs on forces, readiness levels, and equipment programs. The table below shows the results. The assumption is that the top line is locked, but military personnel compensation rises at 1 percent a year and O&M at 2.2 percent a year above inflation. (The budget projections allow 0.4 percent above inflation for military personnel and inflation only for O&M.[64]) The projection assumed that readiness would stay at the FY 2020 level and that modernization programs would remain on track. Special operations forces were held constant since they have been protected historically.

The bottom line is that force structure would get much smaller. Such a scenario would drive force structure to the level of "sequestration" as depicted in Table 1. In reality, the services would make the cuts more "balanced": squeeze readiness, stretch out modernization programs, and cut back munitions inventories, to protect some force structure. However, that is not what the strategy directs.

---

62 Paul Scharre, "Esper's Convenient Lie," *Defense One*, September 18, 2020, https://www.defenseone.com/ideas/2020/09/espers-convenient-lie/168596/. For other examples, see Susanna V. Blume & Molly Parrish, *Investing in Great Power Competition* (Washington, DC: Center for a New American Security, July 9, 2020), https://www.cnas.org/publications/reports/investing-in-great-power-competition; Elbridge Colby, "How to Win America's Next War: War's Sci-Fi Future," *Foreign Policy*, May 5, 2019, https://foreignpolicy.com/2019/05/05/how-to-win-americas-next-war-china-russia-military-infrastructure/; and Christian Brose, *The Kill Chain: Defending America in the Future of High-Tech Warfare* (New York: Hatchet Books, 2020).

63 Democratic Party, *2020 Democratic Party Platform*, 66.

64 Military personnel inflation from *FY 2021 Green Book*, table 5-3; O&M inflation from *FY 2021 Green Book*, table 5-6. Military personnel long-term inflation calculated by comparing inflation in the military personnel account with inflation in the economy as a whole, data from *FY 2021 Green Book*, table 5-6 and 5-1, respectively, 1975-2021.

Table 3: Force Structure Effects of Implementing a Great Power Strategy under Constrained Resources

		FY 2021 Level	FY 2025 Level
Army	Active Component (AC) Personnel	485,900	425,700
	Reserve Component (RC) Personnel	526,300	482,900
	Total BCTs	58	50
Navy	AC Personnel	347,800	318,100
	RC Personnel	58,800	53,400
	Ships	306	293
Marine Corps	AC Personnel	184,100	164,500
	RC Personnel	38,500	37,200
Air Force (includes Space Force)	AC Personnel	327,300	308,100
	RC Personnel	178,400	142,800
	Fighter Attack Aircraft	1,200	1,013

A major unanswered question in this discussion is what qualifies as a "legacy" platform. On this definition hang tens of billions of dollars of acquisition funding and the structure of future forces. Strategists, such as those who criticize the lack of change in the budget, see legacy platforms as those that use old technologies and outdated operational concepts. They would cut manned aircraft, aircraft carriers, and armored vehicles, substituting smaller unmanned and distributed systems.

The military services define legacy as old systems in the inventory. They would retire older systems and buy similar but more modern systems. For example, strategists would urge the Air Force to curtail F-35 procurement and move toward a fleet of unmanned aerial vehicles (UAVs). The Air Force would retire F-16s and A-10s and use the savings to buy more F-35s. Similarly, the Navy is proposing retiring old cruisers and building new destroyers. The Army has proposed reducing procurement of tanks and Bradley Fighting Vehicles while buying a new generation of ground combat vehicles.[65]

Challenge #4:
Strategy Changes That Could Change Force Structure

Strategy drives force structure. Thus, any changes in strategy will change the size and shape of the forces. The NDS received broad support in Congress and the national security community. The challenges that it identified built on what the Obama administration had been discussing after 2014 and on many analyses by outside experts.

Nevertheless, the NDS was not universally acclaimed, particularly by those who want less entanglement in foreign affairs and less spending on defense. Some libertarians and progressives have proposed a strategy of "restraint" and reduced spending that goes with it.

---

65   Tony Bertuca, "DOD Chiefs Try to Sell Congress on a Budget That Would 'Divest to Invest'," Inside Defense, February 26, 2020, https://insidedefense.com/daily-news/dod-chiefs-try-sell-congress-budget-would-divest-invest.

CATO, a libertarian think tank, has consistently rejected a strategy of engagement and forward deployments. As Christopher Preble, CATO's vice president for defense and foreign policy studies, argues: "Admitting that the United States is incapable of effectively adjudicating every territorial dispute or of thwarting every security threat in every part of the world is hardly tantamount to surrender. It is, rather, a wise admission of the limits of American power and an acknowledgment of the need to share the burdens, and the responsibilities, of dealing with a complex world."[66]

CATO's strategy would reduce forward deployments and cut the Army, Air Force, and Marine Corps by a third. The strategy would cut the Navy relatively less (by 25 percent) to retain the ability to deploy globally when needed. Reserves would be reduced less than active-duty forces to maintain a surge capability. These changes would cut about $110 billion per year from the defense budget.[67]

In recent years, a progressive critique of national security strategy and budgets has arisen, reinforcing critiques such as those by CATO. For example, a coalition of progressive groups proposed "utiliz[ing] our military solely for the defense of the people of our country" and cutting $200 billion from the defense budget.[68] A detailed progressive analysis proposed cutting ground (Army and Marine Corps) force structure heavily, reducing readiness through cuts in civilians and contractors, and terminating several nuclear modernization programs and most national missile-defense programs. It would save about $125 billion per year if fully implemented.[69]

Where Is Public Opinion?

Ultimately, the size and shape of the defense effort depend on the level of support from the American people. The chart below shows public attitudes toward national defense.[70] The good news for defense is that there is little support for the notion that the United States is too strong. That opinion barely gets into double digits. The bad news is that support for budget increases or force expansion is weak.

---

66   Christopher A. Preble, "Adapting to American Decline," *New York Times*, April 21, 2018, https://www.cato.org/publications/commentary/adapting-american-decline.

67   Force levels from a think tank budget exercise, results described in Jacob Cohn and Ryan Boone, eds., *How Much Is Enough? Alternative Defense Strategies* (Washington, DC: Center for Strategic and Budgetary Analyses, 2016), http://csbaonline.org/research/publications/how-much-is-enough-alternative-defense-strategies.

68   "Letter to VP Joseph Biden," Demand Progress, May 11, 2020, https://demandprogress.org/50-organizations-urge-biden-trump-adopt-principled-foreign-policy/.

69   Center for International Policy, *Sustainable Defense: More Security, Less Spending – Final Report of the Sustainable Defense Task Force of The Center for International Policy* (Washington, DC: June 2019), http://comw.org/pda/sustainable-defense-more-security-less-spending/.

70   Jeffery M. Jones, "Record High Say US Defense Spending 'about Right'," Gallup Organization, March 16, 2020, https://news.gallup.com/poll/288761/record-high-say-defense-spending-right.aspx.

Chart 5: Public Opinion on National Defense

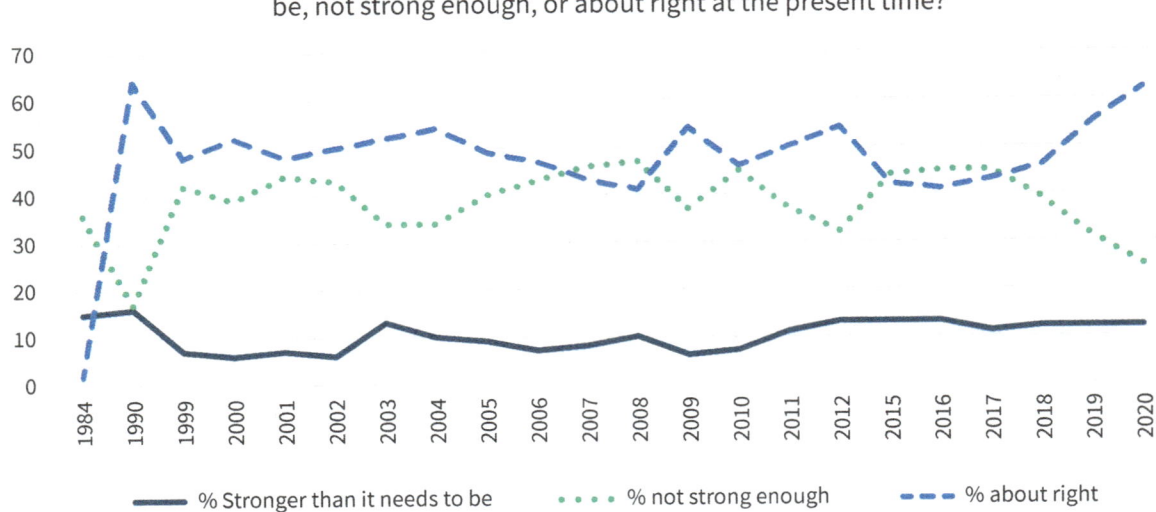

Source: "In Depth: Topics A to Z Military and National Defense," Gallup Organization, https://news.gallup.com/poll/1666/military-national-defense.aspx.

The opinion that the United States is not strong enough began rising in 2012, as the postwar drawdown took effect, and continued rising with the increased threats from Russia, ISIS, and China becoming apparent in 2014.

"Not strong enough" dipped dramatically after 2017 and is now substantially below "about right," likely reflecting satisfaction with the defense buildup and concerns about the Trump administration. Questions about the level of the defense budget elicit similar dynamics.

This level of public opinion would seem to support, though weakly, the path that the Trump administration is on but would not support further large increases. Public opinion could deteriorate if forces become engaged in new conflicts.

Regarding the U.S. role in the world, the public is generally supportive, but there are limits.[71]

- There is strong support for the notion that NATO membership is good for the United States (77 percent versus 15 percent).
- The public is evenly divided about whether the United States should be more or less involved in world affairs (49 percent less involved, 44 percent more involved).
- The public is supportive of the United States taking into account the interests of its allies (54 percent yes, 40 percent no).

---

71 "Large Majorities in Both Parties Say NATO Is Good for the US," Pew Research Center, April 2, 2019, https://www.pewresearch.org/politics/2019/04/02/large-majorities-in-both-parties-say-nato-is-good-for-the-u-s/.

Covid-19: The Wild Card

The pandemic has disrupted the nation's social and economic life and has had a major impact on DOD's operations and industry. The bottom line is that DOD has, so far, weathered the pandemic better than the country overall, as DOD's infection rate is lower and its lethality rate is much lower.[72] The long-term effect on DOD is unclear.

Because the pandemic has had such a major effect on the U.S. society and economy, many speculate it will have a major long-term effect on national security. At a minimum, there will be a replenishment of DOD's medical inventories and some enhancements of dual-use forces (i.e., those that can do both warfighting and humanitarian assistance).

Still, it may be that two years from now, when a vaccine is widely available and economic and social life have returned to some version of a pre-pandemic normal, DOD will retain its current structures and missions. Changes at the federal level could focus on domestic agencies such as FEMA, CDC, and HHS.

On the other hand, polling shows that infectious disease now tops Americans concerns about security. This could drive changes in DOD.

Chart 6: Public Opinion on Threats to the Nation

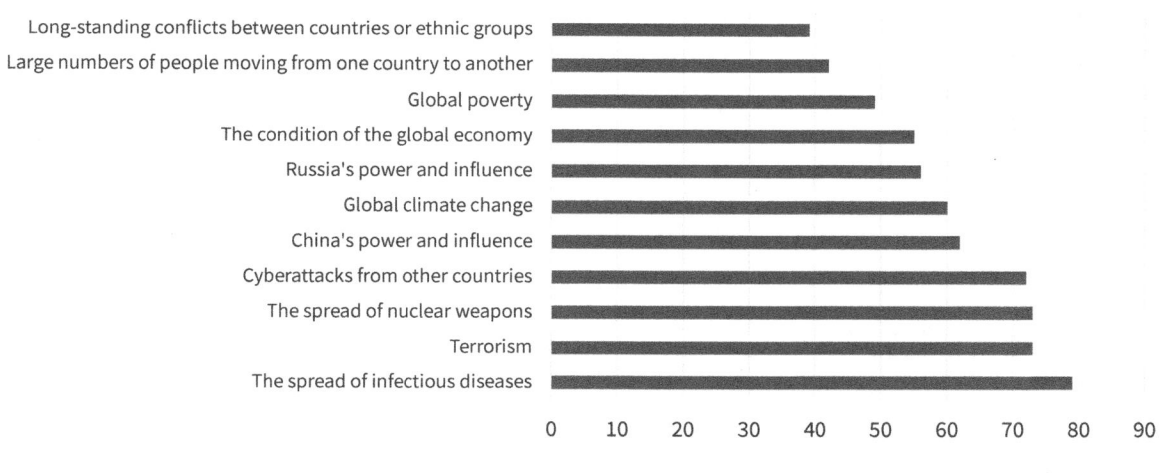

Source: Jacob Poushter and Moira Fagan, "Americans See Spread of Disease as Top International Threat, Along With Terrorism, Nuclear Weapons, and Cyberattacks," Pew Research, April 13, 2020, https://www.pewresearch.org/global/2020/04/13/americans-see-spread-of-disease-as-top-international-threat-along-with-terrorism-nuclear-weapons-cyberattacks/.

One set of arguments holds that because the level of national debt has skyrocketed, and the nation's focus has turned to domestic affairs, the defense budget will go down. Secretary Esper has commented

---

[72] For details on defense and the pandemic, see Mark Cancian and Adam Saxton, "Weekly Covid Response Update," CSIS, https://defense360.csis.org/series/combating-covid-19/.

on this: "[t]here's a concern that [the pandemic] may lead to smaller defense budgets in the future."[73] Indeed, a group of progressives in Congress called for just such a change: "America needs a coronavirus cure, not more war."[74]

Public concerns about future pandemics might drive an effort to expand DOD's role in such national emergencies regardless of the level of the defense budget. This might involve creating new DOD institutions for medical research or greatly expanding those that already exist. It might involve expanding dual-use capabilities, such as building a new generation of hospital ships (which Congress is already contemplating). It might involve reversing the proposed restructuring and shrinking of the military medical community. (DOD has proposed to focus its medical community on "military readiness"—capabilities needed for conflicts—and reducing those capabilities that apply solely or primarily to dependents and retirees.)

Whether this is a good role for DOD is an open question. The military services prefer to focus on the traditional warfighting missions, and domestic agencies exist to provide emergency medical capabilities. However, DOD is often called on in emergencies because of its technical competence and broad set of capabilities.

---

73 Paul McCleary, "Old Weapons under Fire As Covid Debt Rises," Breaking Defense, May 5, 2020, https://breakingdefense.com/2020/05/old-weapons-under-fire-as-covid-debt-rises/.

74 Mark Pocan and Barbara Lee, "Letter to the House Armed Services Committee," U.S. Congress, May 19, 2020, https://pocan.house.gov/sites/pocan.house.gov/files/documents/Pocan-Lee%20Defense%20Spending%20Reduction%20Joint%20Sign-on%20Letter%205-19-20.pdf.

2

Army

The U.S. Army plans slow expansion through FY 2025, but a constrained budget environment will force it to choose between maintaining the units it has and building new kinds of structures. With modernization, the Army has increased production of proven systems and shifted billions into development of high-priority programs to prepare the Army for great power conflict.

KEY TAKEAWAYS

- After a dip in personnel strength in FY 2019, both regular and reserve components have recovered. FY 2021 targets include: regular Army, 485,900; Guard, 336,500; and Army Reserve, 189,800.
- The regular Army and Army Guard project small increases through FY 2025; the Army Reserve will stay essentially level. This represents a substantial reduction to earlier growth plans, but probably the most expansion that can be done in the current budget and security environment.
- New air and missile defense units are entering the force. Security Force Advisory Brigades continue despite their focus on stability operations. Other new kinds of units, such as the widely discussed multidomain brigades, remain mostly conceptual.
- The active-reserve mix has stabilized at 52 percent Guard/Reserve, 48 percent active. There is now less tension between regular Army and its reserve components as a result of closer consultations, higher overall budgets, and shared recruitment challenges.
- Army modernization, which forms the basis for future forces, is a mix of good and bad news: the good news is that the Army continues production of proven systems and has a well-modernized force as a result. More good news is a few new systems are coming out of the research, development, testing, and evaluation (RDT&E) "primordial soup." The bad news is that the Army is still several years away from having a new generation of systems in production to take it into the 2020s and beyond and set it up for potential combat against great power adversaries.

- In an environment of constrained resources, the Army will need to cut existing Brigade Combat Teams (BCTs) if it wants to build new units and procure new systems. So far it has been unwilling to do this.

Force Structure in FY 2021

Table 1: Army End Strength – Regular and Civilians

	Regular Army		Civilian Full-Time Equivalents (000s)
	Brigade Combat Teams	*End Strength*	
FY 2019 Authorized	31	487,500	194,800 (planned)
FY 2019 Actual	31	478,000	197,000
FY 2020 Authorized	31	480,000	194,900 (planned)
FY 2020 Actual	31	485,000	192,100
FY 2021 Request	31	485,900	197,600

Source: Department of the Army, *Army FY 2021 Budget Overview* (Washington, DC: February 2020), Military end strength and force structure on 8, 11, civilian FTEs on 12, https://www.asafm.army.mil/Portals/72/Documents/BudgetMaterial/2021/pbr/Overview%20and%20Highlights/Army_FY_2021_Budget_Overview.pdf.

Regular Army end strength recovered after a dip caused by recruiting and retention difficulties in FY 2019. In that year, the Army aimed for 487,500 but only attained 478,000. It moderated the goal for FY 2020 to 480,000 but was actually able to achieve 485,000. It proposes a small increase of 900 in FY 2021.

The pandemic has affected Army end strength. On the one hand, downturns make recruiting easier. On the other hand, recruiters must do most of their work online and thus have less personal contact. Also, pandemic related precautions such as social distancing limit the throughput in the training establishment. On balance, the effect seems to help end strength since the Army overachieved in FY 2020.

Civilian personnel levels dropped in FY 2020 but will return to their former level.

Table 2: Total Army End Strength – National Guard and Reserve

	Army National Guard		Army Reserve
	Brigade Combat Teams	*End Strength*	*Authorized End Strength*
FY 2019 Authorized	27	343,500	199,500
FY 2019 Actual	27	336,000	190,700
FY 2020 Authorized	27	336,000	189,500
FY 2020 Actual	27	336,000	189,500
FY 2021 Request	27	336,500	189,800

Source: BCT data in Office of the Undersecretary of Defense (Comptroller), *Defense Budget Overview: Fiscal Year 2021 Budget Request* (Washington, DC: Department of Defense, 2020) Appendix A, Table A-4, A-6, https://comptroller.defense.gov/Portals/45/Documents/defbudget/fy2021/fy2021_Budget_Request_Overview_Book.pdf. End strength data in *Army FY2021 Budget Overview*, 8.

End strength for the Army reserve components showed a dip in FY 2019 similar to that seen in the regular forces but not the subsequent recovery. They have stayed at the lower end strength level but seem able to hold that.

Chart 1: Total Army End Strength FY 1999–FY 2021

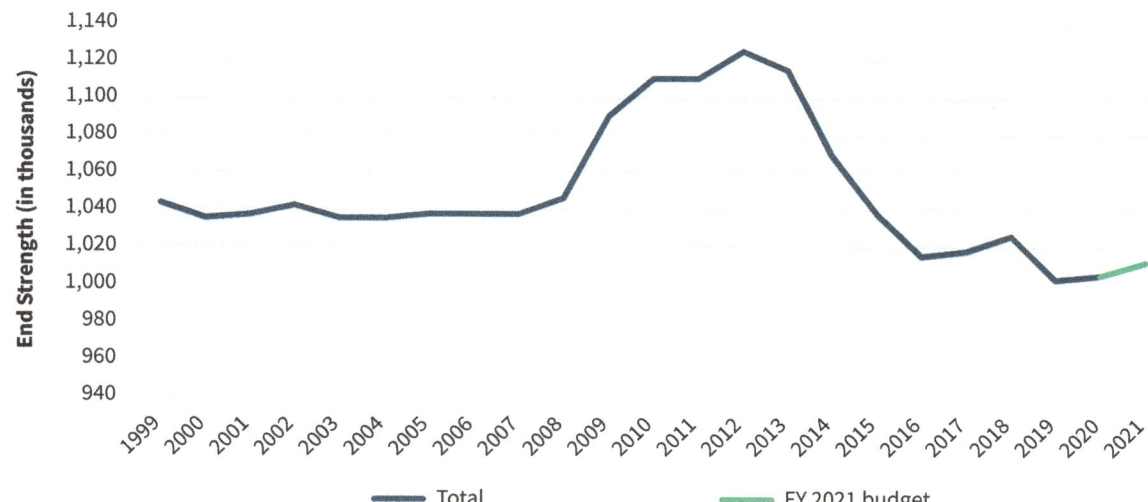

Note: This and several other historical charts begin with the year 1999 because it is before the 9/11 buildup but after completion of the post-Cold War reductions.

Source: Office of the Under Secretary of Defense (Comptroller), *National Defense Budget Estimates for FY 2021* (Washington, DC: Department of Defense, April 2020), Table 7-5: Department of Defense Manpower, 286-288, https://comptroller.defense.gov/Portals/45/Documents/defbudget/fy2021/FY21_Green_Book.pdf; and Office of the Under Secretary of Defense (Comptroller), *PB 21 Budget Roll Out Brief* (Washington, DC: Department of Defense, February 2020), 13.

Chart 1 shows the Army's growth in the 2000s for the wars in Iraq and Afghanistan and its subsequent drop as the wars wound down. The total Army today is 30,000 soldiers below its pre-9/11 level.

The Army had fought hard against plans in the Obama administration to drop to 980,000 soldiers, regular and reserve, or lower. FY 2019 plans called for expansion to 1,040,000 by FY 2023, and Army officials had talked about even higher levels. However, such talk has nearly disappeared as the Army has struggled to maintain its current strength.

There are no major force structure changes in FY 2021. The regular Army maintains 31 Brigade Combat Teams (BCTs), and 11 Combat Aviation Brigades (CABs), with no net change from FY 2020 to FY 2021. The Army National Guard will maintain its current force of 27 BCTs and 8 Combat Aviation Brigades (CABs). The Army Reserve, which consists mostly of support units ("enablers"), retains two Theater Aviation Brigades (TABS).

There is a major difference in the BCT balance between the components. The National Guard is mostly infantry (74 percent). This reduces the need for vehicle maintenance, which is difficult with part-time personnel. The regular Army is more equipment intensive, with 58 percent of BCTs being medium or heavy.

Chart 2: Army BCT Balance by Component

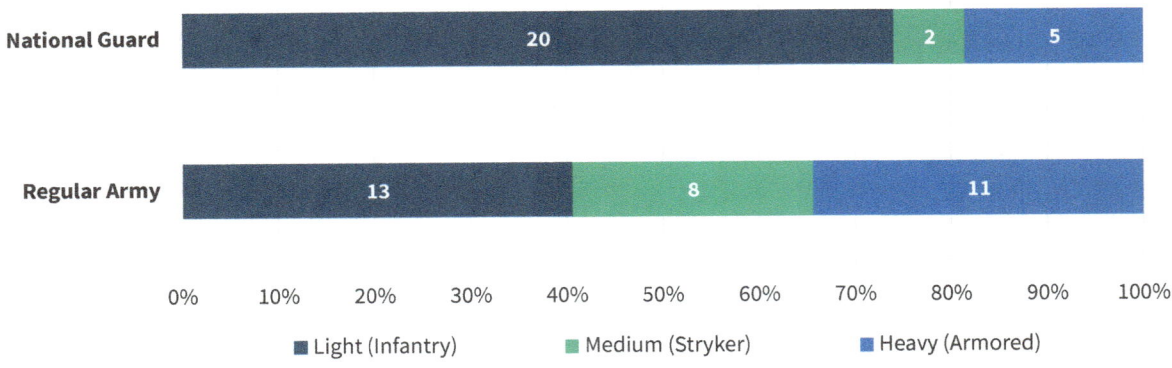

Source: Department of the Army, *Fiscal Year (FY) 2021 Budget Estimates: Operation and Maintenance, Army Justification of Estimates* (Washington, DC: February 2020), 2, https://www.asafm.army.mil/Portals/72/Documents/BudgetMaterial/2021/Base%20Budget/Operation%20and%20Maintenance/OMA_VOL_1_FY_2021_PB_Army_Volume_1.pdf; Department of the Army, *Fiscal Year (FY) 2021 Budget Estimates: Operation and Maintenance, Army National Guard Justification Book* (Washington, DC: February 2020), 35, https://www.asafm.army.mil/Portals/72/Documents/BudgetMaterial/2021/Base%20Budget/Operation%20and%20Maintenance/OMNG_VOL_1_FY_2021_PB_Army_National_Guard_Volume_1.pdf.

As Table 3 shows, the total Army has also been getting heavier, which is unsurprising since it has reoriented itself from a focus on counterinsurgency, which needs infantry, to a focus on great power conflict, which needs firepower.

Table 3: Army BCT Balance by Type

	Light (Infantry)	Medium (Stryker)	Heavy (Armored)
FY 2017	33	9	14
FY 2021	33	9	16

Source: Department of the Army, *Fiscal Year (FY) 2021 Budget Estimates*, 2, Department of the Army, *Fiscal Year (FY) 2021 Budget Estimates*, 35; Department of the Army, *Fiscal Year (FY) 2017 Budget Estimates: Operations and Maintenance, Army Justification of Estimates* (Washington, DC: February 2016), 2, https://www.asafm.army.mil/Portals/72/Documents/BudgetMaterial/2017/base%20budget/operation%20and%20maintenance/Army%20Vol%201%20-%20Justification%20Book.pdf; Department of the Army, *Fiscal Year (FY) 2017 Budget Estimates: Operation and Maintenance, Army National Guard Justification Book* (Washington, DC: February 2016), 52, https://www.asafm.army.mil/Portals/72/Documents/BudgetMaterial/2017/base%20budget/operation%20and%20maintenance/Army%20National%20Guard.pdf.

The Army has finished establishing the Security Force Advisory Brigades (SFABs), five in the regular force and one in the National Guard. SFABs train, advise, assist, enable, and accompany operations with allied and partner nations, thus reducing the burden on BCTs, which would otherwise have to deploy in pieces for this mission. The Army argues that SFABs support the *National Defense Strategy* (NDS) by enabling allies and partners, which is one of the NDS's three major tenets. However, they have principally focused on irregular warfare and stability operations, to which the NDS gives a lower priority. Continuing all six SFABs indicates that the Army is maintaining some balance in its capabilities.

SFABs could also provide the basis for future BCTs if the Army needed to expand.

The Future Size of the Army

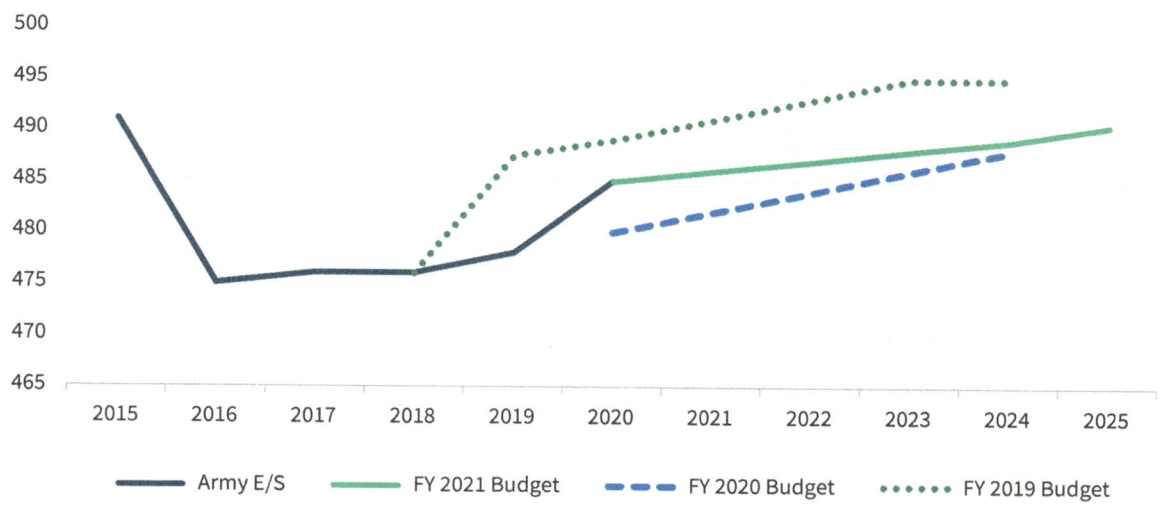

Chart 3: Evolution of Regular Army End Strength Plans, FY 2019–2021 (000s)

As shown in Chart 3, improved recruiting and retention have allowed the Army to get back on a growth slope that is higher than FY 2020, though not as high as what had been projected in FY 2019 and earlier. If the planned growth in the active and reserve components occurs, the Army will get back to its pre-9/11 level. In the long term, the regular Army hopes to get to 495,000.

Three opposing dynamics pull the future size and shape of the Army. One is the guidance in the NDS to focus on great power conflicts with Russia and China. That implies a force equipped with advanced, and likely very expensive, technologies paid for by cuts to structure, if necessary. Another is the day-to-day demand for forces to deploy to Afghanistan, Europe, and elsewhere. That implies a larger force that may not need the most advanced technologies. Finally, difficulties in recruiting and retention, as described earlier, may drive force size regardless of strategy.

The Army continues to note its global engagement: "187,000 soldiers deployed worldwide in 140 countries on six continents."[75] However, neither the Army posture statement nor any budget documents complain about stress. This likely occured because demands in the Middle East have declined substantially from their peak in the 2000s. That was the situation in February 2020. In October, the Army announced a reduction in rotations to combat training centers and in "heel-to-toe deployment rotations" because of "unsustainable operational tempo."[76] What caused this change in attitude toward stress is unclear. Also unclear is the effect it will have on readiness.

---

75 Paul Chamberlain, "Army Fiscal Year 2021 Budget Overview," U.S. Army, February 10, 2020, https://www.asafm.army.mil/Portals/72/Documents/BudgetMaterial/2021/pbr/Overview%20and%20Highlights/Army_FY_2021_Budget_Overview.pdf. The Army posture statement by Secretary Ryan McCarthy and General James McConville has a similar citation.

76 Haley Britzky, "The Army to Cut Down on Rotations to Brigade Level Training Centers to Give Soldiers More Time at Home," Task and Purpose, October 13, 2020, https://taskandpurpose.com/news/army-training-rotations-ausa.

Chart 4: Army Reserve and Army National Guard End Strength

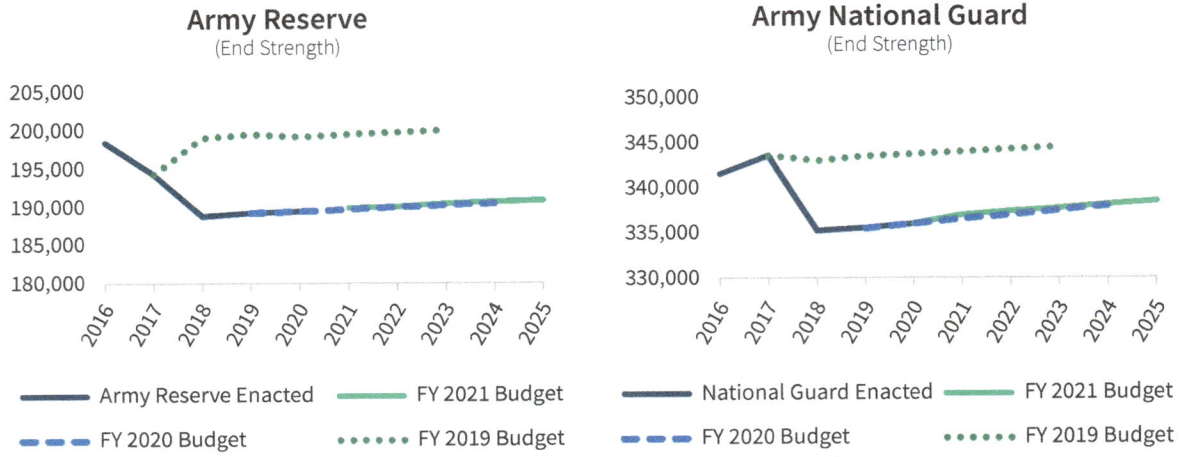

Source: Office of the Undersecretary of Defense (Comptroller), *Defense Budget Overview: Fiscal Year 2019 Budget Request* (Washington, DC: Department of Defense, 2018), 7, https://comptroller.defense.gov/Portals/45/Documents/defbudget/fy2019/FY2019_Budget_Request.pdf; Office of the Undersecretary of Defense (Comptroller), *Defense Budget Overview: Fiscal Year 2020 Budget Request* (Washington, DC: Department of Defense, 2019), 12, https://comptroller.defense.gov/Portals/45/Documents/defbudget/fy2020/fy2020_Budget_Request.pdf; Office of the Undersecretary of Defense (Comptroller), *Defense Budget Overview: Fiscal Year 2021 Budget Request*, 13.

As Chart 4 shows, the Army Reserve had planned to increase to 200,000 and the Army National Guard to 343,000. Instead, both now aim for only small increases to their 2020 end strength.

Rather than increase size, the reserve components have opted to increase readiness. For example, the number of National Guard rotations to Combat Training Centers has continued at four. Nevertheless, both reserve components will suffer from understrength units, as force structure has not declined with the end strength plans.

Readiness is important because the reserve components need to sustain their status as an operational reserve. On average, about 25,000 Army Reserve and Guard personnel are mobilized at any time, mainly supporting operations in Iraq and Afghanistan.[77] With high force demands on the Army continuing, this level of mobilization will likely persist indefinitely.

Balance of Regular and Guard/Reserve Forces

Bottom line up front: the Army as a whole seems to have reached equilibrium at 48 percent regular, 52 percent reserve components, a level attained in FY 2015 and projected to continue through at least FY 2025. Although the active/reserve mix has frequently been a source of tension in the Army, those tensions have eased in recent years as a result of closer consultation arising from a 2016 commission, higher budgets that benefit both components, and the difficulty that both components have in recruiting and retaining additional soldiers.

---

77 "Weekly Reserve Activation Reports," Military Manpower Data Center, [limited distribution, not publicly available].

Nevertheless, given the different cultures, missions, and histories of the two components, the active-reserve mix is a tension that must be managed, not a problem that can be solved.

Tensions between regulars and reservists have existed since the beginning of the United States. This tension is particularly an issue for the Army because it has, by far, the largest reserve component, both in relative and absolute terms. For example, 52 percent of the total Army is in the reserve components, but only 35 percent of the total Air Force, 18 percent of the total Marine Corps, and 15 percent of the total Navy are in reserve components. As Chart 5 shows, Army reserve components (green) are nearly twice the size of all the other reserve components put together (in FY 2021, 525,000 versus 275,000).

As Chart 6 shows, the active/reserve balance has shifted over time. Establishment of the Total Force Policy in 1970, which called for increased reliance on the reserves, the initiation of the Volunteer Force in 1973, which raised the cost of military personnel, and the end of the draft in 1973, which cut off an easy supply of active-duty personnel, caused the ratio to move away from an active-heavy force to parity between the components.

Chart 6: Army Force Mix Ratio 1970–2021

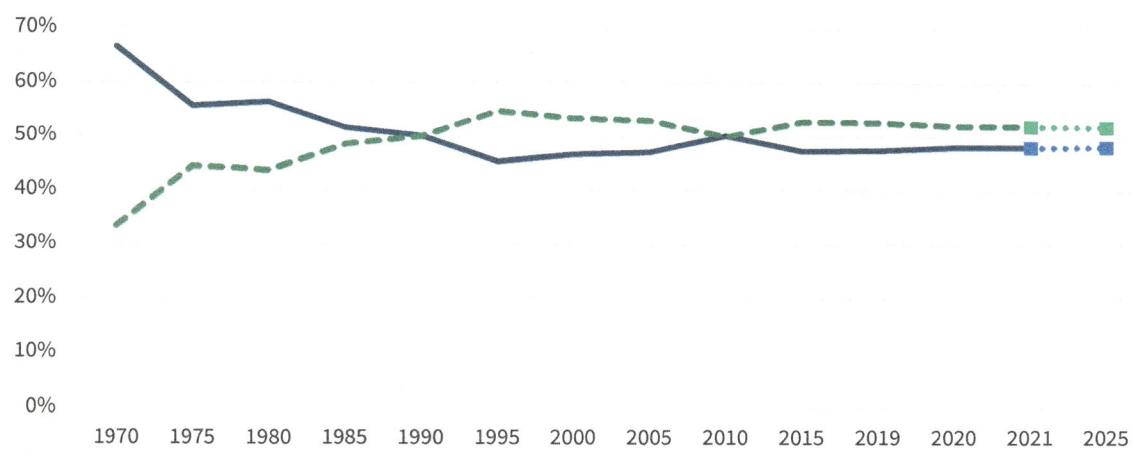

Source: Office of the Under Secretary of Defense (Comptroller), *National Defense Budget Estimates for FY 2021*, Table 7-5, 286-288; and Office of the Under Secretary of Defense (Comptroller), *PB 21 Budget Briefing* (Washington, DC: Department of Defense, Feburary 2020), 13, https://comptroller.defense.gov/Portals/45/Documents/defbudget/fy2021/fy2021_Budget_Request.pdf.

With the end of the Cold War, the ratio changed to a reserve-heavy force as the regular force decreased more rapidly than the reserves.

The ratio reached parity again with expansion of the regular force during the wars in Iraq and Afghanistan but has returned to what appears to be a strategically stable level: 48 percent regular, 52 percent Guard/Reserve. Instead of large growth in either the regular or Guard/Reserve force, the Army, and the Department of Defense in general, has turned to contractors, as discussed in a later section.

Tensions between the components peak during drawdowns, when constrained resources force difficult trade-offs. Thus, there was a crisis in the late-1990s during the post-Cold War drawdown and another in 2014 during the post-Iraq/Afghanistan drawdown. Key to easing recent tensions was the 2016 National Commission on the Future of the Army. The commission looked broadly at all the components and the total Army's needs and published a set of recommendations that all components could accept.[78] The recent budget increases have helped implement the commission's recommendations and eased tensions generally, as the Army does not need to make trade-offs between the components.

However, a budget downturn might bring these tensions to the surface again. Further, a national defense strategy that requires rapid reaction—as the NDS comes close to doing—would also increase tension by moving capabilities from the reserve components to the active components.

The reserves, particularly the National Guard, are politically powerful because of their connection to home-state political establishments. If they feel slighted, they can—and often do—bypass the Army hierarchy and take their concerns directly to Congress.

The Future Structure of the Army: New Kinds of Units

Consistent with the NDS, Army statements focus on great power conflict and moving beyond the regional conflicts of the last 20 years. However, these Army statements place relatively more emphasis on Russia, identifying it as the principal near-term threat, with China as a longer-term threat.[79] That is not surprising since the Western Pacific theater consists mainly of ocean and long distances. The European theater would have greatest need for ground forces with advanced weapons. The Army is not ignoring the Pacific. It is working to develop capabilities that would be applicable there, such as long-range anti-ship missiles. Further, a conflict in Korea would require large U.S. ground forces.

This high-end conflict implies a force, perhaps a smaller force, that has advanced systems for ground combat, fires, and aviation. It also implies a force that has different kinds of capabilities such as cyber, electronic warfare, anti-ship/sea control fires, cruise and ballistic missile defense, and very long-range precision fires. *Creating this force in an environment of constrained end strength will require cutting some existing capabilities, such as BCTs, a step the Army has not yet been willing to take.*

A few new kinds of units are taking shape.

Cyber: Cyber expansion seems to be complete since it has mostly disappeared from Army statements. The Army created cyber units quickly to get this new capability into the field and experiment with it, though there was criticism that the Army did not have enough personnel with the right skills. Although cyber receives a lot of attention, the Army component numbers only several hundred personnel.[80] Longer-term, the Army intends to build integrated intelligence/cyber-electronic warfare units as part of the multidomain forces.

---

78   National Commission on the Future of the Army, *Report to the President and Congress of the United States* (Washington, DC: January 2016), https://fas.org/man/eprint/ncfa.pdf.

79   For example, see "Army FY 2021 Posture Statement" and Chamberlain, "Army Fiscal Year 2021 Budget Overview."

80   Sydney Freedberg, "Army Struggles To Man New Cyber/EW Units: GAO," Breaking Defense, August 16, 2019, https://breakingdefense.com/2019/08/army-struggles-to-man-new-cyber-ew-units-gao/.

Air and missile-defense: These units will be the first new kinds of combat units fielded. The Indirect Fire Protection Capability, designed to defend fixed points against cruise missiles and UAVs, will be fielded in FY 2022. The Maneuver-Short Range Air Defense is being procured now and will be fielded in FY 2023.

Multidomain units: These remain conceptual, although the Army has published concepts and conducted experiments using artillery brigades as the base unit. Multidomain units would integrate space, cyber, air, ground, and maritime "to execute simultaneous and sequential operations using surprise and the rapid and continuous integration of capabilities across all domains to present multiple dilemmas to an adversary."[81] The Army's overall concept is called AimPoint, and the current thinking is that the major changes will occur at higher echelons, division and above.[82]

Pre-positioned equipment: The Army is building an additional set in Europe, thus increasing its rapid reinforcement capability. Extra funding from the European Deterrence Initiative has been key in building/rebuilding pre-positioned unit sets. The Army is examining additional pre-positioning in the Pacific.[83]

The Future Structure of the Army: New Capabilities

Looked at broadly, Army modernization is a "good news, good news, bad news" story: the good news is that the Army continues production of proven systems and has a well-modernized force as a result. More good news is that a few new systems are coming out of the RDT&E "primordial soup." The bad news is that the Army is still several years away from having a new generation of systems in production to take it into the 2020s and beyond and set it up for potential combat against great power adversaries.

MODERNIZING THE CURRENT FORCE

In the near term, the Army is sensibly plugging its most serious capability gaps by upgrading the major systems it has and producing these systems at relatively high rates. As CSIS acquisition experts Andrew Hunter and Rhys McCormick point out, focusing on capabilities through upgrades rather than developing major new systems avoids the technical, budgetary, and political risk of relying on a few costly, high-profile programs.[84]

Thus, the Army FY 2021 budget funds the latest versions of existing systems. These programs run smoothly, produce equipment at known costs and on predictable schedules, and avoid acquisition scandals that in the past embarrassed the Army in front of Congress and the public.

---

81 "Multi-Domain Operations," U.S. Army Training and Doctrine Command, October 4, 2018, https://www.army.mil/standto/2018-10-04.

82 Devon Suits, "Futures and Concepts the Center Evaluates the Future for Structures," Army New Service, April 22, 2020, https://www.army.mil/article/234845/futures_and_concepts_center_evaluates_new_force_structure; and Andrew Feickert, "The Army's AimPoint Force Structure Initiative," Congressional Research Service, May 8, 2020, https://fas.org/sgp/crs/natsec/IF11542.pdf.

83 Sydney Freedberg, Jr., "Army Adding New Arms Stockpile in Europe: Gen. Perna," Breaking Defense, February 4, 2020, https://breakingdefense.com/2020/02/army-adding-new-arms-stockpile-in-europe-gen-perna/.

84 Rhys McCormick and Andrew Hunter, "The U.S. Army's Next Big 5 Must Be Capabilities, Not New Platforms," Defense One, July 25, 2017, https://www.defenseone.com/ideas/2017/07/us-armys-next-big-5-must-be-capabilities-not-new-platforms/139714/?oref=d-river.

Table 4: Major Army Procurement in FY 2021

System	First fielded	Current version	Procurement proposed for FY 2021
Abrams tank M-1	1981	M1A2 SEP V2	89
Bradley Fighting Vehicle M-2/3	1981	M2A4	73
Stryker fighting vehicle	2003	Double V-Hull, 30mm gun	154
Paladin self-propelled howitzer M-109	1963	M109 PIM (A7)	30
Blackhawk UH-60	1978	M model	36
AH-64 Apache	1987	E model	52
CH-47 Chinook	1962	F-model	7

Source: Department of the Army, *Army FY 2021 Budget Overview*, 16.

Two relatively new programs are also in production: the Joint Light Tactical Vehicle, an armored light truck and replacement for the up-armored HMMWVs, and the Armored Multipurpose Vehicle, a replacement for the M113 armored personnel carrier.

The effect of this approach, combined with the large wartime procurements and rebuilds/upgrades funded by Overseas Contingency Operations (OCO) reset during the 2000s, is that the Army's force structure is filled with relatively new equipment. For example, the Apache fleet averages 8 years and the Chinook fleet 10 years.[85] Gone are prewar concerns about aging equipment fleets.

Finally, the Army's FY 2021 budget, like the other services, continues robust funding for munitions, for example, the Guided MLRS rocket, the Hellfire antitank missile, and Patriot missiles (MSE). This reflects preparation for the intense combat that conflict with a great power would entail.

CREATING NEW CAPABILITIES
A long-standing concern about Army modernization is that there are few new systems coming online to replace the existing generation. This was the result of a "triple whammy": a missed procurement cycle due to program failures, a focus on near-term systems for wartime operations, and modernization funding reductions in the postwar drawdown.[86]

The Army has divided its development effort into six major priorities (sometimes known as "the big six"): Long Range Precision Fires (artillery), Next Generation Combat Vehicle (armor), Future Vertical Lift (aviation), Army Network, Air and Missile Defense, and Soldier Lethality (infantry). The Army has added two more capability areas—Assured Positioning, Navigation, and Timing and Synthetic Training Environment—so the modernization effort is now "6+2."

---

85 Congressional Budget Office, *Cost of Replacing Today's Army Aviation Fleet* (Washington, DC: May 2019), Table A-1, https://www.cbo.gov/system/files/2019-05/55180-ArmyAviation.pdf.

86 Rhys McCormick, "The Army Modernization Challenge: A Historical Perspective," CSIS, March 31, 2016, http://fysa.csis.org/2016/03/31/the-army-modernization-challenge-a-historical-perspective. For description of Army acquisition failures, see John M. McHugh, *Army Strong: Equipped, Trained, and Ready, Final Report of the 2010 Army Acquisition Review* (Washington, DC: Department of the Army, January 2011), http://www.rdecom.army.mil/EDCG%20Telecoms/Final%20Report_Army%20Acq%20Review.pdf.

Chart 7 shows funding for the modernization priorities. Most funding is still in R&D, with only air and missile defense and soldier lethality showing significant procurement. Changes from FY 2020 to FY 2021 are modest, except for increases in air and missile defense and soldier lethality to cover procurement.

Chart 7: Funding for Army Modernization Priorities

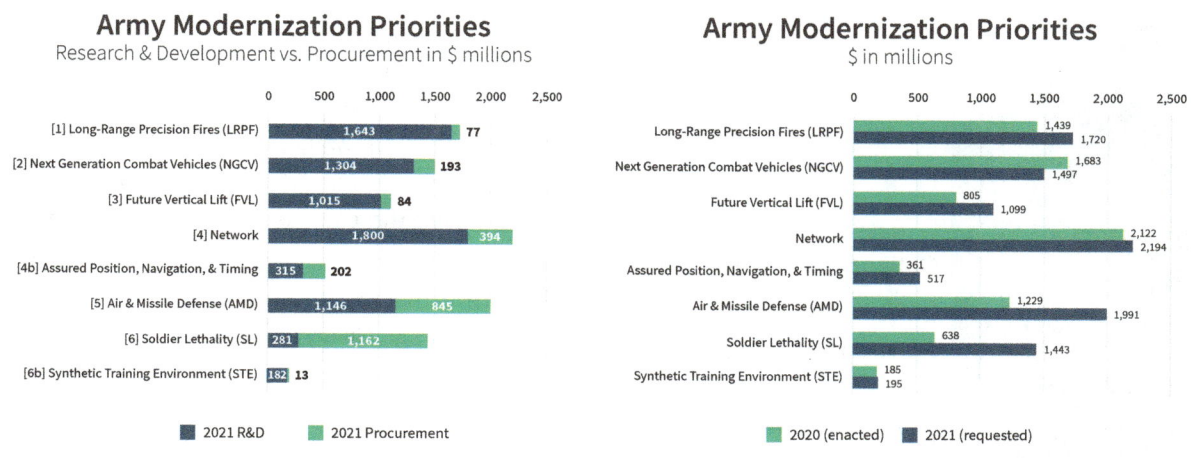

Source: Sydney Freedberg, "Army Boosts Big Six 26% but Trims Bradley Replacement," Breaking Defense, February 10, 2020, https://breakingdefense.com/2020/02/army-boosts-big-six-26-but-not-bradley-replacement/ reprinted with permission. Used with permission from Breaking Defense.

The Army points to 31 systems in development (the RDT&E "primordial soup"), far more than it can afford to procure and field. The Army's chief resource manager warned, "[a]s those 31 signature systems come to maturation and it's time to put things through a production line, that's where we're going to be making some difficult choices."[87]

Shown below are major initiatives in development. The list gives a sense of systems that might enter the force in the future.[88]

---

87   Sydney Freedberg, "Army Needs a Bigger Budget to Build Big Six: Lieut. Gen. Horlander," Breaking Defense, February 18, 2020, https://breakingdefense.com/2020/02/army-needs-bigger-army-budget-to-build-big-6-lt-gen-horlander/. Others have made the same point. Sydney Freedberg, "Shyu to Army: 'You Can't Have It All' with 31 Modernization Priorities," Breaking Defense, December 11, 2019, https://breakingdefense.com/2019/12/shyu-to-army-you-cant-have-it-all-with-31-modernization-priorities/; and Sydney Freedberg, "Army Study Asks: How Much Modernization Can We Afford?," Breaking Defense, June 9, 2020, https://breakingdefense.com/2020/06/army-study-asks-how-much-modernization-can-we-afford/.

88   List comes from Andrew Feickert and Brendan W. McGarry, *Army's Modernization Strategy: Congressional Oversight Considerations*, CRS Report No. R46216 (Washington, DC: Congressional Research Service, February 2020), https://fas.org/sgp/crs/natsec/R46216.pdf.

Table 5: Army Development Priorities

Long Range Precision Fires	Strategic Long-Range Cannon Precision Strike Missile Extended Range Cannon Artillery (ERCA)	Because of the NDS emphasis on long-range precision strike, these programs have received high priority. Several will enter procurement soon. However, they may engender a roles and missions debate with the Air Force because of their range. The fortunes of the artillery have turned around substantially in the last decade. During the stabilization conflicts of the 2000s, artillery was considered a "dead branch walking" because there was less need for firepower.
Next Generation Combat Vehicle	Optionally Manned Fighting Vehicle Robotic Combat Vehicle: 3 variants Armored Multi-Purpose Vehicle (AMPV) Mobile Protected Firepower Decisive Lethality Platform	AMPV is in production. The other programs are further in the future. The ground combat vehicles will likely face some challenges because of their high cost and appearance of being legacy capabilities.
Future Vertical Lift	Future Attack Reconnaissance Aircraft Future Attack Unmanned System Future Long-Range Assault Aircraft	These are major, longer-term programs that will go into production in the late-FY 2020s.
Air and Missile Defense	Maneuver Short-Range Air defense (M-SHORAD) Indirect Fire Protection Capability (IFPC)	Air defense has received a lot of attention recently because of its applicability to great power conflicts. IFPC and M-SHORAD are in production now. Near-term capabilities will use missiles; longer-term capabilities may use directed energy.
Soldier Lethality	Next Generation Squad Weapons – Automatic Rifle Next Generation Squad Weapons – Rifle	The Army is fielding many small improvements in this area. New weapons may use a 6.8mm round (as opposed to the current 5.56 mm) but are still in the testing phase.

3

Navy

Unlike the other services, the Navy has sought to significantly expand its force structure. However, its previous plan to reach 355 ships collapsed because of high costs and the need to incorporate new technologies such as unmanned systems. A new plan incorporates smaller ships and large numbers of unmanned systems.

KEY TAKEAWAYS

- In FY 2021, Navy active-duty personnel would increase by 5,300 to 347,800. Fleet size increases to 306 ships as previously ordered ships arrive, particularly the numerous littoral combat ships (LCS). The Navy continues to plan on significant expansion.

- The 355-ship goal was deemed infeasible because of its high cost. The structure was also criticized for focusing on large and expensive ships, particularly aircraft carriers, and not incorporating unmanned surface and undersea vessels/vehicles.

- When the Navy could not come up with a feasible new plan, Secretary of Defense Esper took over.

- On October 7, Secretary Esper outlined a "500+ ship" future fleet described as "an ever-present, resilient, and dominant fighting force."

- Carriers and large surface combatants (LSCs) may be cut to pay for the unmanned vessels, additional submarines and small surface combatants, and a new class of small amphibious ships. However, many details remain unavailable, and to be real, the plan needs to be incorporated into the president's FY 2022 budget proposal.

- The Navy and the secretary of defense seem to have different interpretations about the future fleet, as has been the case for many years.

- Affordability will be a challenge. The new fleet structure costs about the same as the 355-ship fleet. Esper wants the Navy to find the resources internally and may provide some resources from savings across the Department of Defense (DOD).
- Naval aviation, in contrast to the surface and subsurface fleets, remains focused on manned platforms.
- Ship numbers matter to the Navy because of the high demands for its forces in day-to-day operations for crisis response, allied and partner engagement, and ongoing regional conflicts.

End Strength in FY 2021

Table 1: Navy End Strength – Active, Reserve, and Civilians

	Active Navy	Navy Reserve	Civilian
	End Strength	End Strength	Full-Time Equivalents
FY 2019 Enacted	337,000	59,700	195,000
FY 2020 Enacted	342,500 (340,500 authorized)	60,200 (59,000 authorized)	196,300
FY 2021 Request	347,800	58,800	198,000
Change from FY 2020	+5,300	-1,400	+1,700

Source: Department of the Navy, *Highlights of The Department of the Navy FY 2021 Budget* (Washington, DC: Department of Defense, 2020), Active End Strength data in Figure 2.1, Reserve End Strength data in Figure 2.3, Civilian data in Figure 2.10, includes direct and indirect hires but excludes Marine Corps, https://www.secnav.navy.mil/fmc/fmb/Documents/21pres/Highlights_book.pdf.

The Navy had a good year for recruiting and retention, so its actual active-duty end strength was higher than what had been authorized. (Congress allows the services some leeway.)

Chart 1: Navy Active-Duty Personnel, 1999–2021

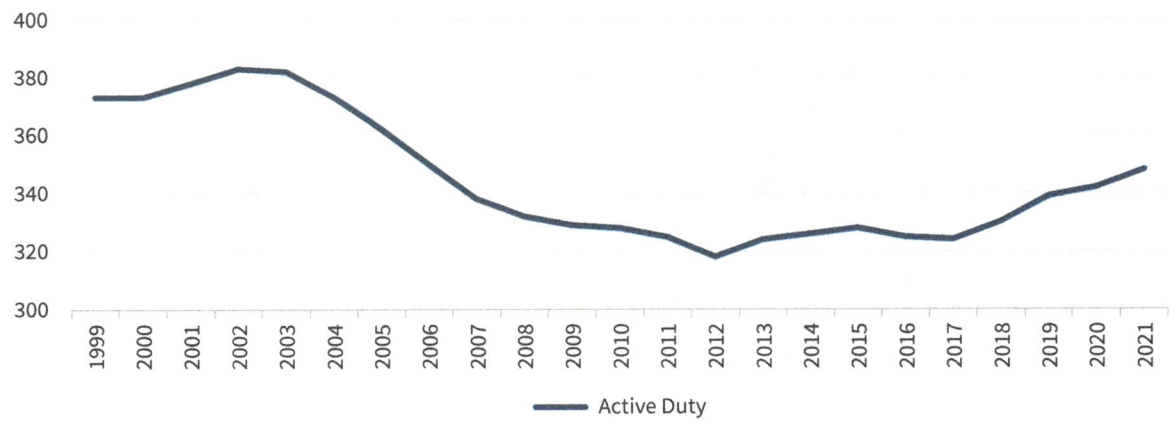

Source: Office of the Under Secretary of Defense (Comptroller), *National Defense Budget Estimates for FY 2021* (Washington, DC: Department of Defense, April 2020), Table 7-5: Department of Defense Manpower, p. 260–262, https://comptroller.defense.gov/Portals/45/Documents/defbudget/fy2021/FY21_Green_Book.pdf; and Office of the Under Secretary of Defense (Comptroller), *PB 21 Budget Roll Out Brief* (Washington, DC: Department of Defense, February 2020), 13, https://www.secnav.navy.mil/fmc/fmb/Documents/21pres/DON_Press_Brief.pdf.

Navy personnel levels have been on a roller coaster, reaching a high of 383,000 in FY 2002 and a low of 318,000 in FY 2012. The number has crept back up, but the Navy is still far below its pre-9/11 size. However, the number of sailors tracks roughly to the number of ships in the fleet (see Chart 2).

Chart 2: Navy Active-Duty Personnel Projections

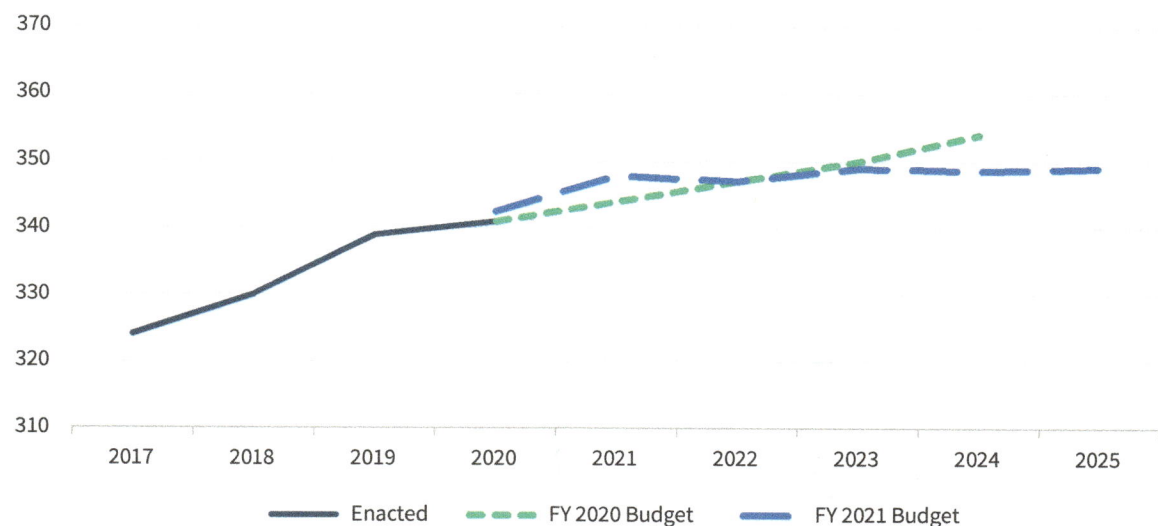

Source: Office of the Under Secretary of Defense (Comptroller), National Defense Budget Estimates for FY 2021 (Washington, DC: Department of Defense, April 2020), Table 7-5: Department of Defense Manpower, p. 260-262, https://comptroller.defense.gov/Portals/45/Documents/defbudget/fy2021/FY21_Green_Book.pdf.

The Navy projects that active-duty end strength will continue to grow, reaching 349,100 by FY 2025. However, unlike its projection last year and for several past years, this projection levels off.

This does not look like a personnel plan for 355 ships or 500+ ships. Indeed, just last year, the Navy said it was 6,200 sailors short in the fleet.[89] Instead, this projection looks like a placeholder designed to save money until a long-term fleet plan is put in place.

---

89   Sam LaGrone, "Fleet Forces: Navy Short 6200 at Sea Sailors Now to Meet New Manning Requirements," USNI News, February 26, 2019, https://news.usni.org/2019/02/26/fleet-forces-navy-short-6200-at-sea-sailors-now-to-meet-new-manning-requirements.

Chart 3: Personnel in Navy Reserve, 1999–2020

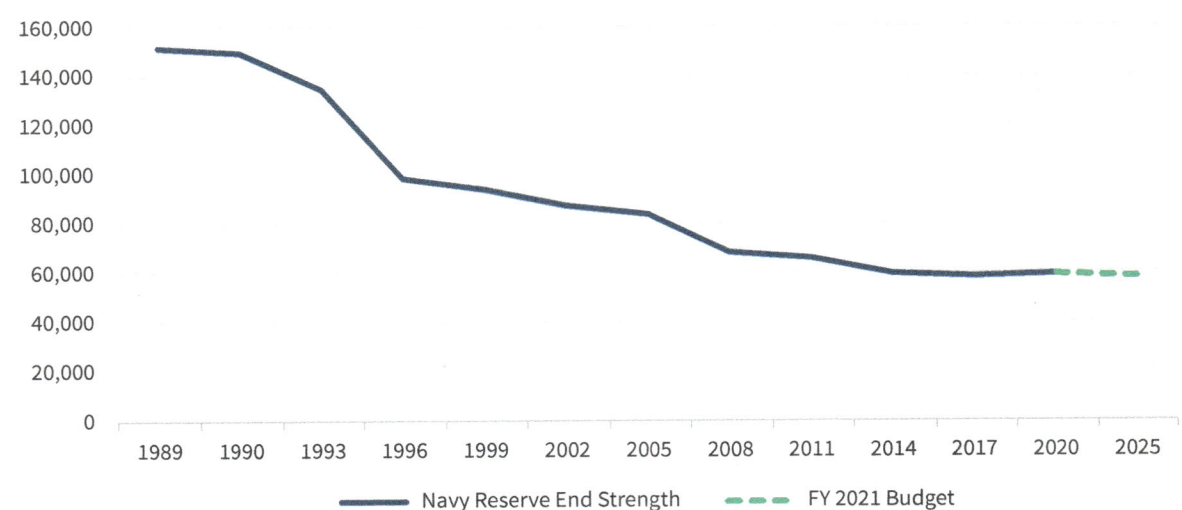

Source: Office of the Under Secretary of Defense (Comptroller), National Defense Budget Estimates for FY 2021 (Washington, DC: Department of Defense, April 2020), Table 7-5: Department of Defense Manpower, p. 260-262, https://comptroller.defense.gov/Portals/45/Documents/defbudget/fy2021/FY21_Green_Book.pdf.

> **[The Navy's personnel] this projection looks like a placeholder designed to save money until a long-term fleet plan is put in place.**

The Navy reserve has been in a long-term decline, unlike other reserve components. Although its end strength has been roughly stable since 2014, by FY 2025 the Navy Reserve will shrink a bit further to 58,000. This long-term decline results from the retirement of all Navy Reserve ships and many Navy Reserve aircraft, so the remaining forces are mainly logistics, support, and staff augmentation. While these have an important role, that role is much narrower than in the reserve components of other services.

The number of civilians increases by 1,700. The Navy, like DOD in general, emphasizes that most civilians work outside Washington and are a critical element of readiness because of the work they do on facilities and maintenance.

Chart 4: Civilian Manpower Work Areas, FY 2021

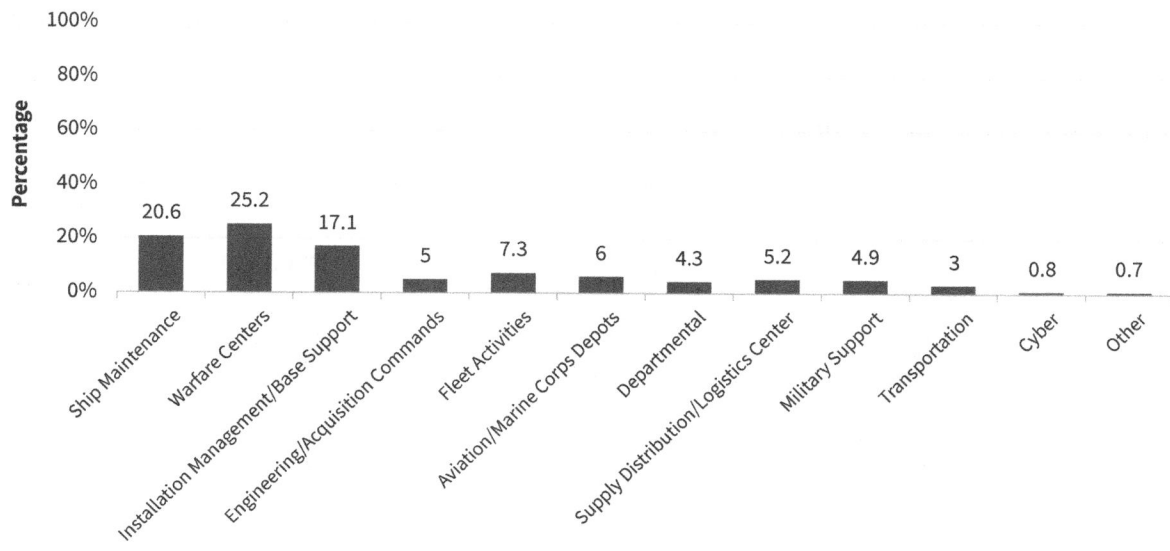

Source: Department of the Navy, *Navy Budget Highlights for FY 2021*.

Fleet Size in FY 2021 and Beyond

Chart 5: Total Navy Active Ships, 1999–2020

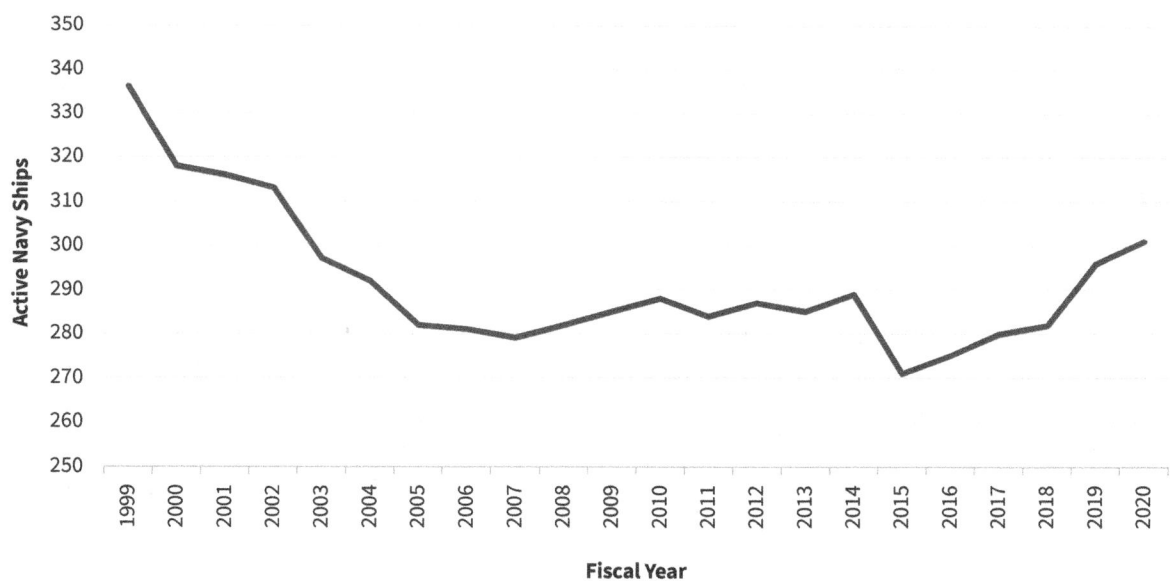

Note: The sharp dip in ship count from 2014 to 2015 was due to the retirement of the last FFG-7 Oliver Hazard Perry-class frigates and to the Navy changing its counting rules briefly in 2014 to include, and then exclude in 2015, patrol coastal craft and hospital ships. Sydney J. Freedberg, Jr., "Outrage On Capitol Hill As Navy Changes Ship-Counting Rules," Breaking Defense, March 11, 2014, https://breakingdefense.com/2014/03/outrage-on-capitol-hill-as-navy-changes-ship-counting-rules/.

Source: Ship count 1999–2016 data from "U.S. Ship Force Levels: 1886 to Present," Naval History and Heritage Command, https://www.history.navy.mil/research/histories/ship-histories/us-ship-force-levels.html#2000. Current and projected ship count from Department of the Navy, *FY 2021 President's Budget*, 5, 15.

After years of shrinkage, the fleet is growing as new ships are delivered, particularly the numerous littoral combat ships (LCSs) and DDG-51 destroyers. (Rightly or wrongly, the ship count is often used as a measure of Navy capacity.[90]) The Navy hit 297 ships by the end of FY 2020 and will reach 306 ships at the end of FY 2021, up from its low point of 271 in 2015.

Chart 6: Ship Count and Tonnage of Navy Battle Force, 1988, 1996, 2019

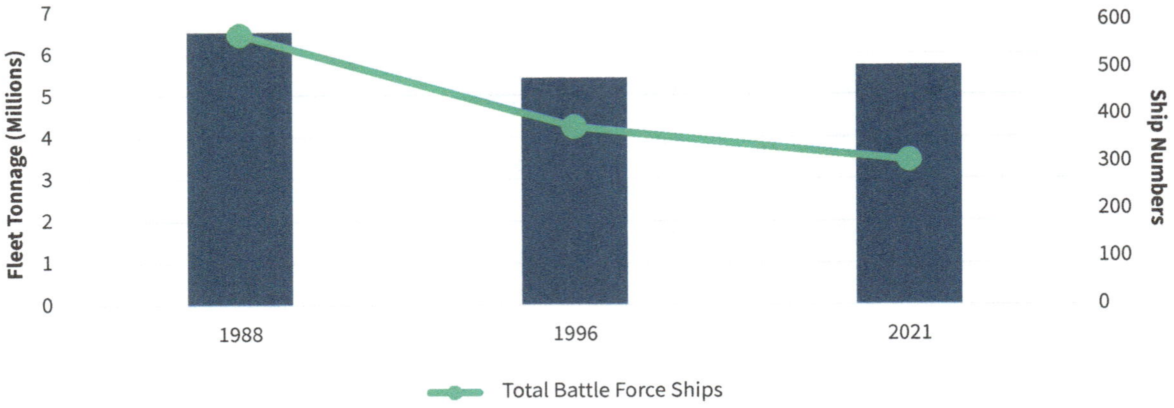

Source: Ship numbers, see previous chart; tonnage from Richard Sharpe, *Jane's Fighting Ships 1988* (New York: Jane's Pub., 1988); Sharpe, *Jane's Fighting Ships 1996* (New York: Jane's Pub., 1996); Stephen Saunders, *Jane's Fighting Ships 2019-2020* (New York: Jane's Pub, 2019); and "U.S. Navy Ships," U.S. Navy, https://www.navy.mil/navydata/our_ships.asp.

After years of shrinkage, the fleet is growing as new ships are delivered, particularly the numerous littoral combat ships (LCSs) and DDG-51 destroyers.

In part, the decline in ship numbers resulted from Navy decisions to buy bigger, and more expensive, ships. As the chart on tonnage shows, today's fleet has 54 percent of the number of ships of 1988 (303 versus 565) but 87 percent of the tonnage. Today's DDG-51 destroyer (Flight IIA) displaces 9,700 tons, twice the tonnage of a 1980s Charles F. Adams-class destroyer and four times the tonnage of a World War II Fletcher-class destroyer (2,500 tons). Indeed, the DDG-51 has the tonnage of a World War II cruiser. The increased size produces greater capability, but ships can only be in one place at a time.

---

90 Admiral James Winnefeld, for one, argues that focus on ship count distorts decisionmaking: James Winnefeld, "Charting a New Course for the U.S. Navy," *Boston Globe*, November 8, 2015, https://www.bostonglobe.com/opinion/2015/11/08/charting-new-course-for-navy/rJeaDKEDlZiXkpKEXIAFlN/story.html.

The Unrelenting Demands of Current Operations

Chart 7: Navy Fleet Size and Deployment Levels

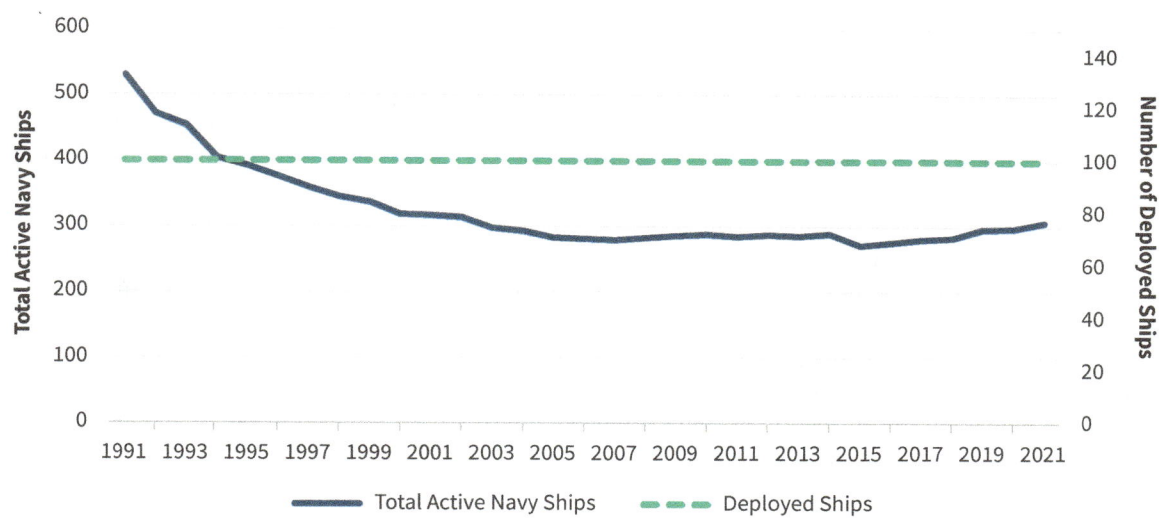

Source: Ship count from Chart 5; deployment levels from Department of the Navy, *FY 2021 President's Budget*, 5.

The average number of ships deployed has remained at the current level of about 100 for three decades, even though the number of ships has declined over time. The need to deploy to Europe, a theater largely ignored since the end of the Cold War, adds to demands. The CENTCOM commander still wants carriers and naval presence.[91] To better cover the Atlantic, the Navy reactivated the Second Fleet headquarters in Norfolk.

The Navy reports that it can fulfill only about half of the theater commanders' requests for Navy ships.[92] Because these theater requests are not resource constrained, it is unsurprising that the requests greatly exceed what is available.

This shortfall engenders a concern that the Navy is too small for the tasks that it is being asked to perform, hence the drive to expand.

On the other hand, the *National Defense Strategy* (NDS) calls for a focus on great power conflict, specifies the need for high-end capabilities, downplays the need for force expansion, and states an intention to reduce day-to-day demands.

---

91 John Grady, "CENTCOM Commander: Middle East Aircraft Carrier Presents Key to Deterring Iran," USNI News, March 11, 2020, https://news.usni.org/2020/03/11/centcom-commander-middle-east-aircraft-carrier-presence-key-to-deterring-iran.

92 John M. Richardson, "Statement of Admiral John M. Richardson," Testimony before the House Committee on Appropriations, Subcommittee on Defense, Hearing on the United States Navy and Marine Corps, 115th Cong., 2nd sess., January 18, 2018, https://docs.house.gov/meetings/AS/AS03/20180118/106784/HHRG-115-AS03-Wstate-RichardsonJ-20180118.pdf.

The Collapse of the 355-Ship Fleet Goal

After candidate Trump, who had called for a 350-ship Navy, won the 2016 election, the Navy did a quick force structure assessment and came up with a new goal of 355 ships.

Compared with the 2014 goal of 308 ships, the Navy's 355-ship goal added numbers in several categories but especially submarines (+18) and large surface combatants (LSCs) (+16). It focused on existing and proven ship types and included none of the nontraditional ships contained in many more recent alternative force structure proposals. The intention was to get ships built quickly, without the delay and risk of development programs.

Both the president and Congress endorsed the Navy's 355-ship goal ("It shall be the policy of the United States to have available, as soon as practicable, not fewer than 355 battle force ships").[93]

However, the 355-ship goal collapsed because of strategy and money. The strategic problem was that it did not explicitly include unmanned systems, which were attracting a lot of attention, and by focusing on large and expensive ships, it did not seem consistent with a developing strategy of dispersed operations for combat in the Western Pacific.

The other problem was that the goal was just too expensive. The Navy's FY 2020 30-year shipbuilding plan calculated spending at $20.3 billion per year through FY 2024 and $26 billion to $28 billion beyond FY 2024, but the Congressional Budget Office (CBO) calculated a cost of $31 billion per year.[94] That was "50 percent larger than the Navy's average funding for shipbuilding over the past five years."[95] The Congressional Research Service came to similar conclusions.[96]

The Navy considered closing this gap between its fleet goal and its resources by extending the life of existing ships by 5 to 19 years.[97] Keeping the hull, mechanical, and engineering systems going this long was possible, given appropriate maintenance. In the past, however, the Navy has retired ships early to free funds for new construction and because of concerns that the combat systems were becoming obsolete. Further, even with service-life extensions, the Navy still needed more money.

Through the fall of 2019 and into the early winter of 2020, the Navy tried but failed to come up with a viable FY 2021 30-year shipbuilding plan. There were too many constraints:[98]

---

93   U.S. Congress, House, *National Defense Authorization Act for Fiscal Year 2018*, HR 2810, 115th Cong., 1st sess., December 12, 2017, Section 1025, https://www.congress.gov/bill/115th-congress/house-bill/2810/text.

94   For Navy costs, see Chief of Naval Operations, *Report to Congress on the Annual Long-Range Plan for Construction of Naval Vessels for Fiscal Year 2020* (Washington, DC: DOD, March 2019), https://www.navy.mil/strategic/PB20_Shipbuilding_Plan.pdf.

95   For CBO costs, see: Eric Labs, *An Analysis of the Navy's Fiscal Year 2020 Shipbuilding Plan* (Washington DC: Congressional Budget Office, October 2019), 3, https://www.cbo.gov/system/files/2019-10/55685-CBO-Navys-FY20-shipbuilding-plan.pdf. Because the Navy did not publish a 30-year shipbuilding plan for the FY 2021 budget, CBO's analysis of the FY 2020 shipbuilding plan is the most recent.

96   Ronald O'Rourke, *Navy Force Structure and Shipbuilding Plans: Background and Issues for Congress*, CRS Report No. RL32665 (Washington, DC: Congressional Research Service, July 2019), https://fas.org/sgp/crs/weapons/RL32665.pdf.

97   Sydney Freedberg, "Keep Ships Longer To Boost Fleet Size: 355 Ships By 2035," Breaking Defense, June 20, 2018, https://breakingdefense.com/2018/06/keep-ships-longer-to-boost-fleet-size-355-ships-by-2035/.

98   For a complete discussion, see Mark Cancian and Adam Saxton, "The Spectacular and Public Collapse of Navy Force Planning," Breaking Defense, January 28, 2020, https://breakingdefense.com/2020/01/the-spectacular-public-collapse-of-navy-force-planning/.

- The Navy suggested getting more money, but the other services pushed back immediately;
- The Navy raised the possibility of changing the way ships are counted, by including in the count unmanned and different kinds of ships, but Congress has always been suspicious, seeing this as a way of cutting the Navy while keeping the appearance of size;
- The Navy proposed changing the 355-ship goal, but that was inflexible having been endorsed by the president and fixed in statute; and
- The Navy proposed finding savings elsewhere in its budget and then shifting these funds to shipbuilding but found this difficult.

With the Navy unable to find a feasible solution, Secretary Esper, in a bureaucratic slap at the Navy, took over development of the Navy's force structure plan.

The Esper Force Structure Assessment

Although DOD had announced its intention to release the plan "in the summer," DOD repeatedly delayed publication, greatly annoying Congress.[99] Finally, on October 7, Secretary Esper presented the outlines of a future fleet. This future fleet, which he called "Battle Force 2045," described the major elements but lacked detail. There was no written product to back up his oral presentation.[100]

> **With the Navy unable to find a feasible solution, Secretary Esper, in a bureaucratic slap at the Navy, took over development of the Navy's force structure plan.**

In developing this future fleet, Esper took inputs from the Navy, the Office of Cost Assessment and Program Evaluation, and a study by the Hudson Institute.[101]

Esper described this as a 500+ ship fleet, including both manned and unmanned vessels/vehicles.[102] He indicated that it would "reach 355 traditional battle force ships prior to 2035."

---

99 Paul McLeary, "EXLUSIVE SecDef Esper Seeks Detente with HASC; New Navy Plan This Summer," Breaking Defense, February 28, 2020, https://breakingdefense.com/2020/02/exclusive-secdef-esper-seeks-detente-with-hasc-new-navy-plan-this-summer/.

100 "Defense Secretary Discusses National Defense Strategy," (event, CSBA, Washington, DC, October 6, 2020), https://www.defense.gov/Watch/Video/videoid/768646/.

101 Brian Clark, Timothy Walton, and Seth Cropsey, *American Seapower at a Crossroads: A Plan to Restore the US Navy's Maritime Advantage* (Washington, DC: Hudson Institute, September 29, 2020), https://www.hudson.org/research/16406-american-sea-power-at-a-crossroads-a-plan-to-restore-the-us-navy-s-maritime-advantage.

102 The Navy and DOD are inconsistent in labeling these as unmanned systems as "vessels" or "vehicles." Generally, unmanned surface ships are described as vessels and unmanned undersea systems are described as vehicles. This report follows this practice, using unmanned surface vessels and unmanned undersea vehicles.

Although Esper did not give a cost, he acknowledged the need for additional resources, calling for shipbuilding funds to rise to the level of the Reagan buildup. He stated that these funds would not come from other services but from the Navy internally and savings from DOD overhead.[103]

CSIS calculated an annual shipbuilding cost of $28.5 billion for this future plan (a total shipbuilding appropriation of about $30.6 billion when other costs, such as small craft and outfitting, are included). Near-term costs would likely be higher to build up to the numbers specified. This was about the level of CBO's analysis of the 355-ship Navy.[104] Savings from procurement of smaller and less expensive ships were offset by larger numbers.

It is important to keep in mind that changes of this magnitude will take decades to implement. The fleet will have mixed ship varieties for many years. Further, this is only a concept. It needs to get into the FY 2022 budget and associated five-year plan with specific numbers for ships and costs. Although the White House is likely to support the plan, that support needs to be manifest in the president's next budget proposal.

The table below was pieced together from his comments and previous news reports. The following section, "The Fleet in FY 2021 and Beyond," contains a detailed description of each ship type and what the Esper proposal would do.[105]

---

103 Paul McLeary, "Navy scours budget to build more ships; SECNAV looks to WWII carriers as model for future," Breaking Defense, October 8, 2020, https://breakingdefense.com/2020/10/navy-scours-budget-to-build-more-ships-secnav-looks-to-wwii-carriers-as-model-for-future/.

104 Congressional Budget Office, *Analysis of the Navy's Fiscal Year 2020 Shipbuilding Plan* (Washington, DC: October 2019), https://www.cbo.gov/system/files/2019-10/55685-CBO-Navys-FY20-shipbuilding-plan.pdf.

105 For a detailed description of Esper's future fleet, see Mark Cancian and Adam Saxton, "Sec. Esper Previews the Future Fleet," CSIS, *Critical Questions*, October 8, 2020, https://www.csis.org/analysis/secretary-esper-previews-future-navy.

Table 2: Future Fleet Structures

Ship Type	Current Fleet	355-Ship Goal	Esper Statement
Aircraft Carriers (CVNs)	11	12	8–11
"Light Carriers"	-	-	6
Attack Submarines (SSNs)	50	66	70–80
Cruise Missile Submarines (SSGNs)	4	-	-
Large Unmanned Undersea Vehicles	-	-	140–240
Large and Medium Unmanned Surface Vessels	-	-	140–240
Large Surface Combatants (CGs/DDGs)	92	104	Unstated, but likely 80–90
Small Surface Combatants (FFs/LCSs/mine warfare)	30	52	60–70
Amphibious Ships	33	38	50–60
Combat Logistics Force	29	32	
Expeditionary Fast Transports and Support Base Ships	34	16	70–90
Command and Support Ships		23	
Ballistic Missile Submarines (SSBN)	14	12	12
Total	297	355	500+

Source: For current fleet size, see Department of the Navy, *Highlights of the Department of the Navy FY 2021 Budget* (Washington, DC: Department of Defense, February 10, 2020) Figure 3.2; for the 355 ship goal, see, EXECUTIVE SUMMARY 2016 Navy Force Structure Assessment (FSA) (Washington, DC: Department of Defense, December 14, 2016), https://news.usni.org/wp-content/uploads/2016/12/FSA_Executive-Summary.pdf.

The Fleet in FY 2021 and Beyond

To understand the future fleet, the place to start is the FY 2021 budget proposal. The president's budget proposed to construct only seven ships in FY 2021: one Columbia-class submarine, one SSN-774 submarine, two DDG-51 destroyers, one FFG(X) frigate, one large amphibious assault ship, and one auxiliary. Congress might add ships in its final bills as it customarily does, another submarine being the most likely addition, but the number of ships funded in FY 2021 will be unusually low compared with recent shipbuilding budgets.

The reason for the low number is that the Navy shipbuilding account declines from $24 billion in FY 2020 to $19.9 billion in FY 2021. One reason for this decline is that the Navy lost money at the last minute of budget preparation as resources shifted from DOD to the Department of Energy's National Nuclear Security Administration for nuclear weapons infrastructure.

The number of ships funded in FY 2021 will be unusually low compared with recent shipbuilding budgets.

Shipbuilding projections in the five-year plan, the Future Year Defense Program (FYDP), average 8.4 new ships per year, down from 11 per year in the FY 2020 projection.

Table 3: Implied Fleet Size for Shipbuilding Rate and Service Life

Ship construction/year	Average life of 30 years	Average life of 35 years	Average life of 40 years
7 (FY 2021 rate)	210	245	280
8.4 (average in FY 2021 five-year plan)	252	294	336

Source: Department of the Navy, *Navy Budget Highlights for FY 2021*.

Table 3 calculates fleet size with different assumptions about building rate and service life. Although building rates will change over the course of decades, the calculation gives insight into the achievability of the goal.

The calculation shows that the fleet never reaches 355 ships. Under most assumptions, the fleet does not even get to 300 ships. Fleet size does reach 336 ships with heroic assumptions about service life. However, the Navy tends to retire ships at 30 or 35 years, as combat systems become obsolete, and service-life extensions do not produce enough additional useful life to make them worthwhile. Assuming a 35-year service life, the Navy would need to build 10.1 ships per year to eventually reach 355 ships.

The good news in the shipbuilding budget is that with the exception of the Columbia-class SSBN and the new FFG(X), Navy shipbuilding programs are in serial production and moving ahead without major issues (assuming the Ford-class carrier can get its ammunition elevators to work). Thus, the Navy avoids the controversies that plagued it in the 2000s when severe problems with the Ford-class carriers, LCSs, and the DDG-1000s brought into question the Navy's ability to effectively manage shipbuilding programs.

This stability will shortly be upset when the new ship types specified by the future force structure begin the acquisition process.

A near-term risk is that the Navy will retire large numbers of ships early to save money to buy a small number of additional new ships. In that case, it will have the worst of both worlds: high costs and smaller numbers.

UNMANNED SHIPS

Discussion begins with unmanned ships, not because they are important in the fleet—none have yet gone beyond the experimental stage—but because they figure so prominently in the new force structure and because so much of the discussion regarding the future fleet centers on this new technology.

Unmanned systems, both surface and undersea, currently exist in various forms from essentially conceptual to working prototypes. None yet constitute a program of record whereby the Navy commits to a certain number and builds all the needed support and infrastructure capabilities. How unmanned systems will operate in the fleet, whether the network can handle the bandwidth, and where unmanned surface vessel (USVs) will be based are all unanswered questions.

The Navy is beginning to incorporate unmanned vessels/vehicles into the fleet to distribute capabilities over more platforms and thereby reduce vulnerability in a great power conflict. Unmanned vessels/vehicles can do work that is too dull and dangerous for manned systems. Unmanned systems may also reduce the number of personnel required or at least move personnel to less vulnerable and less stressful locations.

The Navy is beginning to incorporate unmanned vessels/vehicles into the fleet to distribute capabilities over more platforms and thereby reduce vulnerability in a great power conflict.

The Navy has three programs for seagoing unmanned vessels/vehicles: a large USV, a medium USV, and an extra-large undersea vehicle. Table 4 shows acquisition plans. Funding is nonstandard since these are rapid acquisitions. None are currently funded through the regular shipbuilding account. Funding through the RDT&E appropriation implies that the system is experimental; funding through the Other Procurement account implies that it is a sensor, not a weapon.

The lack of an official program of record for unmanned systems and the nonstandard funding is inconsistent with Esper's plan for major investments. Navy officials have said that concrete plans will be in the FY 2022 budget.[106]

Table 4: Navy Acquisition Plans for Unmanned Surface and Undersea Vessels/Vehicles

	FY 2021	FY 2022	FY 2023	FY 2024	FY 2025	Five-Year Total	Funding
Large USV	2	1	2	2	3	10	RDTE, Navy through FY 2022; in SCN (shipbuilding) FY 2023 and out
Medium USV			1			1	RDTE,N
Extra-Large UUV			2	2	2	6	Other Procurement, Navy

Source: Ronald O'Rourke, Navy Large Unmanned Surface and Undersea Vehicles, CRS Report No. R45757 (Washington, DC: Congressional Research Service, October 2020), 19, https://fas.org/sgp/crs/weapons/R45757.pdf.

The Navy has used Chart 8 to explain its plan for surface ships. Large ships (1,000–2,000 tons, the size of a corvette) will be shooters as well as sensors. A medium-sized unmanned vessel (500 tons, about the size of a current patrol craft) is still in the prototype phase (one was procured in FY 2019

---

106 Thomas Modly, "SECNAV Vector 9," U.S. Navy, January 31, 2020, https://www.navy.mil/Resources/ALNAVs/Message/Article/2235534/secnav-vector-9/.

for experimental purposes) and would only carry sensors, in effect being a disposable scout for the shooters. Note that the fielding of unmanned vessels will reduce the need for LSCs.[107]

Chart 8: Navy Architecture for Unmanned Surface Vessels

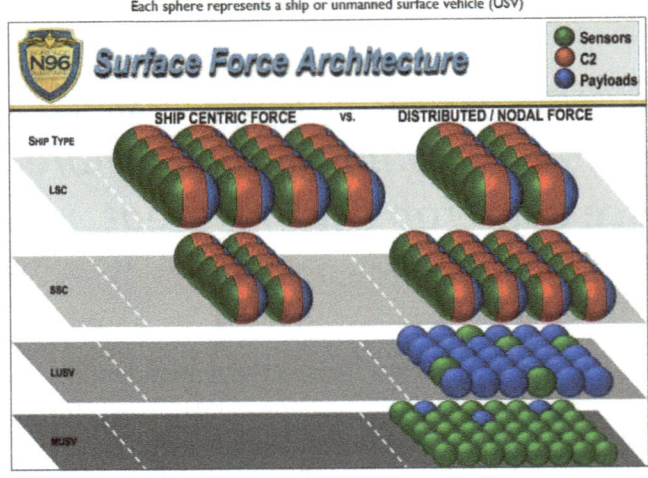

Source: Rear Admiral Casey Moton "Designing & Building the Surface Fleet: Unmanned and Small Combatants," presentation at the conference of the American Society of Naval Engineers (ASNE), June 20, 2019, slide 2. Cited in Ronald O'Rourke, "Future Force Structure Requirements for the United States Navy," House Armed Services Committee, Subcommittee on Seapower and Projection Forces, 116th Cong, 2nd session, June 4, 2020, https://www.congress.gov/116/meeting/house/110772/witnesses/HHRG-116-AS28-Wstate-ORourkeR-20200604.pdf.

Congress has supported the concept of unmanned systems but has been skeptical about the Navy's desire to move quickly before key technologies are proven.

Size is a limitation on USVs. As vessels become larger, they run the risk of becoming too complex for remote operation; small vessels would be appropriate for coastal or harbor operations but become inadequate for ocean seakeeping.

A major limitation of unmanned ships is that they cannot perform many noncombat roles, such as engagement with partners and allies, humanitarian assistance, and gray zone competition.

Chart 9 shows Navy plans for undersea unmanned vehicles (UUVs). The chart is too busy for detailed discussion. The key point is that, unlike surface and air units, subsurface units are seen as complements to manned submarines, not as replacements. For that reason, they are more easily accepted. Many of the systems are small, torpedo-like systems for scouting.

The major undersea system is the Extra Large Unmanned Undersea Vehicle (XLUUV), a 50-ton minisub with a modular payload bay so it can execute a variety of missions. Five are under construction as experimental systems. Additional procurements begin in FY 2023, but in the Other Procurement Navy account, not the shipbuilding account.

---

107   Ronald O'Rourke, *Navy Large Unmanned Surface and Undersea Vehicles*, CRS Report No. R45757 (Washington, DC: Congressional Research Service, October 2020), 19, https://fas.org/sgp/crs/weapons/R45757.pdf.

Chart 9: Navy Plans for Unmanned Undersea Vehicles

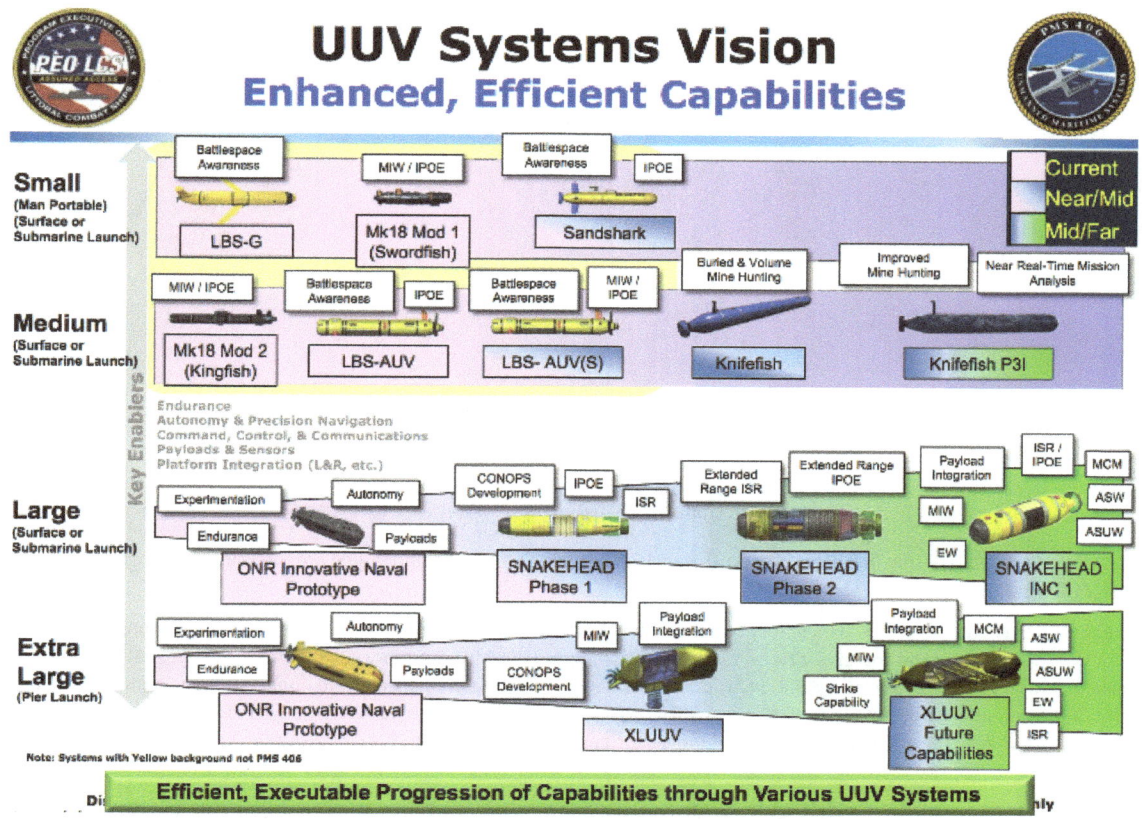

Source: Pete Small, Unmanned Maritime Systems Update (Washington DC: Department of Defense, January 15, 2019), 2, https://www.navsea.navy.mil/Portals/103/Documents/Exhibits/SNA2019/UnmannedMaritimeSys-Small.pdf?ver=2019-01-15-165105-297.

CARRIERS

Chart 10: Projected Carrier Fleet Size, FY 2020–FY 2045

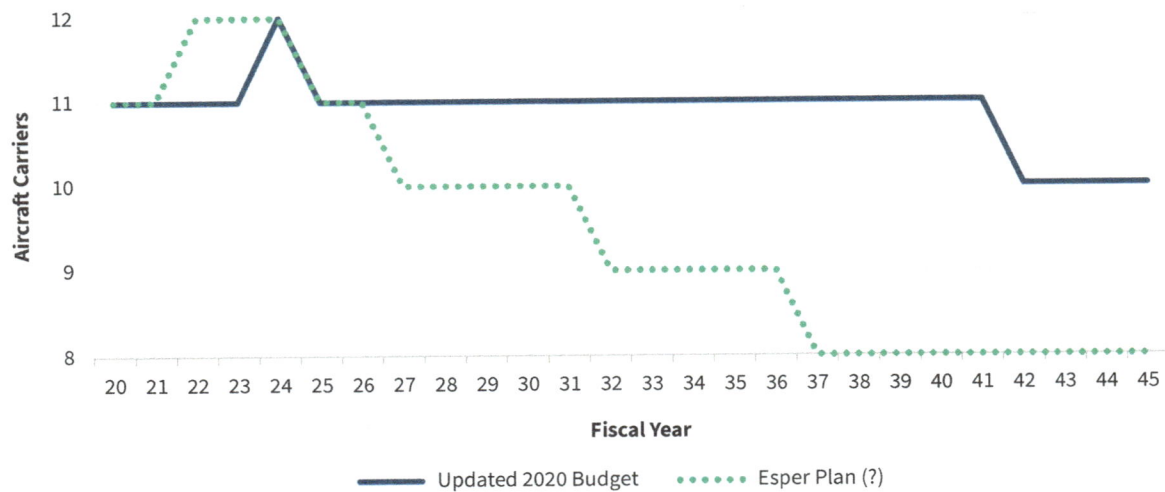

Note: This and subsequent ship inventory charts use data from last year's 30-year shipbuilding program since no program has been published for FY 2021.

Source: Data from Long-Range Naval Inventory tables in the Chief of Naval Operations, Report to Congress on the Annual Long-Range Plan for Construction of Naval Vessels for Fiscal Year 2019 (Washington, DC: DOD, February 2018), https://www.secnav.navy.mil/fmc/fmb/Documents/19pres/LONGRANGE_SHIP_PLAN.pdf; and Chief of Naval Operations, Report to Congress on the Annual Long-Range Plan for Construction of Naval Vessels for Fiscal Year 2020 (Washington, DC: DOD, March 2019), https://www.navy.mil/strategic/PB20_Shipbuilding_Plan.pdf. The updated 2020 budget removes the early retirement of the USS Harry Truman in 2024.[108]

The size of the carrier force drives Navy force structure and budgets for two reasons: carriers and their escorts take up most of the shipbuilding budget, and providing aircraft for the carriers takes most of the aviation budget.

Congress established a requirement for a minimum operational carrier force of 11. The Navy's 2016 Force Structure Assessment established a goal of 12, but this is nearly impossible to achieve because of the long lead time needed to build carriers.[109]

> *The size of the carrier force drives Navy force structure and budgets . . .*

---

108 Occasional one-year dips or spikes in carrier numbers in 2027, 2040, and 2045 have been removed to better portray the long-term differences in the respective shipbuilding plans.

109 Ronald O'Rourke, *Navy Ford Class (CVN-78) Aircraft Carrier Program: Background and Issues for Congress*, CRS Report No. RS20643 (Washington, DC: Congressional Research Service, August 2020), https://fas.org/sgp/crs/weapons/RS20643.pdf.

Although Secretary Esper gave a range of 8 to 11, he implied that the number would go down. Press reports indicated that the secretary's staff had recommended 9 carriers.[110] However, Admiral Gilday later stated, "[w]hen the report comes out, you'll see the same numbers for the supercarrier force."[111] The Navy and the Office of the Secretary of Defense seem to be in different places here.

Aircraft carriers have long been criticized by strategists because of their high cost and perceived vulnerability. Many strategists see large aircraft carriers as "legacy" systems. A recent House Armed Services Committee study tentatively suggested to "shift funding from a single aircraft carrier and instead use multiple unmanned aerial vehicles."[112]

However, the highly visible usefulness of aircraft carriers for day-to-day crisis response and regional conflicts gives them a lot of support.[113] Pushed by Congress and a highly attractive offer from Huntington Ingals Industries, the carrier builder, the Navy executed a two-carrier procurement in January 2019.[114] This double procurement had the effect of locking in carrier construction for a decade.

Faced with an institutional, political, and industrial need to continue building large nuclear-powered aircraft carriers, the Navy has periodically proposed retiring old carriers early, instead of doing a midlife extension, and will likely propose the same in the future. However, Congress rejected both previous proposals to do this, for the USS *George Washington* (CVN-74) and USS *Harry Truman* (CVN-75), and the Navy quickly backed down. The incongruity of buying new carriers while retiring old ones early was hard to justify. Further, such an approach constituted the highest-cost strategy for carrier procurement, since a year of operational life gained from a midlife extension is much less costly than a year gained from new construction.[115]

Chart 10 assumes that the Navy continues to build nuclear aircraft carriers every five years (five-year "centers," to use the Navy term, because funding is spread over eight years) but retires the next three Nimitz-class carriers early, consistent with what it has tried to do recently. If Congress refuses to go along, then the carrier levels will stay at the level of the FY 2020 plan. The Navy could propose building carriers on a slower timeline, for example, on eight year "centers," but carrier advocates have prevailed against such a slowdown in the past.

---

110 David Larter, "Defense Department Study Calls for Cutting Two of the U.S. Navy's Aircraft Carriers," Defense News, April 20, 2020, https://www.defensenews.com/naval/2020/04/20/defense-department-study-calls-for-cutting-2-of-the-us-navys-aircraft-carriers/.

111 "CNO ADM. Michael Gilday," Defense One Podcast, October 14, 2020, https://www.defenseone.com/ideas/2020/10/ep-79-cno-adm-michael-gilday/169236/.

112 House Armed Services Committee, *Future of Defense Task Force Report 2020* (Washington, DC: U.S. House, September 23, 2020), 67, https://armedservices.house.gov/_cache/files/2/6/26129500-d208-47ba-a9f7-25a8f82828b0/6D5C75605DE8DDF0013712923B4388D7.future-of-defense-task-force-report.pdf.

113 Examples of the carrier debate this year: Talbot Manvel, "Aircraft Carriers: Bigger Is Better," U.S. Naval Institute, *Proceedings*, September 2020, https://www.usni.org/magazines/proceedings/2020/september/aircraft-carriers-bigger-better. And the response, Philip Pournelle, "Overemphasis on efficiency can endanger the fleet," U.S. Naval Institute, *Proceedings*, Letter to the editor, October 2020. Also, Loren Thompson, "Claims of Aircraft Carrier Vulnerability Are False, but the Versatility Is Real," *Forbes*, June 9, 2020, https://www.forbes.com/sites/lorenthompson/2020/06/09/claims-of-aircraft-carrier-vulnerability-are-false-but-the-versatility-is-real/#73c7a6ab591a.

114 For an extended discussion of the carrier debate, see Mark Cancian, *U.S. Military Forces in FY 2018: The Uncertain Buildup* (Washington, DC: CSIS, October 2017), p. 62, https://www.csis.org/analysis/us-military-forces-fy-2018.

115 Mark Cancian, "Penny Wise and Pound Foolish: The Navy's Carrier Construction Strategy," U.S. Naval Institute, *Proceedings*, March 2019, https://www.usni.org/magazines/proceedings/2019/march/penny-wise-and-pound-foolish-navys-carrier-construction-strategy.

"Light" carriers: The idea of a "light" carrier—something smaller than the large CVN—has been around for decades. Recently, a RAND study indicated that such carrier options might be attractive.[116] Several commentators, such as Senator John McCain in 2017, proposed building smaller carriers on the America-class landing helicopter assault (LHA) design. In 2019, then-undersecretary Thomas Modly stated that the $13 billion cost of a Ford-class carrier was "unsustainable," thus reinforcing the case for a lighter alternative.[117]

Esper's future Navy has "up to six" light carriers to supplement the CVN "supercarriers," as he called them. He raised the possibility of using the USS *America* "as a model." The assumption in this CSIS analysis is that these light carriers are repurposed helicopter carriers, not new builds. Currently there are 11 helicopter carriers intended for amphibious missions and classed as amphibious ships (an "L" designator). However, they have large flight decks from which the short takeoff and landing version of the F-35 (B model) can fly. Strategists have long proposed using these ships as aircraft carriers for non-amphibious missions such as power projection and sea control.

Admiral Gilday muddied the waters by talking about the light carrier as the "aviation combatant of the future," noting that the time horizon was 2045. This implies a specifically designed ship far in the future, a concept that seems entirely different from the near-term capability that Esper implied.[118]

LARGE SURFACE COMBATANTS

Chart 11: Projected Large Surface Combatants, FY 2020–FY 2045

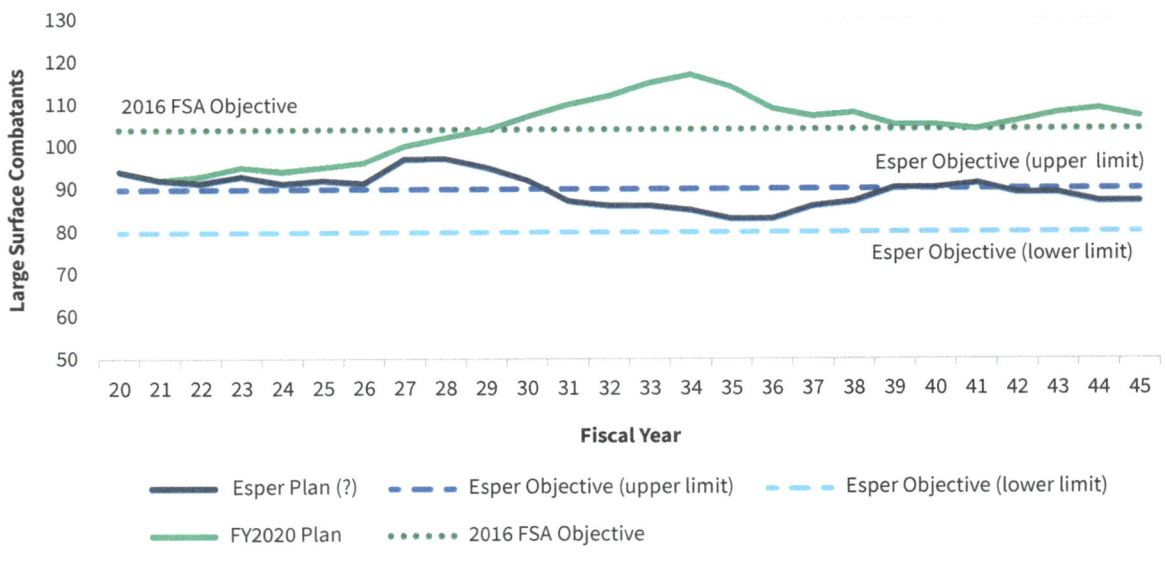

Note: Lines for the "Esper plan" are estimates, hence the question mark. This is the same for the following charts.

Source: Chief of Naval Operations, *Report to Congress on the Annual Long-Range Plan for Construction of Naval Vessels for Fiscal Year 2020* (Washington, DC: DOD, March 2019), https://www.navy.mil/strategic/PB20_Shipbuilding_Plan.pdf.

---

116 Bradley Martin and Michael McMahon, *Future Aircraft Carrier Options* (Santa Monica, CA: RAND Corporation, 2017), https://www.rand.org/pubs/research_reports/RR2006.html.

117 Justin Katz, "Modly: $13B carriers are not affordable, but what's next is not clear," Inside Defense, February 14, 2019, https://insidedefense.com/daily-news/modly-13b-carriers-are-not-affordable-whats-next-not-yet-clear.

118 Patrick Tucker, "Chief of Naval Operations Outlines Plans for Drones, Many Carriers," Defense One, October 13, 2020, https://www.defenseone.com/policy/2020/10/chief-naval-operations-outlines-future-drones-minicarriers/169204/.

Large surface combatants (LSCs) are destroyers and cruisers. Historically, these constituted the backbone of the service fleet. However, as indicated in Chart 8, the fielding of unmanned vessels may reduce the number of LSCs even as they increase the number of small-scale combatants. Indeed, the Navy's director of surface warfare said, "the future force mix is one that favors a ratio of small surface ships and unmanned surface vessels."[119] Although Esper did not discuss large combatants, other sources put the number for the future fleet at 80 to 90.[120] This is substantially below the goal in the 355-ship fleet (104 LSCs) but about where the fleet is today (92).

DDG-51 Destroyers: The program is on track, with 85 currently funded or delivered. Ships built since 2010 incorporate a ballistic missile defense capability. The most current version is the Flight III configuration with a more powerful radar, called the AN/SPY-6 Air and Missile Defense Radar.

In April 2018, the Navy announced that it wanted to extend the service lives of all DDG-51s to 45 years—an increase of 5 or 10 years over previous plans—in order to reach the numbers required for the 355-ship goal. However, the Navy recently announced plans to retire the first four DDG-51s rather than upgrade them, thus putting in question its extended life plan.[121]

The FY 2020 plan showed the Navy procuring 13 DDG-51s from FY 2021 to FY 2025, a level sufficient to maintain a fleet of 85. The FY 2021 plan shows procurement of only 9 over the same period. The Navy's plan may be to reduce production of these ships until the inventory gets down to the target levels.

DDG-1000 Zumwalt Destroyers: These three stealthy, high-technology destroyers (at 14,500 tons, larger than Ticonderoga-class cruisers and, indeed, the size of pre–World War I battleships) are still having problems. The total buy was cut in the 2000s from 32 to 3, with 47 percent cost growth. The lead ship was commissioned in 2016, but delivery was delayed to late 2020 because of a series of serious engineering casualties. The other two ships have now been delivered, but neither has made a deployment. Further, the ships' 155mm guns, originally a primary justification for the ship, have become ineffective with cancellation of the long-range munition that they were to fire.[122]

CG-47 Cruiser Modernization: The Navy proposes to modernize only 7 of the 11 newest cruisers, not all 11 as had been the plan last year. Concerned about a shrinking ship inventory, Congress has repeatedly balked at retiring these chips in the past. Esper's plan likely assumes retirement of these cruisers since there is no need to expand the LSC force.

Next generation LSC: Shipbuilding plans continue to show some version of a next-generation LSC ("DDG Next") but in the future beyond the FYDP-period, indicating that such plans are in flux.

---

119 Jason Sherman, "New Future Surface Combatant Fleet Analysis Validates Contribution of Medium, Large USVs," Inside Defense, January 22, 2020, https://insidedefense.com/daily-news/new-future-surface-combatant-fleet-analysis-validates-contribution-medium-large-usvs.

120 David Larter, "Defense Department Study Calls for Cutting Two of the Navy's Aircraft Carriers," Defense News, April 20, 2020, https://www.defensenews.com/naval/2020/04/20/defense-department-study-calls-for-cutting-2-of-the-us-navys-aircraft-carriers/.

121 Mallory Shelborne, "Navy Cancels DDG 51 Service Life Extensions," Inside Defense, March 9, 2020, https://insidedefense.com/daily-news/navy-cancels-ddg-51-service-life-extensions.

122 Ronald O'Rourke, *Navy DDG-51 and DDG-1000 Destroyer Programs: Background and Issues for Congress*, CRS Report No. R32109 (Washington, DC: Congressional Research Service, July 28, 2020), https://fas.org/sgp/crs/weapons/RL32109.pdf.

The projection assumes that the CG-47 class retires without modernization and that the service lives of the DDG-51s are not extended. The projection stays above the Esper target because so many previously ordered ships deliver but falls into the target zone as decommissionings increase.[123]

SMALL SURFACE COMBATANTS
Chart 12: Projected Small Surface Combatants, FY 2020–FY 2045

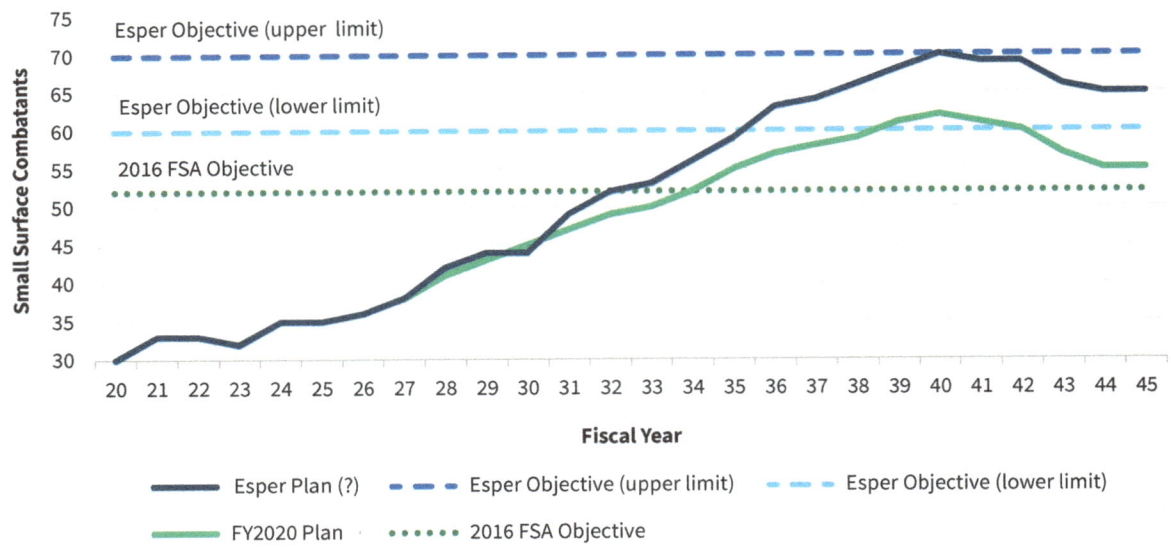

Source: Chief of Naval Operations, *Report to Congress on the Annual Long-Range Plan for Construction of Naval Vessels for Fiscal Year 2020.*

Small surface combatants (SSCs) are frigates, LCSs, and mine countermeasures ships.[124]

Although smaller and less capable than cruisers and destroyers, they cost half as much.

During the Cold War, SSCs had a wartime mission of escorting convoys. This mission disappeared after the Cold War, and SSCs went out of favor. However, interest has renewed in an environment of a great power competition where adversaries can reach out extended distances and threaten U.S. sea lines of communication. SSCs are also useful for providing a more distributed naval force structure to operate within an adversary's defensive zone. They can operate in shallower waters such as the South China Sea and provide a secondary benefit of increasing total fleet numbers, therefore allowing the Navy to be present in more places globally.

In Secretary Esper's future force, the goal for SSCs increases from 52 to between 60 and 70. This force will consist of LCSs and the follow-on frigates.

Because LCSs with mine countermeasure modules are now entering the fleet, the Navy proposes to phase out the mine countermeasures ships (MCM-1 Avenger-class), retiring all by 2024, a one-year delay from last year's plan. This class of ship disappears from the fleet, replaced by sensors on other ships such as LCSs.

---

123 My thanks to Eric Labs of the Congressional Budget Office for this projection of LSCs.

124 The Navy includes patrol craft in this category but not in the battle force inventory and so are excluded here. The general rule is that ships must be able to deploy overseas on their own to count, and patrol craft are too small.

The LCS classes are now entering the fleet in large numbers, typically two to three per year. However, performance of the LCS classes is widely regarded as disappointing, and production has now ended. The Navy proposes retiring the first four ships instead of upgrading them.

Replacing the LCS program is a follow-on frigate program, FFG(X), that will be multi-mission, like the earlier FFG-7 class, and not single-mission like the LCSs. The first ship was authorized in FY 2020 and another ship is proposed for FY 2021. To speed introduction of the class and to reduce risk, both driven by the experience of the LCS program, bidders were required to use an existing design. A team led by Fincantieri/Marinette Marine won the competition with a European design. Using a foreign design is highly unusual and reflects the Navy's desire for speed and risk reduction.

The Navy's FY 2020 shipbuilding plan showed procurement of two FFG(X)s every year from FY 2021 to FY 2029. However, the FY 2021 five-year plan shows one in FY 2021 and FY 2022 and two per year after that. This phasing will delay entry of larger numbers into the fleet but is prudent given the difficulties typically encountered with new ship classes.[125] Eventually, however, production will need to increase if the fleet is to reach the goals set out by Esper. The projection assumes a "2-3-2-3" profile beginning FY 2024.

The phasing may mitigate technical risk, but there is also risk of cost growth. The CBO places the cost per ship at potentially 40 percent higher than the Navy is currently estimating. That would be a major challenge for the program.[126]

---

125 Ronald O'Rourke, *Navy Constellation (FFG-62) Class Frigate (Previously FFG[X]) Program: Background and Issues for Congress*, CRS Report No. R44972 (Washington, DC: Congressional Research Service, July 2020), https://fas.org/sgp/crs/weapons/R44972.pdf.

126 Eric Labs, *The Cost of the Navy's New Frigate*, Congressional Budget Office, October 2020, https://www.cbo.gov/system/files/2020-10/56669-New-Frigate-Program.pdf.

AMPHIBIOUS SHIPS

Chart 13: Projected Amphibious Assault Ships, FY 2020–FY 2045

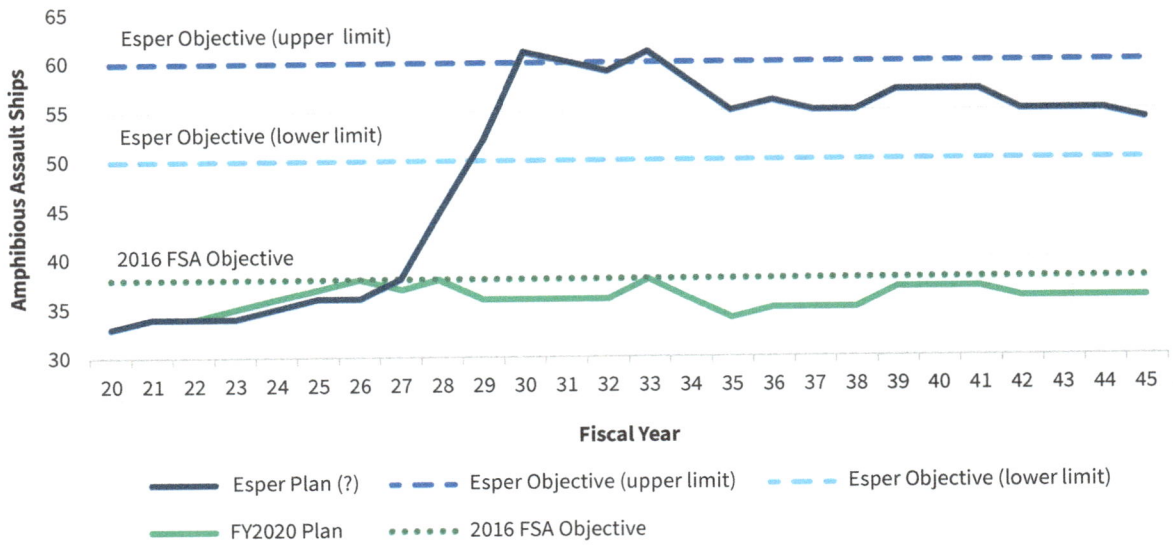

Source: Chief of Naval Operations, *Report to Congress on the Annual Long-Range Plan for Construction of Naval Vessels for Fiscal Year 2020.*

Plans for the amphibious fleet have been thoroughly disrupted in the last year. For many years, the Navy and Marine Corps goal was 38 large ships—landing helicopter assault/decks (LHAs/LHDs), dock landing platforms (LPDs), dock landing ships (LSDs). This goal was calculated by the need to launch an amphibious operation of two Marine expeditionary brigades (17 ships each) plus a 10 percent margin for maintenance.

General Berger, in his commandant's guidance (described in detail in the Marine Corps chapter) rejected this methodology. He argued that large amphibious ships appear vulnerable in a great power conflict, and the ability of the Navy and Marine Corps to execute a classic landing in the high-threat environment foreseen by the NDS seemed doubtful: "Visions of a massed naval armada nine nautical miles off-shore in the South China Sea preparing to launch the landing force in swarms of ACVs, LCUs, and LCACs are impractical and unreasonable."[127]

Instead, he proposed smaller amphibious ships that would be more distributed, with the loss of any individual ship less catastrophic. This would reverse a long-standing trend toward larger and more capable ships, which are more efficient for moving Marine forces and for peacetime presence but expensive and limited in number.

Navy and Marine Corps officials have floated 28 to 30 as a possible fleet size for these small amphibious ships, tentatively called a "light amphibious warship," with first funding in FY 2023. These would indeed be small, carrying 30 to 40 crew and 70 Marines. This would make them about the size of

---

127 General David Berger, *Commandant's Planning Guidance* (Washington, DC: Department of the Navy, 2019), 5, https://www.hqmc.marines.mil/Portals/142/Docs/%2038th%20Commandant%27s%20Planning%20Guidance_2019.pdf?ver=2019-07-16-200152-700.

a World War II landing craft infantry (LCI), much smaller than the De Soto County-class tank landing ship (LSTs) of the 1960s to 1990s and even smaller than World War II LSTs.[128]

The future amphibious fleet projection in Chart 13 shows the implication of the Navy's tentative construction program: 3 in FY 2023, 6 in FY 2024, 10 in FY 2025, and 9 in FY 2026 (commissioning assumed to be two years after funding). The projection assumes that 6 of the LHAs/LHDs are subtracted from the amphibious fleet and attributed to the carrier fleet. That brings the total down into the target range.

The FY 2021 budget continues buying large amphibious ships. It proposes buying one LPD flight II (the second in the class) and buying one every two years in the longer term.

The large deck helicopter carriers, LHA-6-class, are still in the five-year program, with the next one planned for FY 2023. Congress added advance procurement funds for a ship in FY 2020, but these funds were diverted to construction of the border wall. The implication of Esper's comments is that these would be America-class ships, optimized for aviation.[129]

If up to six LHAs/LHAs are diverted to operations as light carriers, the amphibious force will look very different in the future.

ATTACK SUBMARINES

Chart 14: Projected Attack Submarine Fleet (SSNs and SSGNs), FY 2020–FY 2049

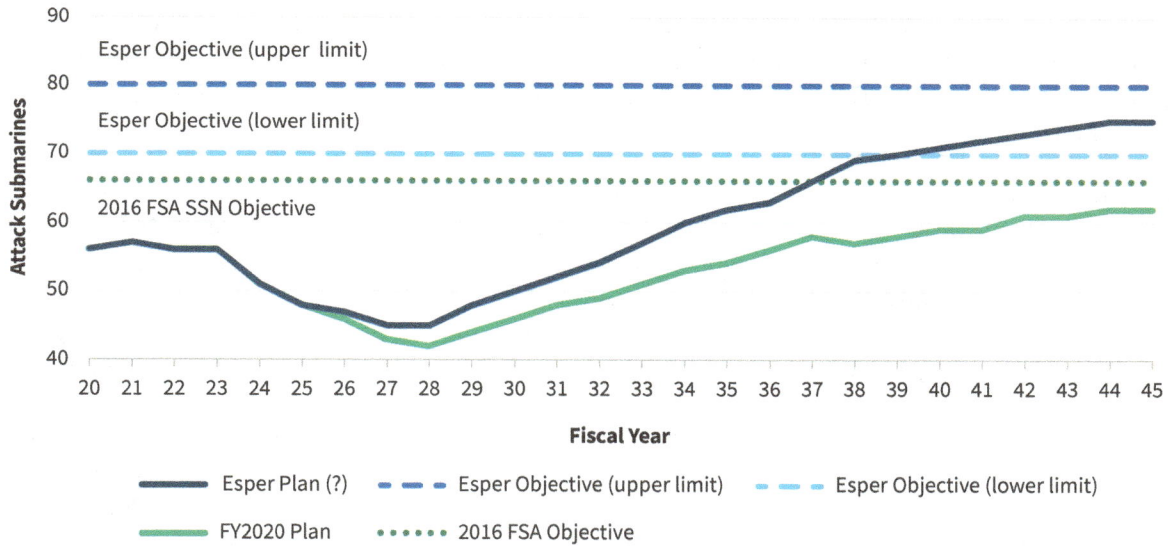

Source: Chief of Naval Operations, *Report to Congress on the Annual Long-Range Plan for Construction of Naval Vessels for Fiscal Year 2020.*

---

128 Paul McLeary, "If It Floats, It Fights: Navy's New Small Ship Strategy," Breaking Defense, August 28, 2020, https://breakingdefense.com/2020/08/if-it-floats-it-fights-navys-new-small-ship-strategy; and Joseph Trevithick, "Navy Wants to Buy 30 New Light Amphibious Warships to Support Radical Shift in Marine Ops," The Drive, May 5, 2020, https://www.thedrive.com/the-war-zone/33299/navy-wants-to-buy-30-new-light-amphibious-warships-to-support-radical-shift-in-marine-ops.

129 Ronald O'Rourke, *Navy LPD-17 Flight II and LHA Amphibious Ship Programs: Background and Issues for Congress*, CRS Report No. R43543 (Washington, DC: Congressional Research Service, October 2020), Table I., p. 8, https://fas.org/sgp/crs/weapons/R43543.pdf.

Attack submarines (SSNs) receive strong support from strategists because their firepower and covertness are useful in great power conflicts. Thus, they are likely to receive strong support in the next administration, whether that is a Trump or Biden administration. However, submarines are expensive (about $3.3 billion each in the current version), so increasing production is difficult.

Secretary Esper's goal is 70 to 80, higher than the old goal of 66. He implies that this is the highest shipbuilding priority.

In the near term, the attack submarine fleet is stable. Numbers stay in the fifties, and the Navy planned to build new boats at the rate of two per year. That plan was disrupted in the FY 2021 budget proposal, where the number of new attack submarines dropped to one. That occurred because of a last-minute shift of $2 billion from DOD to the National Nuclear Security Administration to pay for upgrades in the nuclear weapons infrastructure. However, Congress seems disinclined to go along, with the House version of the National Defense Authorization Act (NDAA) putting a second submarine back in and the Senate version providing supportive sentiments and some money.

The greater problem is long term. Numbers dip in the late-2020s and early-2030s, bottoming at 42 boats as Los Angeles-class boats built during the 1980s retire.[130] Secretary Esper said that the new plan intends to extend the service life of additional older submarines, but the Navy tends to retire old ships early in order to buy new ships.

This prospective submarine shortfall will happen at a time when Russian and Chinese submarines are becoming more capable and active.[131] Retirement of the Ohio-class SSGNs in the late-2020s, which greatly reduces the undersea strike capability, exacerbates the numbers shortfall, although the missile compartments of the newest Virginia-class submarines, with the Virginia Payload Module, will mitigate the capability shortfall.

The obvious solution is to build more submarines, but having two submarine construction programs operating simultaneously puts pressure on both the shipbuilding account and the submarine industrial base.[132] The FY 2020 Navy 30-year shipbuilding plan showed a capacity for three total submarines per year, attack (SSN) or ballistic missile (SSBN) submarines, although the Navy did not always fund to the total capacity. Esper called for building three Virginia-class submarines per year in addition to SSBNs as soon as possible, but the industrial base will need a lot of funding and lead time to get to that level of production.

The Esper projection in Chart 14 assumes additional submarines in FY 2022 and FY 2023, with a level of three SSNs per year achieved in FY 2026, just outside the five-year period. Delivery is six years from funding. Production returns to two submarines per year in FY 2038 so the inventory does not overshoot. It also assumes that additional older submarines will be extended for an additional 10 years.

---

130 Chief of Naval Operations, *Report to the Congress on Annual Long-Range Plan for Construction of Naval Vessels for Fiscal Year 2020* (Washington, DC: March 2019), https://media.defense.gov/2020/May/18/2002302045/-1/-1/1/PB20_SHIPBUILDING_PLAN.PDF.

131 For example, Kathleen H. Hicks et al., *Undersea Warfare in Northern Europe* (Washington, DC: CSIS, July 2016), https://www.csis.org/analysis/undersea-warfare-northern-europe.

132 Ronald O'Rourke, *Navy Virginia (SSN-774) Class Attack Submarine Procurement: Background and Issues for Congress*, CRS Report No. RL32418 (Washington, DC: Congressional Research Service, September 2020), https://fas.org/sgp/crs/weapons/RL32418.pdf.

The dotted line on the chart shows the problem. The Navy cannot build enough new submarines quickly enough to significantly mitigate the trough. What it can do is accelerate the rate at which it gets to its target level.

BALLISTIC MISSILE SUBMARINES

Chart 15: Projected Ballistic Missile Submarine Fleet (SSBNs), FY 2020–FY 2045

Source: Chief of Naval Operations, *Report to Congress on the Annual Long-Range Plan for Construction of Naval Vessels for Fiscal Year 2020*.

The Columbia-class SSBN program—which will replace the existing Ohio-class submarines—continues as planned. The FY 2021 budget proposes authorization for the first ship. Because the program is high priority, enjoys strong bipartisan support, and has no schedule slack, it will likely be unaffected by any changes in future shipbuilding plans. The Esper plan, for example, maintains the same goal of 12.

The budget cost is substantial—$4.4 billion in FY 2021 ($4 billion procurement plus $400 million RDT&E)—and has nearly doubled from FY 2020.[133] Affordability of the $100 billion program, long identified as a challenge for Navy shipbuilding, has become a near-term, rather than long-term, issue.

There have been proposals to find other funding mechanisms for the Columbia-class, for example, through a National Sea-based Deterrence Fund. However, none have resulted in substantially increasing funds for Navy shipbuilding.[134]

---

133 Office of the Under Secretary of Defense Comptroller, *Program Acquisition Cost by Weapon System for FY 2021* (Washington, DC: Department of Defense, February 2020), 6-3, https://comptroller.defense.gov/Portals/45/Documents/defbudget/fy2021/fy2021_Weapons.pdf.

134 Ronald O'Rourke, *Navy Columbia Class (SSBN-826) Ballistic Missile Submarine Program: Background and Issues for Congress*, CRS Report No. R41129 (Washington, DC: Congressional Research Service, October 1, 2020, https://fas.org/sgp/crs/weapons/R41129.pdf.

CBO has questioned the cost estimates, noting that cost per ton for submarines has been higher than what the Navy is planning. CBO's cost estimate is 10 percent, or $700 million, higher per Columbia-class submarine than the Navy's estimate. The Government Accountability Office has similarly questioned DOD's cost estimate.[135] So far, the Navy has not changed any cost estimates.

Any substantial cost growth here will severely disrupt other elements of the shipbuilding plan and hence the future fleet.

Naval Aviation Modernization: The Future Air Wing

It has been said that the U.S. Navy comprises a complete military itself: a navy (with its ships), an army (with the Marine Corps), and an air force (with its air wing). Because naval aircraft provide the striking power of the aircraft carrier, the central weapon system in the U.S. Navy, aviation plays a larger role in the U.S. Navy than it does in other navies.

In FY 2021, naval aviation (Navy and Marine Corps) proposes to procure 121 aircraft of all kinds, down from 163 in FY 2020. Naval aviation is in generally good shape. Inventories have been stable, the average age for most elements is good, and the Navy has been buying enough aircraft to maintain its inventory. That is the good news.

The bad news is that the Navy needs to increase aircraft procurement in the future to maintain current inventories, faces ever higher costs to maintain its aircraft inventory, and has been slow to field unmanned aerial vehicles (UAVs).

Inventories have been stable, the average age for most elements is good, and the Navy has been buying enough aircraft to maintain its inventory. That is the good news.

---

135 Labs, *Navy's Fiscal Year 2020 Shipbuilding Plan*, 19-21; Government Accountability Office, *Columbia-Class Submarine Overly Optimistic Cost Estimate Will Likely Lead to Budget Increases* (Washington, DC: April 2019), https://www.gao.gov/products/GAO-19-497.

FY 2021 Procurement

Table 5: Department of the Navy Aircraft Procurement in FY 2021

Fixed Wing	FY 2021 (Proposed)	First Procurement	Last Procurement
F-35C (CV)	21	2011	-
F-35B (STOVL)	10	2008	-
FA-18E/F	24	1995	2021
E-2D Advanced Hawkeye	4	2014	2023 (planned)
P-8A	-	2010	2020
KC-130J	5	2005	-

Rotary Wing			
CH-53K (HLR)	7	2018	-
MV-22B / CMV-22B	9	1997	2022 (planned, small buys in 2023 and 2024)
AH-1Z /UH-1Y	-	2004	2019
TH-57 Replacement/TH-73	36	2022 (planned)	-
VH-92A	5	2021	2023

UAV			
MQ-4C Triton	0	(2023 production restart)	-
MQ-25 Stingray	0	(2023 planned)	-
MQ-8B/C	0	2005	2020
MQ-9A Reaper (USMC)	0	2020	2020
Total	**121**		

Source: Department of the Navy, *Highlights of the Department of the Navy FY 2021 Budget, Office of Budget* (Washington, DC: Department of Defense, March 12, 2020), Figure 4.3, https://www.secnav.navy.mil/fmc/fmb/Documents/21pres/Highlights_book.pdf; Navy Fact Files, https://www.navy.mil/Resources/Fact-Files/; Year of first/last procurement is the budget year.

For many years, naval aviation has been procuring mature systems with predictable costs and schedules (with the significant exception of the F-35). As Table 5 shows, that stability is coming to an end. Long-established production lines have recently finished or soon will (gray highlighted); new systems will replace them.

Particularly striking is the plan to end F-18 production after nearly 40 years. This is a change from last year's plan, which continued to buy F-18s at least through FY 2024. F-35 production does not increase to make up for the lost F-18 production. The planned end to F-18 procurement may reflect an expectation of having to fill fewer carrier decks. Although there is a next-generation fighter in development ("Next Generation Air Dominance"), procurement is not expected until the 2030s. (See Air Force chapter for further discussion.)

The other challenge is that the total number of aircraft procured goes down. In the FY 2020 budget, the average number of aircraft procured per year in the five-year plan was 130. In the FY 2021 plan, it is 107.

Table 6: Aircraft Inventory Replacement Rate

Number of Aircraft Procured	Total Inventory to Be Replaced	Years Required to Replace Inventory
121 (FY 2021 procurement)	3,933	33 years
107 (FY 2021 five-year plan average)		37 years
157 (Rate required for 25-year average service life)		25 years

Source: FY 2021 procurement numbers from *Highlights of The Department of the Navy FY 2021 Budget*.

Table 6 shows the number of years required to replace the current aircraft inventory at various procurement rates. The FY 2021 and five-year average procurement rates result in very old fleets. The rate would need to increase to 157 aircraft procured per year to get to a target of 25 years.

The bottom line is that if the Navy does not start buying more aircraft, either the fleet gets smaller or the fleet gets older.

THE HIGH COST OF STABLE INVENTORIES
Chart 16: Department of the Navy Aircraft Inventory

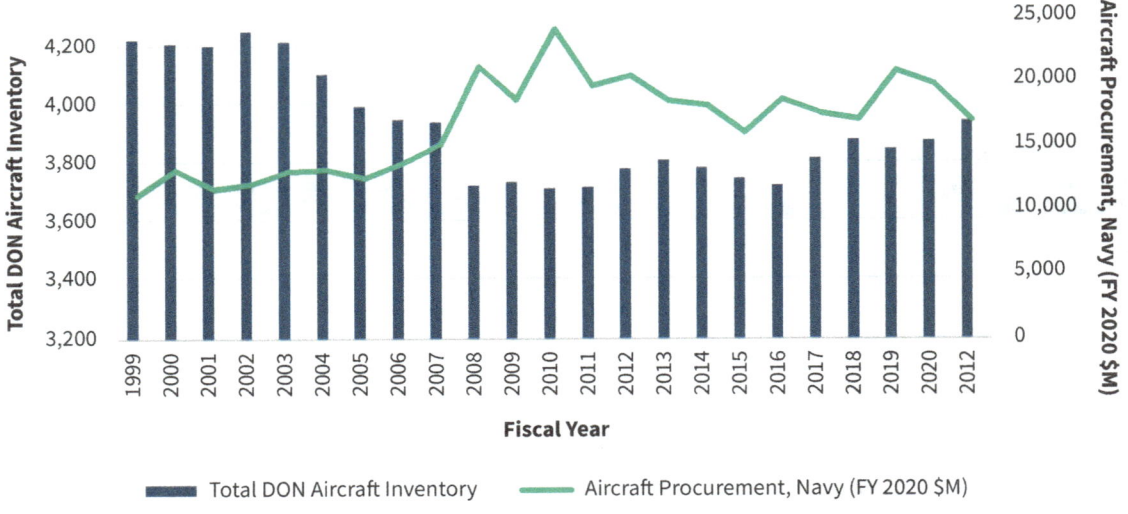

Source: Department of the Navy, *FY 2017 Budget Estimates Data Book* (Washington, DC: Department of Defense, April 2016), 64, https://www.secnav.navy.mil/fmc/fmb/Documents/17pres/FY17_Data_Book.pdf; Updated with data from Department of the Navy, *Highlights of the Department of the Navy FY 2019* (Washington, DC: Department of Defense, 2018), https://www.secnav.navy.mil/fmc/fmb/Documents/19pres/Highlights_book.pdf; and Department of Defense, *Fiscal Year (FY) 2021 Budget Estimates: Justification Book Volume 1 of 3: Aircraft Procurement, Navy* (Washington, DC: March 2019), https://www.secnav.navy.mil/fmc/fmb/Documents/20pres/APN_BA1-4_BOOK.pdf.

Threatening the long-term health of Navy aviation (and Marine Corps and Air Force aviation, as described later) is the high cost of sustaining fleet numbers. As the chart above shows, funding for procurement of naval aviation has increased by about 50 percent since the early-2000s to maintain a smaller inventory.

The reason is that each generation of aircraft costs more than the generation before it. For example, the E-2C costs $116 million per aircraft (in FY 2021 dollars) when last procured in the early-2000s. Its replacement, the E-2D, has more powerful radar and enhanced command linkages but costs $227 million (FY 2021 dollars).[136]

THE (SLOW) FIELDING OF UAVS: TRITON AND MQ-25

Chart 17: Navy and Air Force Large UAV Inventories

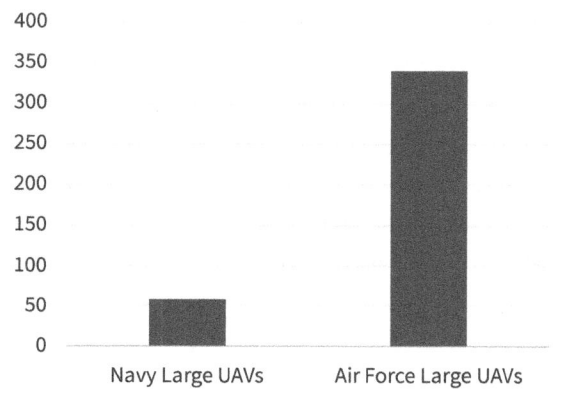

Source: Department of the Air Force, *Air Force Budget Highlights for FY 2021* (Washington, DC: DOD, 2020), appendix, https://www.saffm.hq.af.mil/Portals/84/documents/FY21/SUPPORT_/FY21%20Budget%20Overview_1.pdf; and *Department of Defense Fiscal Year (FY) 2021 Budget Estimates Aircraft Procurement, Navy, Book 2*, line 59 (p. 841-860) and line 65 (p.981-1001), https://www.secnav.navy.mil/fmc/fmb/Documents/21pres/APN_BA5_BOOK.pdf.

The Navy's FY 2021 procurement of large UAVs (0) is the same as the Air Force's (0)—a problem for both services—but the Navy's UAV inventory (58, MQ-8 and MQ-4) is far behind the Air Force's (340, MQ-9 and RQ-4). This reflects the Navy's relative emphasis on manned systems and, to some, a lack of interest in unmanned systems. The Navy's tepid action with unmanned aviation systems stands in contrast to its bold action with unmanned surface and subsurface systems.

In his shipbuilding speech, Secretary Esper made an interesting side point about naval aviation. He said that the plan for the future fleet included unmanned ship-based aircraft for "all types, fighters, refuelers, early warning, and electronic attack aircraft." This is a significant development because the Navy's near-term plans are for UAVs to have only support rules, not to be shooters.

---

136 Procurement funding only; E-2D costs from "E-2D Advanced Hawkeye Aircraft Selected Acquisition Report," Department of Defense, Dec 2018, https://www.esd.whs.mil/Portals/54/Documents/FOID/Reading%20Room/Selected_Acquisition_Reports/FY_2018_SARS/19-F-1098_DOC_29_E-2D_AHE_SAR_Dec_2018.pdf. E-2C costs from Obaid Younossi et al., *The Eyes of the Fleet: An Analysis of the E-2C Aircraft Acquisition Options* (Santa Monica, CA: RAND Corporation, 2002), https://www.rand.org/content/dam/rand/pubs/monograph_reports/2009/MR1517.pdf. Escalation factors from Undersecretary of Defense (Comptroller), *National Defense Budget Estimates for FY 2021* (Washington, DC: Department of Defense, April 2020), https://comptroller.defense.gov/Portals/45/Documents/defbudget/fy2019/FY19_Green_Book.pdf.

> *The Navy's tepid action with unmanned aviation systems stands in contrast to its bold action with unmanned surface and subsurface systems.*

Despite Secretary Esper's endorsement, the future for Navy unmanned aircraft does not look much better. The MQ-8C Fire Scout, though a significant improvement over the "B" model, continues to have performance problems, having been declared "not operationally effective" by testers.[137]

The MQ-4C Triton long-range surveillance UAV (a relative of the Air Force's RQ-4 Global Hawk), which began production in FY 2020, pauses production until FY 2023. This is a change from the Navy's previous plan to procure two per year. The system received some notoriety when the Iranians shot down one of the prototypes in June 2019.

The MQ-25 is the Navy's first carrier-capable unmanned aircraft, growing out of a series of experimental programs such as the Unmanned Carrier Launched Aerial Surveillance and Strike (UCLASS) program. In 2017, the Navy announced its plan to develop the aircraft as a tanker with some intelligence, reconnaissance, and surveillance (ISR) capabilities, rather than as a strike platform. The program remains stable, with first procurement planned for FY 2023. Nevertheless, controversy lingers about the program because many observers see it as having been sidelined to a support mission when it should constitute a frontline attack capability. Secretary Esper's comments will add to that controversy.[138]

Munitions as an Element of Strategy: Range and Precision

The Navy's warfighting problem is that it built platforms designed for regional conflicts and for operating close to the adversary. Its ships are highly capable but large and few. Its tactical aircraft are very short ranged. So, the Navy's challenge—and that of the other services, to a lesser degree—is how to use these existing systems against an adversary that can build a formidable defensive zone (often called an anti-access/area denial, or A2/AD, zone).

One Navy solution is to put long-range precision munitions on existing weapons systems, both ships and aircraft. That allows assets to stay out of the most dangerous area but still participate in the fight. Thus, the Navy has developed an "offensive missile strategy." Although the details are classified, the strategy purports to sustain current inventories, increase the capabilities of existing weapons, and develop new weapons.

---

137 Justin Katz, "DOT&E Says Fire Scout Is 'Not Operationally Effective'," Inside Defense, February 4, 2020, https://insidedefense.com/daily-news/dote-says-fire-scout-not-operationally-effective-reveals-navy-created-tiger-team.

138 Called "strategic malpractice" in Robert Martinage and Shawn Brimley, "The Navy's New Museum Drone and Strategic Malpractice," War on the Rocks, April 28, 2015, http://warontherocks.com/2015/04/the-navys-new-museum-drone-and-strategic-malpractice. Similar criticisms have come from Bryan McGrath of the Hudson Institute and Jerry Hendrix of the Center for New American Security.

One Navy solution [to the problem of operating close to the adversary] is to put long-range precision munitions on existing weapon systems, both ships and aircraft.

The president's FY 2021 budget maintains a high level of munitions procurement, comparable to the purchasing rate last year even though Navy procurement resources decreased. Key munitions actions include:

- For ships, buying the latest version of tactical Tomahawk (Block IV) and an over-the-horizon missile for LCSs;

- For aircraft, buying the Long Range Anti-Ship Missiles (LRASM), essentially an adaptation of the Air Force's JASSM, and the Joint Standoff Weapon – Extended Range (JSOW-ER);

- For longer-term capability, $1 billion to develop the Conventional Prompt Strike (CPS), a hypervelocity missile, as well as continuing development of the Offensive Anti-Surface Warfare (OASuW) Increment 2 missile and a Next-Generation Land Attack Weapon;[139] and

- The budget does cut procurement of Small Diameter Bomb II, an airdropped land-attack munition, likely reduced because of the less intense bombing campaigns in the Middle East. The budget also cuts procurement of the LCS surface-to-surface missile module, likely because of a reduced LCS buy and a changing missile mix.

---

139 Megan Eckstein, "Navy Investing in Researching Next-Generation Missiles, Enhancing Current Ones," USNI News, April 15, 2019, https://news.usni.org/2019/04/15/navy-investing-in-researching-next-generation-missiles-enhancing-current-ones; and Statement of Honorable James F. Geurts, Lieutenant General Steven Rudder, and Rear Admiral Scott Conn, Senate Armed Services Committee, Seapower Subcommittee, 116th Cong., 1st sess., April 10, 2019, https://www.armed-services.senate.gov/imo/media/doc/Geurts_Rudder_Conn_04-10-19.pdf. In addition, other systems, such as stealthy long-range unmanned strike platforms, have been advocated by others as means to argue the Navy's ability to penetrate A2/AD environments. Jerry Hendrix, *Filling the Seams in U.S. Long-Range Penetrating Strike* (Washington, DC: Center for a New American Security, August 2018), https://www.cnas.org/publications/reports/filling-the-seams-in-u-s-long-range-penetrating-strike.

4

Marine Corps

The Marine Corps begins a major restructuring to develop capabilities for great power conflict after two decades of conducting counterinsurgency ashore. The budget cuts units and personnel to pay for these new capabilities. However, many commentators worry that the restructuring will make the Marine Corps too narrowly focused.

KEY TAKEAWAYS
- General Berger's new guidance aims to restore the Marine Corps to its naval roots after two decades of operations ashore, invest in capabilities focused on great power conflict in the Pacific, and divest unneeded forces.
- To pay for this, the Marine Corps' active-duty end strength begins a decline to about 172,000, the level before the wars in Iraq and Afghanistan.
- Despite a continuing high operational tempo, the Marine Corps is pursuing modernization over expanding force structure.
- Ground forces would gain long-range precision fires but give up three infantry battalions, tanks, and some counterinsurgency capabilities. Most artillery would convert from cannon to missile units
- UAVs would increase in number, but the Marine Corps is far behind the Air Force in this regard and the Marine Corps' UAV development program is in disarray.
- The amphibious fleet will include large numbers of light amphibious warships (LAWs). These will provide more distributed capabilities that can implement the Marine Corps' intention to be a "stand in" force that can operate inside an adversary's defensive bubble. The trade-off is that, because of the LAWs small size, they will not be able to support the customary level of global forward deployments, which may decline as a result.

- The restructuring has been criticized for focusing too much on a maritime campaign in the Western Pacific, ignoring other global conflicts, and relying on unproven operational concepts.

The FY 2021 budget is an interim step as the Marine Corps seeks to implement a major restructuring. This restructuring would shed capabilities designed for counterinsurgency and sustained operations ashore and cut a slice across the entire Marine Corps to pay for new capabilities. Because the restructuring plan came out after the FY 2021 budget, full implementation is expected in the FY 2022 budget and its associated five-year plan.

End Strength in FY 2021

Table 1: Marine Corps – Active, Reserve, and Civilians

	Marine Corps Active Duty *Authorized End Strength*	Marine Corps Reserve *Authorized End Strength*	Civilian Full-Time Equivalents
FY 2020 Enacted	186,200	38,500	22,594
FY 2021 Request	184,100	38,500	22,896
Change	-2,100	0	+302

Source: Department of the Navy, *Highlights of The Department of the Navy FY 2021 Budget* (Washington, DC: 2020), Active duty end strength data in Figure 2.6; Reserve end strength data in figure 2.7; Civilian data in Figure 2.10, https://www.secnav.navy.mil/fmc/fmb/Documents/21pres/Highlights_book.pdf.

In FY 2021, the Marine Corps decreases active-duty end strength by 2,100. This is the first increment of a larger decrease to pay for the commandant's restructuring.

Marine Corps Reserve end strength stays level at 38,500, where it has been for many years. On the one hand, the retention and recruitment challenges of expanding are too great. (The Marine reserves got into some trouble in the past when they tried to expand to over 40,000.) On the other hand, the demands of maintaining a full division-wing structure prevent it from getting much smaller. General Berger's guidance hints at some changes in the future: "We will explore the efficacy of fully integrating our reserve units within the Active Component, as well as other organizational options." However, that is still pending.[140]

Marine Corps civilians increase slightly, as with Department of Defense (DOD) civilians overall, reflecting the focus on rebuilding readiness and the substitution of civilians for military personnel in support activities. Marine Corps civilian strength levels have been relatively level for several years. One notable point is that the number does not go down, at least yet, as the active-duty force gets smaller.

---

140 David Berger, *Commandant's Planning Guidance: 38th Commandant of the Marine Corps* (Arlington, VA: 2019), https://www.hqmc.marines.mil/Portals/142/Docs/%2038th%20Commandant%27s%20Planning%20Guidance_2019.pdf?ver=2019-07-16-200152-700.

Chart 1: Marine Corps Active-Duty End Strength 1999–2025 (000s)

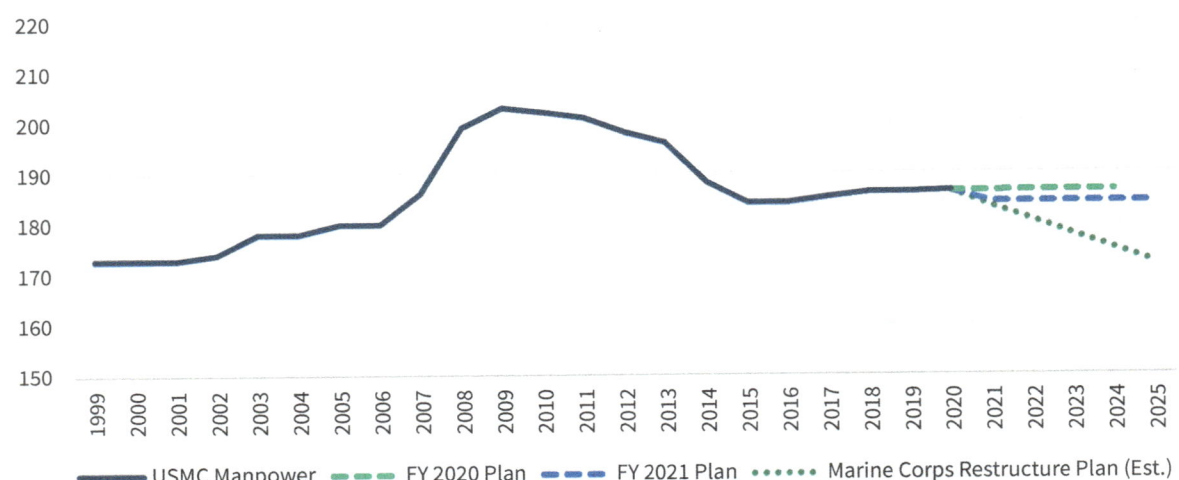

Source: Office of the Under Secretary of Defense (Comptroller), *National Defense Budget Estimates for FY 2021* (Washington, DC: Department of Defense, April 2020), Table 7-5, https://comptroller.defense.gov/Portals/45/Documents/defbudget/fy2021/FY21_Green_Book.pdf; and Office of the Under Secretary of Defense (Comptroller), *PB 21 Budget Roll Out Brief* (Washington, DC: Department of Defense, February 2020), 13, https://www.saffm.hq.af.mil/Portals/84/documents/FY21/SUPPORT_/FY21%20PB%20Rollout%20Brief_1.pdf?ver=2020-02-10-114941-800.

Not so long ago, the Marine Corps had talked about expanding the active-duty force to 194,000. That level would have allowed the Marine Corps to build new capabilities without sacrificing the old. However, flat budgets required some trade-offs.

The projection in the FY 2021 budget shows a small decrease compared to the FY 2020 projection. However, last year, General Berger said: "If provided the opportunity to secure additional modernization dollars in exchange for force structure, I am prepared to do so."[141] His restructuring plan, which came out after the budget was published, described cutting active-duty end strength by "about 12,000" to pay for the new capabilities envisioned. That would take the active-duty Marine Corps down to 172,000, a reduction that will likely be incorporated into the FY 2022 budget.

Even at that level, the Marine Corps would be coming out of the wars at about the same level (172,000) that it went in (172,600).

The McKenzie Group of 2013 (named after its leader, then-Lieutenant General Kenneth F. McKenzie, now General McKenzie, commander of CENTCOM) argued that forward presence and crisis response were the Marine Corps' primary force drivers because of the strain that deployments put on the force. This may have also been a reflection of the time, at least in part driven by 10 years of high wartime operational tempo (OPTEMPO).[142]

---

141 Ibid., 6.

142 Brian Buggeman and Ben Fitzgerald, *Crisis Response: Institutional Innovation in the United States Marine Corps* (Washington, DC: Center for a New American Security, Nov 2015), https://www.cnas.org/publications/reports/crisis-response-institutional-innovation-in-the-united-states-marine-corps.; Robert Neller, "Posture of the Department of the Navy," Testimony to the Senate Armed Services Committee, 116th Cong., 1st sess., April 9, 2019, https://www.armed-services.senate.gov/imo/media/doc/Neller_04-09-19.pdf.

In any case, that argument has disappeared. General Berger did not mention high OPTEMPO or personnel stress in his annual posture statement to Congress.[143] That is a change from statements pre-2016, when the commandants routinely cited the stress of multiple deployments.

A New Force Structure

When General Berger became commandant, he issued planning guidance with four major themes: to reestablish the Marine Corps' naval roots after years of operations ashore in Iraq and Afghanistan; to build structure and weapons for great power conflict, particularly in the Pacific; to eliminate legacy capabilities that did not fit with a new concept; and to maintain a high level of individual warfighting prowess.[144] These themes were consistent with the *National Defense Strategy* (NDS) and previously published Marine concepts such as Expeditionary Advance Base Operations and Littoral Operations in a Contested Environment. The Marine concepts envision a shift to distributed operations and the Marine Corps contributing to sea control in a naval campaign through shore-based aircraft and fires, not just by projecting power ashore.

In March 2020, the Marine Corps announced the specifics of the restructuring in *Marine Corps 2030*.[145] The sections below contain details.

Unlike the Navy's proposed restructuring, General Berger stated, "I seek no additional resources for this effort."[146] Thus, the restructure cuts many force elements to create savings to acquire new capabilities. Implementation will be a 10-year effort, though some changes, such as the retirement of tanks, have taken place immediately. The document and General Berger's statements since its issuance emphasize that this is an ongoing process with continued experimentation and wargaming. In particular, the logistics structure, reserves, and elements of aviation are unresolved.

The restructuring maintains the three active-duty Marine Expeditionary Forces (MEFs): I and II MEFs located in the continental United States (California and North Carolina, respectively) and III MEF on Hawaii, Okinawa, and mainland Japan. Today, the MEFs are nearly identical, though they have minor variations, and III MEF is a bit smaller because of its overseas basing. However, *Marine Corps 2030* notes that the MEFs may not be identical in the future.

The restructuring also maintains the reserve division-wing team, headquartered in New Orleans but spread over the entire country. (The reserve division-wing team lacks the headquarters to make it an MEF. Since the reserves are employed at lower unit levels, such a headquarters is not needed.) The Marine Corps reserve, like the Army National Guard but unlike the other reserve components, mirrors

---

143 David Berger, "Posture of the Navy," Statement before the Senate Armed Services Committee, March 5, 2020, https://www.armed-services.senate.gov/imo/media/doc/Modly--Gilday--Berger_03-05-20.pdf.

144 U.S. Marine Corps, *Marine Corps Operating Concept* (Washington, DC: Department of the Navy, September 2016), https://www.mccdc.marines.mil/Portals/172/Docs/MCCDC/young/MCCDC-YH/document/final/Marine%20Corps%20Operating%20Concept%20Sept%202016.pdf?ver=2016-09-28-083439-483; "Littoral Operations in a Contested Environment," U.S. Marine Corps and U.S. Navy, 2017, https://www.candp.marines.mil/Concepts/Subordinate-Operating-Concepts/Littoral-Operations-in-a-Contested-Environment/; and "Expeditionary Advance Base Operations," U.S. Marine Corps, 2018, http://www.candp.marines.mil/Concepts/Subordinate-Operating-Concepts/Expeditionary-Advanced-Base-Operations/.

145 U.S. Marine Corps, *Force Design 2030* (Washington, DC: March 2020), https://www.hqmc.marines.mil/Portals/142/Docs/CMC38%20Force%20Design%202030%20Report%20Phase%20I%20and%20II.pdf?ver=2020-03-26-121328-460.

146 Berger, "Posture of the Navy."

the organization of the active-duty force. No capabilities reside disproportionately in the Marine Reserve (except the small civil affairs community, which is almost entirely in the reserves).

General Berger's guidance and restructuring barely mention cyber and special operations, which raises questions about how they fit into his new concept for the Marine Corps. Both had been uncomfortable fits, with cyber Marines being hard to recruit and special forces Marines siphoning top talent from the regular line units.[147]

If fully implemented, the restructuring would also have a major cultural impact on the Marine Corps. Hitherto, the infantry has been the centerpiece of the Marine Corps and the principal instrument by which it wins battles. Its mission has been clear: "locate, close with, and destroy the enemy."[148] Under this restructuring, the Marine Corps would win battles using long-range fires from artillery and aviation. The infantry role would be mostly defensive, to protect these long-range fire assets.[149]

Ground Forces

Table 2 lays out the major changes that the restructuring would make to Marine Corps ground forces. The Marine Corps emphasizes that experimentation is ongoing, so additional changes are likely. In particular, the Marine Corps is still formulating plans for logistics and the reserves. (For a detailed assessment of *Marine Corps 2030*, see Mark Cancian, "The Marine Corps' Radical Shift Towards China."[150])

---

147 For the case against these units, see, for example, Dakota L. Wood, *Rebuilding America's Military: The United States Marine Corps – Refocusing the Corps on Its Primary Mission: Contributing to the Prosecution of Naval Campaigns* (Washington, DC: Heritage Foundation, March 21, 2019), https://www.heritage.org/sites/default/files/2019-03/SR211_0.pdf.

148 The full infantry mission statement: "The mission of the [infantry] is to locate, close with, and destroy the enemy by fire and maneuver, or repel the enemy's assault by fire and close combat." From U.S. Marine Corps, *The Marine Rifle Squad*, MCWP 3-11.2 (Washington, DC: 2002), 1-1, https://www.marines.mil/Portals/1/Publications/MCWP%203-11.2%20Marine%20Rifle%20Squad.pdf.

149 Philip Athey, "Steely Eyed Killers No More: What Will the Corps' Culture Look like under the New Force Design?," *Marine Corps Times*, September 18, 2020, https://www.marinecorpstimes.com/news/your-marine-corps/2020/09/18/passive-defenders-or-steely-eyed-killers-what-will-the-corps-culture-look-like-under-new-force-design/. David Barno and Nora Bensahel make a similar argument for the Army in "The Headwinds Looming for the U.S. Army," War on the Rocks, October 27, 2020, https://warontherocks.com/2020/10/the-headwinds-looming-for-the-u-s-army/.

150 Mark Cancian, "The Marine Corps' Radical Shift Towards China," CSIS, *Commentary*, March 25, 2020, https://www.csis.org/analysis/marine-corps-radical-shift-toward-china.

Table 2: Marine Corps Ground Force Structure

	Current Structure	Proposed Structure
Infantry	24 active-duty infantry battalions	21 active-duty infantry battalions, each about 15 percent or 125 marines smaller
	8 reserve infantry battalions	6 reserve infantry battalions
Fire support	21 cannon batteries; 7 rocket batteries	5 cannon batteries; 21 missile/rocket batteries
Tanks	7 tank companies	0 tanks, no capability retained
Bridge companies	3 bridging companies (active and reserve)	0 bridging companies
Law enforcement (military police) units	3 battalions	0 battalions

Infantry: The cut of three infantry battalions appears to be a bill payer. The press release says that the remaining battalions will be more "mobile" and reportedly "commando-like."[151] That implies deleting some of the heavy weapons such as mortars and anti-tank missiles. On the other hand, in *Marine Corps 2030*, which came out later, the commandant says, "I am not confident that we have adequately assessed all of the implications of the future operating environment on the proposed structure of our future infantry battalion." He directs further experimentation, so the organization of the infantry battalion is not a closed issue.

Cutting infantry battalions allows proportional cuts in supporting capabilities—in aviation, logistics, and fire support—thus creating enough savings to pay for new capabilities.

The infantry has long been the heart of the Marine Corps, so, if implemented, this would be a major institutional as well as force structure change. The three active-duty divisions would have 27 infantry battalions at full strength. The infantry battalions have been getting smaller over time, totaling about 1,050 Marines up until the mid-1980s. This change will take them down to about 725. Thus, the total number of Marines in infantry battalions goes from 28,350 in the early 1980s to 15,200 in the future, a cut of 47 percent for a Marine Corps of about the same size.

Fire support: The artillery community will be roughly the same size after the restructuring, but it will be dramatically different. Some of the new batteries will be HIMARS, which fire long-range guided and unguided missiles at land targets. Some will be a new system that fires tactical Tomahawk anti-ship missiles. Because of their guided munitions, missile and rocket batteries can hit ground targets and ships at long range. However, they do not support the infantry with massed and area fires as cannon batteries do. This shift is a statement that the Marine Corps does not expect to face adversary armies close-up on the ground but will instead fight maritime campaigns at long distances.

Tanks: This has been the most visible change. Tanks have been part of the Marine Corps since World War II and have fought in every conflict since then. As with changes to the artillery, it is a dramatic

---

151 "Press Release: Marine Corps Announces New Force Design Initiatives," U.S. Marine Corps, Marine Corps Combat Development Command, press release, March 23, 2020, https://insidedefense.com/sites/insidedefense.com/files/documents/2020/mar/03232020_fd.pdf.

statement that the Marine Corps does not plan to participate in ground conflicts in the future as it did in, for example, Desert Storm or the 2003 invasion of Iraq.

Bridge companies: These companies are useful for ground combat maneuver but not on islands.

Law enforcement battalions: These units are useful for counterinsurgency but would have little role in a Pacific maritime campaign. The fact that the Marine Corps retains no capability here shows the focus on the Western Pacific scenario and a determination not to get involved in future counterinsurgency campaigns.

Aviation Forces and Challenges

Table 3 shows the current aviation structure and proposed changes under *Force Design 2030*.

Table 3: Marine Corps Aviation Force Structure

	Current Structure	Proposed Structure
Rotary wing—tiltrotor	17 squadrons	14 squadrons
Rotary wing—light attack	7 squadrons	5 squadrons
Rotary wing—heavy	8 squadrons, currently transiting from aging CH-53Es to CH-53K	5 squadrons
Fixed wing—fighter attack (F-18, F-35)	18 total squadrons; planned acquisition: 353 F-35Bs (STOVL version) and 67 F-35Cs (carrier version)	No change to number of squadrons, but number of F-35s per squadron reduced from 16 to 10.
C-130 cargo aircraft	3 squadrons	4 squadrons
Unmanned aviation systems (UAVs)	3 squadrons unarmed ISR	Add 3 armed UAV squadrons,

Source: U.S. Marine Corps, *Force Design 2030* (Washington, DC: March 2020), https://www.hqmc.marines.mil/Portals/142/Docs/CMC38%20Force%20Design%202030%20Report%20Phase%20I%20and%20II.pdf?ver=2020-03-26-121328-460.

Tiltrotor: The restructuring cuts three squadrons because they mainly support infantry, which is getting smaller. The reduction may create some stress on the remaining squadrons since MV-22s have been used heavily. The Marine Corps has purchased all 360 MV-22 aircraft, so it is unclear where the cut aircraft will go, perhaps retained for the training base (which has used older models) and future attrition.

Rotary wing—light attack: The Marine Corps' light-attack helicopters (AH-1Zs) are most useful against enemy armor and infantry. Although the helicopters have enough range to participate in sea control, they lack a long-range stand-off weapon and need to get close to their target. Because the Marine Corps recently completed the buy of these aircraft, they will likely go into storage for later use. The reduced size and role for attack helicopters raises questions about whether the Marine Corps will participate in the Army's Future Attack Reconnaissance Aircraft program.

Rotary wing—heavy: The stated reason for the cut is that with less heavy equipment and less infantry, there is less need for heavy-lift helicopters. However, it is likely that General Berger also considered the high cost to maintain these large and expensive helicopters. The cut of three squadrons implies a one-third cut to the replacement CH-53K program, which is just entering production.

Fixed-wing fighter attack: The reduction in aircraft per squadron implies a cut of about 45 F-35s when training and maintenance overhead are included. As a key reason for the reduction, the restructuring report points to a pilot shortage and the Marine Corps' inability to fix the shortage. However, the commandant's guidance also signaled a willingness to trade off expensive and manned fixed-wing aircraft for UAVs. Nevertheless, General Berger indicates that the changes are not settled: "I am not convinced that we have a clear understanding yet of F-35 capacity requirements for the future force." He reinforced the point in a later media roundtable.[152] Cutting F-35s will be controversial because of the program's strong support in Congress, which has annually added aircraft to the budget.

C-130 cargo aircraft: This increase likely recognizes the need to support geographically widespread teams in distributed operations. Because C-130 aircraft can land on rough airfields, they can supply forces in austere, forward locations. The increase would therefore be for the cargo mission and not for the refueling mission since the number of Marine aircraft overall would decline.

UAVs: The Marine Corps has fallen far behind Air Force and Army in fielding armed UAVs as a result of its focus on manned aircraft such as the F-35. This change is long overdue but apparently delayed further by waiting for a developmental system. See the discussion below.

Chart 2: Marine Corps Aircraft Inventory by Type

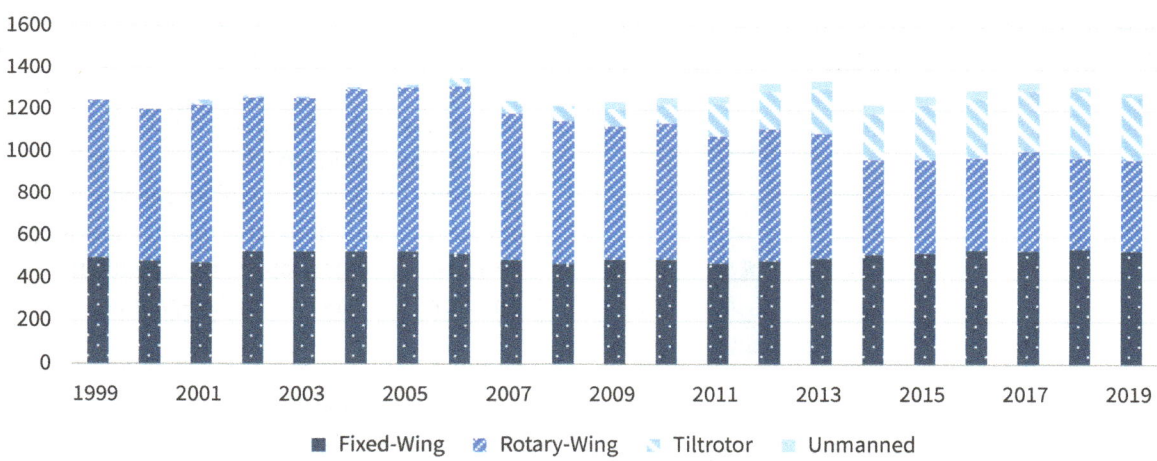

Source: Data from successive editions of International Institute for Strategic Studies, *Military Balance* (London, UK: Routledge, 1999-2019), https://www.iiss.org/publications/the-military-balance. Supplemented by U.S. Marine Corps, *2019 Marine Corps Aviation Plan* (Washington, DC: 2019), https://www.aviation.marines.mil/portals/11/2019%20avplan.pdf.

Marine aircraft inventories have increased for the last few years. The rotary-wing fleet has mostly been recapitalized with the MV-22 and UH/AH-1 procurements, so it is modern and relatively young. The CH-53K program will complete that recapitalization. The fixed-wing fleet is in the process of recapitalization with the F-35. So, despite the high cost of contemporary aircraft, Marine aviation is in pretty good shape, unlike the Air Force.

---

152 Megan Eckstein, "Marines Won't Cut F 35 Buy Total for Now but External Review May Change That," USNI News, April 1, 2020, https://news.usni.org/2020/04/01/marines-wont-cut-planned-f-35-buy-totals-for-now-but-external-review-could-change-that.

The effect of Marine Corps 2030 on aircraft inventories is unclear. It will cut rotary-wing, tiltrotor, and fixed-wing fighter attack but increase UAVs and C-130s. Since the forces being supported get smaller, the aviation inventory will likely also get smaller.

Lag in Fielding UAVs

The Marine Corps, having led the way on UAVs in the 1980s, now lags far behind the other services. General Berger vows to change this, saying that "starting with POM-22 [the Marine Corps will] develop a much broader family of unmanned systems."

The Marine Corps considered acquiring MQ-9 Reapers as an interim capability. It bought two MQ-9 Reapers in FY 2020 budget and was going to request another three in FY 2021 but did not. Instead, the Marine Corps is waiting for the USMC-developed large UAV (called MUX) because of its shipboard capabilities. However, the program is being restructured, having collapsed from having too many requirements piled on it. The Marine Corps hopes to have a family of systems with something fielded in the FY 2023 timeframe but the program is unsettled.[153]

This is a cautionary tale about letting the requirements process opt for the perfect (MUX) over the good (MQ-9).

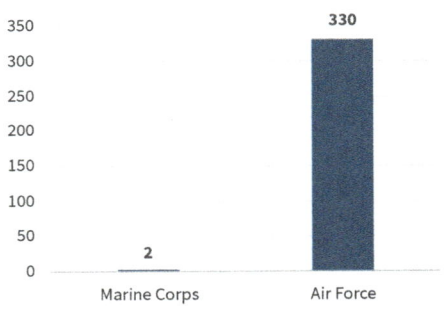

Chart 3: Marine Corps v. Air Force Armed UAVs in FY 2020

Source: *Highlights of The Department of the Navy FY 2021 Budget* (Washington, DC: Department of the Navy, February 2020), Figure 4-3, https://www.secnav.navy.mil/fmc/fmb/Documents/21pres/Highlights_book.pdf; and Department of the Air Force, *Budget United States Air Force Fiscal Year 2021 Budget Overview* (Washington, DC: March 2019), 38, Appendix, https://www.saffm.hq.af.mil/Portals/84/documents/FY21/SUPPORT_/FY21%20Budget%20Overview_1.pdf?ver=2020-02-10-152806-743.

The fate of the Marine Corps' RQ-21 Blackjack is unclear. Fielding has been completed to four operational squadrons, having experienced difficulties in development and a reduction in planned quantities to 21.[154] Located at regiment/MEU level, it will be capable of operating both ashore and from L-class ships. It performs reconnaissance and surveillance functions but has no attack capability.

However, *Force Design 2030* seems to indicate uncertainty about the future of the MQ-21 fleet. "We need to transition from our current UAS platforms to capabilities that can operate from ship, from shore, and be able to employ both collection and *lethal* [emphasis added] payloads."[155]

---

153 Megan Eckstein, "Marines Ditch MUX Ship-based Drone to Pursue Large Land-Based UAS, Smaller Ship Board Vehicle," Naval Institute News, March 10, 2020, https://news.usni.org/2020/03/10/marines-ditch-mux-ship-based-drone-to-pursue-large-land-based-uas-smaller-shipboard-vehicle.

154 Defense Operational Test and Evaluation, *RQ-21A Blackjack Unmanned Aircraft System* (Washington, DC: Department of Defense, January 2016), http://www.dote.osd.mil/pub/reports/FY2015; and Justin Katz, "Marine Corps Manpower Shift Leads to Reduction in RQ-21 FY-19 Request," Inside Defense, February 16, 2018, https://insidedefense.com/insider/marine-corps-manpower-shift-leads-reduction-rq-21-fy-19-request.

155 U.S. Marine Corps, *Force Design 2030*, 9.

The Marine Corps also fields a wide variety of smaller UAVs (RQ-11, -12, -20) for tactical reconnaissance and targeting and is experimenting aggressively with integrating such capabilities into small unit operations. None of these systems have attack capabilities, however.

Like the Navy, the Marine Corps has focused on manned aircraft and is far behind the Army and the Air Force in fielding UAV capabilities. General Berger wants to go in a different direction, but the Marine Corps MUX program is in disarray, and he faces decades of aviation culture built around manned aircraft.

Reaction to Marine Corps 2030

The proposed restructuring has been met with both support and doubts. Support comes from strategists who see China as the primary threat and would focus defense efforts tightly on that adversary. They endorse the new technologies and operational concepts.[156]

Doubts arise from five primary concerns.[157]

- The focus on China downplays the possibility of conflicts elsewhere. Since World War II, the United States has fought many regional conflicts but never a great power conflict. Thus, James Webb, former senator, former secretary of the Navy, and Marine combat veteran, criticized a narrow focus on China: "If history teaches us anything in combat, it is that the war you get is rarely the war that you game . . . [The restructuring] could permanently reduce the long-standing mission of global readiness that for more than a century has been the essential reason for [the Marine Corps'] existence as a separate service."[158]

- The new warfighting concepts are unproven. The restructure assumes that in a conflict with China, Marine forces could move into the Chinese defensive bubble, survive, and be supported. That briefs well but may not work in a contested environment where logistics need to move forward continuously and adversary firepower can strike isolated Marine outposts.[159]

---

156 For example, T.X. Hammes, "Building a Marine Corps for Every Contingency, Clime, and Place," War on the Rocks, April 15, 2020, https://warontherocks.com/2020/04/building-a-marine-corps-for-every-contingency-clime-and-place/; Jake Yaeger, "Expeditionary Advanced Maritime Operations: How the Marine Corps Can Avoid Becoming a Second Land Army in the Pacific," War on the Rocks, December 26, 2019, https://warontherocks.com/2019/12/expeditionary-advanced-maritime-operations-how-the-marine-corps-can-avoid-becoming-a-second-land-army-in-the-pacific/; Benjamin Jensen, "The Rest of the Story: Evaluating the US Marine Corps Force Design 2030," War on the Rocks, April 27, 2020, https://warontherocks.com/2020/04/the-rest-of-the-story-evaluating-the-u-s-marine-corps-force-design-2030; and Jeff Cummings, Scott Cuomo, Olivia Garard, and Noah Spataro, "Getting the Context of Marine Corps Reform Right," War on the Rocks, May 1, 2020, https://warontherocks.com/2020/05/getting-the-context-of-marine-corps-reform-right/.

157 Raising all the concerns, Tanner Greer, "The Tip of the American Military Spear Is Being Blunted," Foreign Policy, September 29, 2020, https://foreignpolicy.com/2020/07/06/us-marines-strategy-military-tip-spear-china-congress/; Paul McHale, "A Critical Assessment of Marine Commandant David Berger's Planning Guidance and Force Design 2030," privately circulated; and Mark Cancian, "Don't Go Too Crazy, Marine Corps," War on the Rocks, January 8, 2020, https://warontherocks.com/2020/01/dont-go-too-crazy-marine-corps/.

158 James Webb, "The Future of the US Marine Corps," The National Interest, May 8, 2020, https://nationalinterest.org/feature/future-us-marine-corps-152606; and Dan Goure, "Will Commandant Burger's Planning Guidance Mean the End of the Marine Corps?," Real Clear Defense, December 13, 2019, https://www.realcleardefense.com/articles/2019/12/13/will_commandant_bergers_planning_guidance_mean_the_end_of_the_marine_corps_114919.html.

159 Walker Mills, Dylan Phillips-Levine, and Colin Fox, "Cocaine Logistics for the Marine Corps," War on the Rocks, July 22, 2020, https://warontherocks.com/2020/07/cocaine-logistics-for-the-marine-corps/.

- A force design for one kind of operation cannot necessarily conduct a different kind of operation successfully. Thus, a Marine Corps designed for an island campaign against China in the Western Pacific will be poorly designed for conflicts elsewhere, particularly regional conflicts that might occur in Korea or the Middle East. The U.S. Army of the 1960s that was designed to fight the Soviets on the plains of Germany was poorly positioned to fight insurgents in the jungles of Southeast Asia.[160]
- Conflicts against China and Russia are likely to operate in the gray zone and are not high-intensity and kinetic. The new force design is not well suited for these demands because of reductions to counterinsurgency capabilities and the reorientation of training to focus exclusively on a high-end fight.[161]
- All warfighting requires close-in firepower. The new structure focuses on long-range precision fire, but the need for close-in fires, including tanks and cannon artillery, has not gone away.[162]

Marine Air-Ground Task Forces

The Marine Corps has long prided itself on being able to task organize—that is, to put existing units together into temporary groups for a particular purpose. The Marine Corps has a standard set of task force templates for what it calls Marine Air-Ground Task Forces (MAGTFs). Each of the standard templates has four elements: a command element, a ground combat element, an aviation element, and a logistics element. The largest, a Marine Expeditionary Force (46,000–90,000 Marines), is built around the Marine division and air wing. The middle-sized force, the Marine Expeditionary Brigade (4,000–16,000 Marines), is built around an infantry regiment and air group. The smallest, the Marine Expeditionary Unit (MEU, about 2,200 Marines), is built around an infantry battalion and composite squadron.[163]

Two new task forces have received attention: special-purpose MAGTFs (SP-MAGTFs) and littoral combat regiments.

SP-MAGTFs: Although not new, SP-MAGTF units represent a different capability for the Marine Corps. Traditionally, the smallest unit that the Marine Corps deployed was an MEU. To provide rapid response and persistent presence in AFRICOM and CENTCOM and periodic theater engagement in SOUTHCOM, the Marine Corps established these land-based special-purpose units, which are smaller than the MEU. That made them both more agile and easier to deploy, though at the cost of logistics and firepower.

---

160   Mark Stout, "Archives: World War I and the Lesser Included Threat," War on the Rocks, December 5, 2014, https://warontherocks.com/2014/12/warchives-world-war-i-and-the-lesser-included-threat/; and Ben Wan Beng Ho, "Shortfalls in the Marine Corps EABO Concept," Naval Institute, *Proceedings*, July 2020, https://www.usni.org/magazines/proceedings/2020/july/shortfalls-marine-corps-eabo-concept.

161   John Vrolyk, "Insurgency, Not War, Is China's Most Likely Course of Action," War on the Rocks, December 19, 2019, https://warontherocks.com/2019/12/insurgency-not-war-is-chinas-most-likely-course-of-action/.

162   Jared Simonelli, "Declawing the Tiger: Rebuttal of the Decision to Phase out Marine Tank Battalions," The Strategy Bridge, August 4, 2020, https://thestrategybridge.org/the-bridge/2020/8/4/declawing-the-tiger-a-rebuttal-of-the-decision-to-phase-out-marine-tank-battalions; and Sebastien Roblin, "One for the Books: Marine Corps Sherman Tanks Have a Brutal Fight at Tarawa Atoll," National Interest, August 11, 2020, https://nationalinterest.org/blog/buzz/one-books-marine-corps-sherman-tanks-had-brutal-fight-tarawa-atoll-152131.

163   U.S. Marine Corps, *Expeditionary Operations*, Doctrinal Publication 3 (Washington, DC: 1998), 69–77, https://www.marines.mil/Portals/1/Publications/MCDP%203.pdf?ver=2019-07-18-093631-287.

The Marine Corps appears to be reconsidering the mission and staffing of SP-MAGTFs, using deployed MEUs when these are in the region and regular units to meet specific taskings. This eases the burden of creating new special-purpose units, even relatively small ones.

Marine Littoral Regiment (MLR): This new kind of unit would deliver anti-ground and anti-ship fires and be able to survive inside an adversary's (e.g., China's) defensive bubble. These new units harken back to a World War II capability, Marine defense battalions, which were designed to protect forward bases from naval and air attack. The Marine Corps is experimenting in Hawaii using troops stationed there. MLRs tentatively consist of a combat team, an air-defense battalion, and a logistics unit, though their exact structure and numbers are unclear at this point.[164]

Also unclear is whether MLRs will be permanent or task-organized units. MLRs look a lot like a specialized MEU, though they are not characterized that way.

Guam and Pacific Force Stationing

This is a classic good news (Australia) and bad news (Okinawa/Guam/Japan) story.

Okinawa/Guam/Japan: The Marine Corps is engaged in a long-term effort to ease the burden of its force footprint on Okinawa by moving forces to Guam, though also to mainland Japan, Hawaii, and the mainland United States. The current plan is for the number of Marines on Okinawa to be halved, to 11,500, by 2027.[165]

The government of Japan is paying for much of the massive facility construction on Guam, and construction is going forward, though the timeline has slipped repeatedly.[166] In September, the Marine Corps christened a new base, Camp Blaz, named for a Marine general of Guamanian descent. Apparently only 1,300 Marines will be permanently stationed on Guam, with another 3,700 coming to the island as a rotational force. This is a change from the original expectation that all troops would be permanently stationed on Guam.[167]

The re-stationing effort also involves building a new air facility—called the Futenma replacement facility—in the less inhabited northern area of Okinawa at Camp Schwab. This project continues to have difficulties, with the completion date pushed out again, to 2030, and the price skyrocketing. It appears unlikely that this will ever be completed.[168]

---

164 Megan Eckstein, "Marines Testing Regiment at Heart of Emerging Island Hopping Future," USNI News, June 4, 2020, https://news.usni.org/2020/06/04/marines-testing-regiment-at-heart-of-emerging-island-hopping-future; and Sean Snow, "New Marine Littoral Regiment, Designed to Fight in Contested Maritime Environment, Coming to Hawaii," *Marine Corps Times*, May 14, 2020, https://www.marinecorpstimes.com/news/your-marine-corps/2020/05/14/new-marine-littoral-regiment-designed-to-fight-in-contested-maritime-environment-coming-to-hawaii.

165 Emma Chanlett-Avery, Christopher T. Mann, and Joshua A. Williams, "U.S. Military Presence on Okinawa and Realignment to Guam," Congressional Research Service, April 9, 2019, https://fas.org/sgp/crs/row/IF10672.pdf.

166 "U.S. to start moving Okinawa-based marines to Guam in 2024," *Japan Times*, April 27, 2017, https://www.japantimes.co.jp/news/2017/04/27/national/politics-diplomacy/u-s-start-moving-okinawa-based-marines-guam-2024/#.WZw_qsa1vct.

167 Seth Robson, "Marines Activate Camp Blaz on Guam," *Stars & Stripes*, September 30, 2020, https://www.stripes.com/news/pacific/marines-activate-camp-blaz-on-guam-the-corps-first-new-base-since-1952-1.647005.

168 Matthew Burke and Aya Ichihashi, "Marine Airfield Relocation on Okinawa to Take 16 Years Longer and Cost $5.4 billion More Than Originally Projected," *Stars & Stripes*, May 29, 2020, https://www.stripes.com/news/pacific/marine-airfield-relocation-on-okinawa-to-take-16-years-longer-and-5-4-billion-more-than-originally-projected-1.631642.

The entire re-stationing effort is a cautionary tale to those seeking to move U.S. forces around the globe. Although there are strong strategic reasons for such posture changes, executing them can be extremely challenging in the real world of local politics, regional tensions, and the inevitable difficulties involved with large-scale construction projects.

Australia: By contrast to the slow and controversial moves on Okinawa and Guam, the Marine Corps' rotational deployments to Darwin, Australia continue into their tenth year without controversy, with six-month rotations on the ground of about 1,200 personnel each year. Rotations restarted after a pause during the pandemic. The rotations have continued through changes of administration in both Australia and the United States, so the politics look settled. The disadvantage is that the forces are a great distance from any likely conflict (2,500 miles from the South China Sea).

Amphibious Ships, Alternative Platforms, and Global Deployments

Amphibious ships: The Navy chapter described how the amphibious fleet will lose some of its high-end ships, potentially up to six helicopter carriers (LHAs/LHDs) repurposed to be "light carriers" that complement the "supercarriers (CVNs)." The Navy might curtail the number of LPD's flight I and II, although it has not released specifics. Instead, the amphibious fleet will add 28 to 30 light amphibious warships (LAWs). Each LAW would carry 75 Marines. Because such a ship is much smaller than anything in the current or recent inventory, it will change the way Marines organize and train for amphibious operations. It is also unprecedented in recent amphibious ship design in that it is intended for relatively short voyages, transit from point A to point B, and not for long-term deployments.

Alternative platforms: The Navy and Marine Corps may use non-amphibious ships, such as Maritime Prepositioning Force ships (TAK-Es), high-speed vessels (Expeditionary Fast Transports, or EPFs), and mobile landing platforms/afloat forward staging bases (now called Expeditionary Sea Base, or ESB, and Expeditionary Transfer Dock, or ESD). General Berger used them extensively when he was the Marine commander in the Pacific, but the concept does not appear in his guidance.[169]

Global deployments: The total numbers will go up, but the number of ships capable of global deployments will go down. This new amphibious fleet will not sustain the current structure of seven MEUs (one in Japan, three on the West Coast, three on the East Coast) and their long-standing forward deployments.

---

169 Robert D. Holzer and Scott C. Truver, "The U.S. Navy In Review," U.S. Naval Institute, *Proceedings*, May 2017, https://www.usni.org/magazines/proceedings/2017-05/us-navy-review.

5

Air Force

The Air Force continues the development and procurement of next-generation aircraft to meet the demands of great power conflict. Fielding of new aircraft has been enough to arrest the increase in fleet age. However, the Air Force is not buying enough new aircraft to sustain its force structure, so it seeks to retire older aircraft.

KEY TAKEAWAYS
- Air Force military personnel levels, active and reserve component, increase slightly in FY 2021 and over the five-year period but remain essentially level. The largest increases are among civilians.
- Like the other services, the Air Force faces high day-to-day operational tempo while at the same time preparing to meet the demands of great power conflict.
- Aircraft inventories and fleet aging have stabilized in the near term.
- However, the Air Force is not buying enough new aircraft to maintain the inventory over the long term. Increasing procurement to the levels needed to sustain the inventory will require historically high costs.
- Instead, the Air Force plans to close this gap by retiring older aircraft and shrinking the force, possibly substantially. However, Congress has been reluctant to do this in the past.
- Given these circumstances, the Air Force is backing away from its 25 percent expansion goal to reach 386 operational squadrons.
- The FY 2021 budget procures no unmanned aircraft, so the unmanned fleet has plateaued at 6 percent of the force.

- Nuclear forces require a greater share of the Air Force budget as Reagan-era systems reach the end of their service lives, and as a result, nuclear modernization generates some opposition.
- The Space Force continues to take shape, so far entirely from Air Force elements.

End Strength in FY 2021

Table 1: Air Force End Strength – Active and Civilians

	Air Force Active		Civilian Full-Time Equivalents
	Combat Coded Squadrons	Authorized End Strength	
FY 2020 Enacted	40	332,800	172,100
FY 2021 Request	40	333,700	174,600
Change	0	-100	+2,500

Note: Combat coded squadrons = fighter and bomber squadrons with a wartime mission; Air Force is moving toward a new sizing metric—operational squadrons—which includes fighters, bombers, airlift, intelligence/surveillance/reconnaissance (ISR), command and control (C2), special operations, space, cyber, missile, and personnel recovery squadrons. By that metric, there are currently 301 squadrons.

Source: Department of Defense, *United States Air Force Budget Overview Fiscal Year 2021* (Washington, DC, April 2020), 5, https://www.saffm.hq.af.mil/Portals/84/documents/FY20/FY2020%20Air%20Force%20Budget%20Overview%20Book%20Final%20v3.pdf?ver=2019-03-13-082653-843; Squadron and civilian data from Office of the Under Secretary of Defense (Comptroller), *Defense Budget Overview* (Washington, DC: April 2020), 2–8, A-4, 5, https://comptroller.defense.gov/Portals/45/Documents/defbudget/fy2021/fy2021_Budget_Request_Overview_Book.pdf.

Table 2: Air Force End Strength – Reserve and Air National Guard

	Air Force Reserve		Air National Guard	
	Combat Coded Squadrons	Authorized End Strength	Combat Coded Squadrons	Authorized End Strength
FY 2020 Planned	3	70,000	21	107,100
FY 2021 Request	3	70,100	21	107,700
Change	0	+100	0	+600

Source: Department of Defense, *United States Air Force Budget Overview Fiscal Year 2021*, 5. Squadron data from Office of the Under Secretary of Defense (Comptroller), *Defense Budget Overview*, A-3.

All three components maintain the same major elements of the force structure. Changes in personnel levels are small.

A bright spot is active/reserve relations. By working closely with its reserve components, and giving them at least a small end strength increase, the Air Force has avoided the internal conflicts that had marred earlier budgets and required a 2014 force structure commission to make peace.[170]

---

170 National Commission on the Structure of the Air Force, *Report to the President and Congress of the United States* (Washington, DC: January 2014), https://policy.defense.gov/Portals/11/Documents/hdasa/AFForceStructureCommissionReport01302014.pdf.

Another bright spot is that the pandemic is solving the Air Force's long-standing and, until recently, severe pilot shortage. With the commercial travel industry in deep recession, the airlines have stopped hiring, so pilots are staying in the service.

Chart 1: Air Force – Active End Strength, 1999–2021

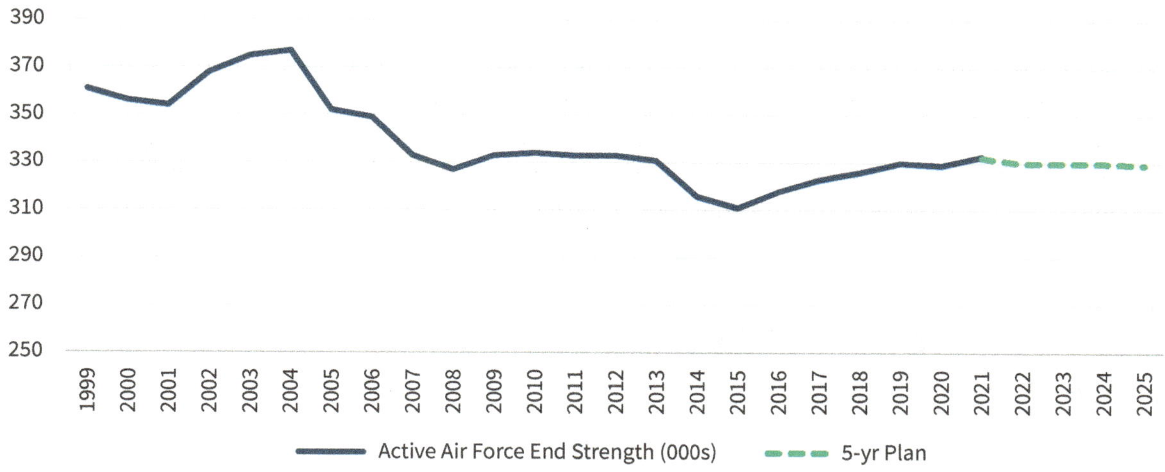

Source: Office of the Under Secretary of Defense (Comptroller), *National Defense Budget Estimates for FY 2021* (Washington, DC: April 2020), Table 7-5: Department of Defense Manpower, 260–262, https://comptroller.defense.gov/Portals/45/Documents/defbudget/fy2021/FY21_Green_Book.pdf.

As the chart above shows, end strength rose in the wake of the invasions of Afghanistan and Iraq. After 2004, however, the Air Force adopted a strategy of retiring older aircraft and reducing personnel to shift funds to modernization. Active-duty end strength fell from a high of 377,000 to a low of 316,000. Critics argued that this decrease had harmed readiness and gutted the pilot inventory.[171] Thus, the Air Force began increasing end strength in FY 2016.

Personnel levels will stay at about the FY 2021 level through FY 2025. This is likely a hedge against an uncertain budget future. The Air Force is reluctant to add personnel that it cannot sustain but is not at the point of major cuts either. However, the Air Force budget documents reveal no details.

Indeed, this lack of information permeates the Air Force FY 2021 budget documents. Although there is extensive data about the budget year, there is almost no description of what might happen in the future for personnel or force structure. This contrasts with previous years, where the budget documents had some explanation of what would happen during the five-year planning period. Further, the Air Force's two major development programs, the B-21 bomber and the Next Generation Air Dominance aircraft, are classified programs about which little is known publicly.

---

171 Mike Benitez, "Air Force in Crisis, Part II: How Did We Get Here?," War on the Rocks, March 8, 2018, https://warontherocks.com/2018/03/air-force-in-crisis-part-ii-how-did-we-get-here/.

Operational Tempo: Gone as a Stated Concern

Like the other services, the Air Force notes how busy it is. In the annual posture statement, Secretary Barrett and General Goldfein stated that "over 28,000 Airmen deployed worldwide last year . . . flew more than 75,000 strike sorties, employed more than 11,000 weapons in Iraq, Syria, and Afghanistan, and conducted more than 27,000 airlift and refueling sorties across U.S. Central Command."[172]

Despite the description of high activity, any mention of stress resulting from these operations is gone. RAND noted that "since the 1990s, the US military has operated at a tempo more akin to war than peace" and found that "prolonged operations are driving contemporary [Air Force] capacity shortfalls" and that these would continue in the four notional futures that RAND analyzed.[173] Nevertheless, comparing the Air Force's statement about operations this year with statements in previous years, the level seems to have gone down from the height of the bombing campaigns against ISIS in Syria/Iraq and against the Taliban in Afghanistan.

Force Structure in FY 2021 and Beyond

Chart 2: Air Force – Aircraft Inventory

Source: Department of Defense, *United States Air Force Budget Overview Fiscal Year 2021*, 6.

The Air Force has stabilized its force structure at about 5,500 aircraft, after a sharp decline from 2002 to 2009. The Air Force has maintained its inventories by allowing the average aircraft age to increase (to 29.2 years).[174]

---

172 U.S. Air Force, *USAF Posture Statement Fiscal Year 2021* (Washington, DC: March 2020), https://www.armed-services.senate.gov/imo/media/doc/Barrett--Goldfein_03-03-20.pdf.

173 Alan Vick, Paul Dreyer, and John Speed Myers, *Is the Air Force Flying Force Large Enough? Assessing Capacity Demands in for Alternative Futures* (Santa Monica, CA: RAND Corporation, 2018), https://www.rand.org/pubs/research_reports/RR2500.html.

174 Numbers measured by Total Active Inventory (TAI), that is, aircraft assigned to operating forces, as well as for test and maintenance. It includes primary, backup, and attrition reserve aircraft.

This happened because the Air Force took a procurement holiday in the late-1990s and, for its numerous fighter/attack aircraft, planned to move directly to an all fifth-generation force fleet. This plan collapsed in the early-2000s when the F-22 buy was curtailed at 187 aircraft, and the F-35 program was delayed many years because of development problems.

Thus, Stephen Kosiak, a long-time budget commentator, has argued that these trends [shrinking inventories and aging fleets] arise from deliberate choices: "[H]istorical trends in the US military's force structure and modernization plans are largely the result of policy and programmatic choices made by DOD and service leadership. Contrary to widely held belief . . . the size and shape of today's forces are not simply a byproduct of budgetary or other pressures beyond DOD's control."[175]

The good news is that fleet aging overall has nearly stopped as new aircraft enter the force. The bad news is that the procurement cost of just maintaining the current inventory will rise far above historical aircraft procurement budget levels through the 2030s.

> **The good news is that fleet aging overall has nearly stopped as new aircraft enter the force. The bad news is that the procurement cost of just maintaining the current inventory will rise far above historical aircraft procurement budget levels through the 2030s.**

Although the Navy and Army also face challenges with aircraft aging and maintaining their aircraft fleets, the Air Force is in far worse shape regarding aging and the slow acquisition of replacements.[176]

---

[175] Steven M. Kosiak, *Is the US Military Getting Smaller and Older? And How Much Should We Care?* (Washington, DC: Center for a New American Strategy, June 2017), https://s3.amazonaws.com/files.cnas.org/documents/CNASReport-SmallerOlderMilitary-Final.pdf.

[176] Edward Keating, *The Cost of Replacing the Department of Defense's Current Aviation Fleet* (Washington, DC: Congressional Budget Office, January 2020), https://www.cbo.gov/system/files/2020-01/55950-CBO-DoD-aviation.pdf; for analysis of the Air Force fleet specifically, see Edward Keating, David Arthur, and Adebayo Adejeji, *The Cost of Replacing Today's Air Forces Fleet* (Washington, DC: Congressional Budget Office, December 2018), https://www.cbo.gov/system/files/2018-12/54657-AirForceAviationFunding.pdf.

Chart 3: Air Force – Aircraft Average Age and Inventory

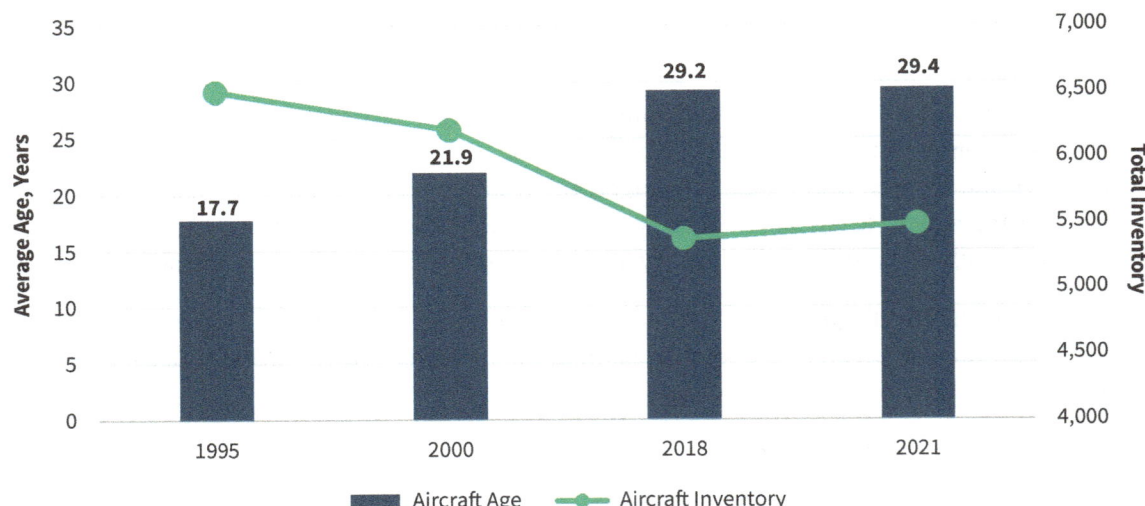

Source: Air Force Association, "USAF Almanac 2020," *Air Force Magazine* 103, no. 6 (June 2020): 63, https://www.airforcemag.com/app/uploads/2020/06/June2020_Fullissue5.pdf; Air Force Association, "USAF Almanac 2001," *Air Force Magazine* 84, no. 5 (May 2001): 55–58, http://www.airforcemag.com/MagazineArchive/Magazine%20Documents/2001/May%202001/0501facts_figs.pdf; and Air Force Association, "USAF Almanac 1996," *Air Force Magazine* 79, no. 5 (May 1996): 56–60, http://www.airforcemag.com/MagazineArchive/Magazine%20Documents/1996/May%201996/0596facts_figures.pdf. 2000 and 1995 years calculated by averaging the average age of the active, reserve, and air national guard fleet aircraft.

Some fleets are in relatively good shape: the transport fleet (21 years, on average) because of acquiring C-17s and C-130s, the special operations fleet (12 years) because of its high priority, and the UAVs/RPVs (6 years) because of large wartime purchases. Other fleets are old: fighter/attack (29 years old), bomber (42 years), tanker (49 years), helicopter (32 years), and trainers (32 years).[177] All the older fleets (except for some specialty aircraft) have programs in place for modernization, but the programs have been delayed, are expensive, and may take years to implement fully.

Unfortunately, the FY 2021 procurement level is far too low to sustain the Air Force's current inventory. In FY 2021, the Air Force proposes to procure 106 aircraft.

Assuming a 30-year service life, this will sustain an inventory of 3,180 aircraft.

> 106 aircraft procured in FY 2021 x 30-year service life = 3,180 total inventory

The current inventory is 5,387. To sustain that inventory requires nearly doubling the number of aircraft acquired per year.

> 5,387 target inventory ÷ 30-year service life = 180 aircraft acquired per year

Even if aircraft service life were extended to 40 years, the Air Force would still need to buy substantially more aircraft.

> 5,387 target inventory ÷ 40-year service life = 135 aircraft acquired per year

---

177 Fleet age numbers current as of September 30, 2019, from Air Force Association, "Air Force and Space Force Almanac 2020," *Air Force Magazine* 103, no. 6 (June 2020), 63, https://www.airforcemag.com/issue/2020-06/.

> *Some fleets are in relatively good shape . . . other fleets are old. All the older fleets . . . have programs in place for modernization, but the programs have been delayed, are expensive, and may take years to implement fully.*

The bottom line is that to sustain its current inventory, the Air Force will have to buy many more aircraft or less expensive aircraft. Alternatively, the Air Force will need to greatly reduce its aircraft inventory and sharply cut its force structure.

Divest to Invest

The Air Force has two reasons to reduce its aircraft inventory and associated force structure. First, as described above, is its inability to maintain the structure with the number of aircraft that it has been able to procure recently and in the foreseeable future. Second is its desire to make a wide variety of (expensive) investments in advanced systems, aircraft, weapons, sensors, and networks that would be suitable for conflict with a great power.

General Charles Q. Brown, the new Air Force chief of staff, expressed this in his first communication to Air Force personnel: "Our airmen need us to integrate and accelerate the changes necessary to explore new operational concepts and bring more rapidly the capabilities that will help them in future fights." Thus, he talks about "ruthless prioritization," implying the elimination of many older systems.[178] Air Force budget documents foreshadow a large future force structure cut: "The Air Force is planning for less legacy force capacity to begin investing additional manpower into capabilities for tomorrow's high-intensity conflict against near-peer competitors."[179]

> *General Charles Q. Brown, the new Air Force chief of staff . . . talks about "ruthless prioritization," implying the elimination of many older systems.*

For this reason, the Air Force has repeatedly proposed to retire aircraft. The proposed retirements for FY 2021 are modest (see Table 4). Congress, however, has often balked at retirements, noting that the Air Force says it is already too small for the tasks it has been given. When the Air Force proposed

---

178 Charles Q. Brown, Jr., "Accelerate Change or Lose," U.S. Air Force, August 2020, https://www.airforcemag.com/app/uploads/2020/08/CSAF-22-Strategic-Approach-Accelerate-Change-or-Lose-31-Aug-2020.pdf.

179 Department of the Air Force, *Fiscal Year FY 2021 Budget Estimates, Military Personnel Appropriation* (Washington, DC: February 2020), 6, https://www.saffm.hq.af.mil/Portals/84/documents/FY21/MILPER_/FY21%20Air%20Force%20Military%20Personnel_1.pdf?ver=2020-02-10-091310-847.

eliminating the A-10 fleet, for example, Congress opposed such an action, putting explicit prohibitions in the FY 2015 NDAA and proposed FY 2021 NDAA.[180]

A recent CSIS report laid out the savings that the Air Force might achieve by retiring certain aircraft fleets. The fleets most likely to be retired are the KC-10 tanker, the B-1 and B-2 bombers, the A-10 close air support aircraft, the E-8C surveillance aircraft, the U-2 spy plane, and the E-3 airborne warning and control plane. The report argued that the greatest savings arose when entire fleets were eliminated, thus eliminating the fixed costs of a training and maintenance infrastructure.

However, the report also noted that such retirements would leave gaps in Air Force capabilities. Retiring the B-2 bombers, for example, would leave the United States without a stealthy penetrating bomber until the B-21 was fielded in strength.[181]

These force structure trade-offs drive a series of strategic choices about airpower:

- **What kinds of conflicts should the Air Force prepare for: those against great powers or a spectrum of air environments, including those with less-demanding environments?** In lower threat air environments, such as North Korea, the Air Force can use legacy aircraft extensively. For conflicts against great powers such as China and Russia, with their sophisticated air defenses, the Air Force would need to focus exclusively on advanced capabilities.

- **How can airpower achieve the greatest effects?** Will the greatest effects come from attacks close to friendly front lines—that is, through close air support and battlefield interdiction? The ground forces are strong advocates here, arguing that these effects are immediate and tangible.[182] Airpower advocates argue that the greatest effect comes from the deep attack of strategic targets. The Air Force has historically leaned toward the latter for a variety of organizational and doctrinal reasons.[183]

- **What is the value of stealth in modern air warfare?** Stealth—needed to penetrate heavily defended airspaces—is expensive to develop, procure, and sustain.[184] Further, there is an operational penalty. Proponents argue that the cost and performance trade-offs are worthwhile

---

180 Carl Levin and Howard P. 'Buck' McKeon National Defense Authorization Act for Fiscal Year 2015, https://www.congress.gov/bill/113th-congress/house-bill/3979; Senate Armed Services Committee, National Defense Authorization Act for Fiscal Year 2021, https://www.congress.gov/bill/116th-congress/senate-bill/4049.

181 Todd Harrison, "How the Air Force Can Save $30 Billion," CSIS, November 12, 2019, https://aerospace.csis.org/wp-content/uploads/2019/11/How-the-Air-Force-Can-Save-30-Billion.pdf.

182 Scott Beauchamp, "An Infantryman's Defense of the A-10," Task and Purpose, February 29, 2016, http://taskandpurpose.com/infantrymans-defense-10.

183 The literature on close air support versus strategic attack is extensive. For a recent example, see Phil Haun and Colin Johnson, "Breaker of Armies: Airpower in the Easter Offensive and the Myth of Linebacker One and Two in the Vietnam War," *International Security* 40, no. 3 (Winter 2015/16): 139–78, https://www.mitpressjournals.org/doi/abs/10.1162/ISEC_a_00226?journalCode=isec.

184 Technically not "stealth" but "low observability" since nothing is actually invisible. The additional cost of stealth is difficult to estimate since aircraft are bought in different quantities, have different characteristics beyond stealth, and costs can include different elements (such as development). One data point is from the Navy, which is buying both fourth generation F-18E/Fs and fifth generation F-35s. The average recurring procurement cost of F-35B/Cs over the life of the program is about 30 percent more than an F-18 in FY 2020. Adding non-recurring costs for manufacturing and development would greatly increase the cost differential.

because of rising air threats.[185] Opponents argue that only a small part of the fleet needs to be stealthy, while the rest can be non-stealthy.[186]

The answers to these questions go far beyond this report, but the questions show that there are difficult strategic decisions behind inventory numbers.

The Air Force Expansion Proposal: Fading Away

Not surprisingly, given the Air Force's difficulty in maintaining the current fleet size, its proposal for expansion is fading away.

> *Not surprisingly, given the Air Force's difficulty in maintaining the current fleet size, its proposal for expansion is fading away.*

In 2018, then-secretary of the Air Force Heather Wilson proposed a 25 percent increase in force structure, describing it as "the Air Force we need" (see Chart 5).[187] This would increase the Air Force from 312 operational squadrons to 386. Much of the growth would be in enabling capabilities such as tankers, special forces, space, and especially command and control (C2) and intelligence, surveillance, and reconnaissance (ISR), which provide the precision targeting that long-range munitions require.

---

185 For example, Jeff Harrigian and Max Morosko, "Fifth Generation Air Combat: Maintaining the Joint Force Edge," Mitchell Institute for Aerospace Studies, The Mitchell Forum, no. 6, July 2016, http://docs.wixstatic.com/ugd/a2dd91_bd906e69631146079c4d082d0eda1d68.pdf; and Loren Thompson, "Trump Defense Team inherits Bad Ideas About Air Power from The Obama Years," Forbes, February 2, 2017, https://www.forbes.com/sites/lorenthompson/2017/02/01/trump-defense-team-inherits-bad-ideas-about-air-power-from-the-obama-years.

186 For example, Mike Pietrucha, "The U.S. Air Force and Stealth: Stuck on Denial Part I," War on the Rocks, March 24, 2016, http://warontherocks.com/2016/03/stuck-on-denial-part-i-the-u-s-air-force-and-stealth; and Mike Benitez, "Stealth Is King, the World Is Flat," War on the Rocks, May 19, 2016, https://warontherocks.com/2016/05/stealth-is-king-the-world-is-flat/.

187 Chuck Broadway, "SecAF Wilson provides Air Force update," U.S. Air Force, September 17, 2018, https://www.af.mil/News/Article-Display/Article/1635645/secaf-wilson-provides-air-force-update/ (full speech linked here: https://spacepolicyonline.com/wp-content/uploads/2018/09/SECAF-AFA-Speech-FInal-Sep-17-2018-AF-We-Need.pdf).

Chart 4: Air Force Expansion by Mission Category

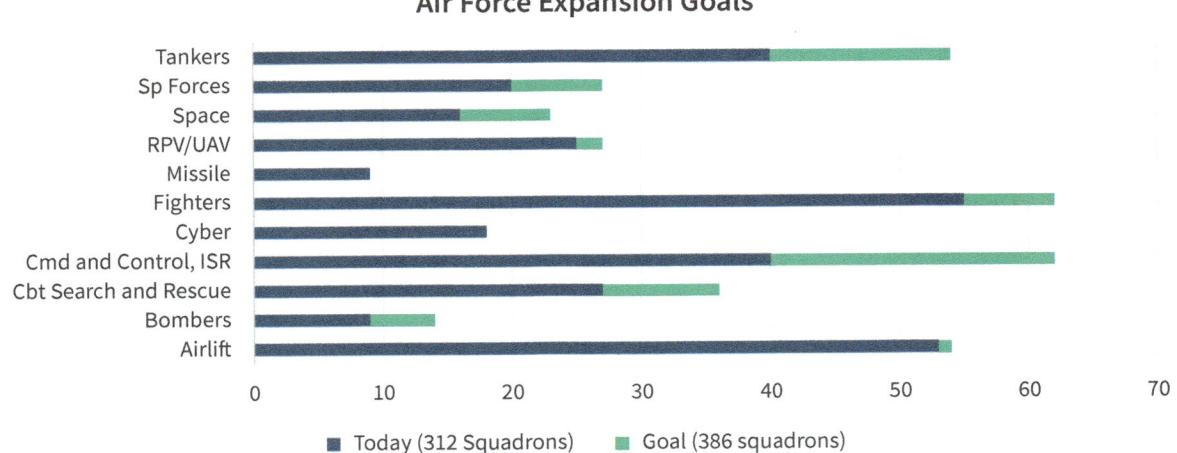

Source: Air Force, *Restoring Readiness: FY2020 Posture* (Washington, DC: April 2019), https://www.af.mil/Portals/1/documents/5/FY20_Posture_Statement.pdf?ver=2019-04-04-092535-083&timestamp=1554384341518.

In 2019 and 2020, the Air Force reaffirmed this goal. General Goldfein discussed it explicitly and at length in his FY 2020 posture statement. It disappeared from the FY 2021 posture statement.[188] This was unsurprising since the Air Force has taken no steps to reach this expansion goal, unlike the Navy and its 355-ship goal. When General Charles Brown, the new Air Force chief of staff, was asked about it, he said that 386 squadrons were indeed what the Air Force needed to execute the strategy, but the goal had been a resource unconstrained answer to a congressional question. Instead, he talked about achieving the required "capability," not necessarily the numbers.[189]

All of this might be written off as another exercise in fiscally unconstrained planning, but the tension between the expansion goal and the Air Force's desire to shrink to save money for modernization will provide a lever for those in Congress and elsewhere who are reluctant to retire older aircraft.

The State of the Fleets

In general, the Air Force has programs in place to modernize the individual fleets, but this modernization has been delayed and will take time, and as a result, today's aging fleets will be around for a long while. Nevertheless, each fleet faces its own circumstances and therefore deserves individual consideration.

---

188 U.S. Air Force, *USAF Posture Statement Fiscal Year 2021*.
189 "Ep. 76: Air Force Chief of Staff Gen. Charles Q. Brown, Jr.," Defense One podcast, September 24, 2020, https://www.defenseone.com/ideas/2020/09/ep-76-air-force-chief-staff-gen-charles-q-brown-jr/168745/.

The Bomber Force

The bomber force consists of B-52s, B-1s, and B-2s. The long-range plan is for the B-21 Raider to replace the B-1s and B-2s. The B-52s will continue in service at least into the 2040s and maybe beyond. The last B-52 pilot has probably not yet been born.

Since no new aircraft are being produced, the bomber force continues to age (currently 43 years on average), though various upgrade programs keep the aircraft flying and operationally relevant, for example, new engines for the B-52s and a new defensive system for the B-2s. The Air Force would like to divest some of the B-1s early but has run into congressional opposition.

The B-21 Raider program continues in development, with budget demands seeming to stabilize: $2.9 billion in FY 2020 and $2.8 billion in FY 2021 and remaining at that level through FY 2025. Because the B-21 has a mid-2020s fielding date ("Initial Operating Capability"), the legacy B-52s, B-1s, and B-2s will comprise the bomber force for many years to come. Details are uncertain, however, because the B-21 remains a classified program.

The Fighter Force

The fighter/attack force has been the central element of the Air Force since the end of the bomber era in the early-1960s. It therefore requires detailed examination.

The average age of the fighter/attack force has increased from 8 years at the end of the Cold War in 1991 to 26 years today, while numbers have decreased from 4,000 in 1991 to 1,981 (total) today. Kosiak's observation is applicable here. Both fleet aging and reduced numbers result from an Air Force decision to cease production of fourth-generation aircraft (F-15s and F-16s) in the 1990s and instead wait for production of the fifth-generation (F-22s and F-35s). This was the opposite of the Navy's decision to continue production of the F-18. Unfortunately, production of the F-22 was curtailed at 187 aircraft during the budget drawdown in the late-2000s, and the F-35 was delayed many years from its original schedule.

F-35s: The Air Force again requests 48 aircraft in FY 2021, about the same as for the last four years, although Congress routinely increases the buy (to 62 in FY 2020) out of a concern that the aircraft are being fielded too slowly. According to the procurement budget documents, 48 will be the long-term procurement level, rather than the 60 aircraft per year that the Air Force had intended.[190]

After several years of making good progress in maturing technologies, the aircraft are operational, but the program has still not achieved the planned levels of reliability and capability. The FY 2019 annual report of the director of Operational Test and Evaluation (DOT&E) (the latest available of such reports) noted: "The Joint Strike Fighter (JSF) program continues to carry 873 unresolved deficiencies . . .. Although the program is working to fix deficiencies, new discoveries are still being made, resulting in only a minor decrease in the overall number of deficiencies." Reliability and maintainability metrics remain below goals. Operational testing continues.[191]

---

190 Department of Defense, *FY 2021 Budget Justification Book: Aircraft Procurement, Air Force* (Washington, DC: February 2020), 1-1, https://www.saffm.hq.af.mil/Portals/84/documents/FY21/PROCUREMENT_/FY21%20Air%20Force%20Aircraft%20Procurement%20Vol%20I_1.pdf?ver=2020-02-10-145310-973.

191 Director of Operational Test and Evaluation, *FY 2019 Annual Report* (Washington, DC: Department of Defense, January 2020), 19-32, https://www.dote.osd.mil/Portals/97/pub/reports/FY2019/dod/2019f35jsf.pdf?ver=2020-01-30-115432-173.

Fielding of new F-35s is beginning to ease the aging of the fleet (as will production of F-15EXs). Nevertheless, at 48 aircraft per year, it would take another 28 years to reach the F-35 inventory objective of 1,763—or through FY 2049. Even at 60 aircraft per year, the Air Force goal, it would take 22 years—or through FY 2043. The average age of the fighter/attack fleet will therefore remain high for a long time, perhaps indefinitely.

F-15EX: A major change in the FY 2020 budget was that the Air Force proposed buying a new version of the F-15E dual-role aircraft, the F-15EX. Although the procurement cost is only about 10 percent lower than the F-35s currently (in part a result of the F-35s higher production rate), the sustainment cost of an F-15EX is projected to be about 40 percent lower; therefore, the fleet will be more sustainable. Further, the time needed for units to transition from legacy aircraft to the F-15EX is much shorter than the two years needed for the more complicated transition to the F-35A. Thus, the Air Force will have more squadrons available for operations.

The proposal has been controversial, with many airpower advocates criticizing any procurement of fourth-generation aircraft as a step backward. However, Congress has gone along with the plan.[192]

Numerically, this is a minor shift since the Air Force proposes to buy only 12 F-15EXs in FY 2021 and 144 in total.[193] During the five-year period, the Air Force will buy 3.5 times as many F-35s. Nevertheless, it is a major shift in acquisition strategy and opens the possibility for a larger shift in the future.

A-10s: The Air Force has surrendered to the will of Congress (and to real-world operations) by re-winging the A-10 fleet and extending fleet life into the late-2030s rather than retiring the fleet in the near term.[194]

F-15s and F-16s: Although the Air Force plans to retire large numbers of older F-15s and F-16s, the slow rate of acquiring new aircraft requires sustaining some of these fleets for many years. F-16s still provide 40 percent of the Air Force fighter fleet. In FY 2021, the Air Force proposes $616 million for F-16 modifications and upgrades, particularly for advanced radars. For the F-15, it proposes to spend $349 million for a variety of upgrades, particularly for an improved radar. Spending will continue at these levels throughout the five-year period.

OA-X: This off-the-shelf light-attack aircraft (called "OA-X") has disappeared as an Air Force program. The concept was that such an aircraft would be better suited for missions in low-threat environments because it would be less expensive to operate, reduce wear on high-end aircraft, and have more focused training. After conducting several tests and experiments, the Air Force terminated notions of an acquisition program. The posture statement says the Air Force will continue involvement to help coalition partners. SOCOM will continue the program under "armed overwatch."[195]

---

192 John Tirpak, "F-15EX: Careful What You Don't Ask for," *Air Force Magazine*, April 2019, http://www.airforcemag.com/MagazineArchive/Pages/2019/April%202019/F-15EX-Careful-What-You-Dont-Ask-For.aspx.

193 DOD, *FY 2021 Budget Justification Book: Aircraft Procurement*, 1-17.

194 Stephen Losey, "A-10 re-winging completed, will keep Warthog in the air until late 2030s," *Air Force Times*, August 13, 2019, https://www.airforcetimes.com/news/your-air-force/2019/08/13/a-10-re-winging-completed-will-keep-warthog-in-the-air-until-late-2030s/.

195 Air Force, *Air Force Posture Statement*, 12; Courtney Albon, "GAO Dismisses Light Attack Aircraft Protest as USAF Opts Not to Proceed with the Program," Inside Defense, February 14, 2020, https://insidedefense.com/daily-news/gao-dismisses-light-attack-aircraft-protest-usaf-opts-not-proceed-program.

Next Generation Air Dominance (NGAD): Coming up over the horizon is NGAD, the next-generation fighter/attack program for both the Navy and Air Force. Funding in the FY 2020 budget reaches $1 billion. The program received a lot of attention recently when the Air Force reported that a "full-scale flight demonstrator" flew. This indicated that the program might be further along than had been thought. However, the Congressional Research Service pointed out that this was not a "prototype," which would indicate a mature program ready for production.[196]

The Air Force's stated intention is to field new aircraft faster, emphasizing continuous development, a shorter service life, and rapid fielding of new capabilities. If successful, this would break with half a century of practice. However, because of the secrecy surrounding the program, little is known. The budget justification books show research, development, testing, and evaluation (RDT&E) rising to $2.7 billion in FY 2025 but no procurement in the five-year plan (at least in the published documents).[197]

How this program shakes out will profoundly affect the shape of the future Air Force and, indeed, may determine whether manned aircraft are a dying capability or whether they have decades of continuing relevance.

NGAD will raise a key question: what does "legacy" mean when talking about weapon systems? As discussed in the overview chapter of this military forces report, the military services define legacy as old systems in the inventory.[198] They would retire older systems and buy similar but more capable systems. Strategists, on the other hand, see legacy platforms as those that use old technologies and outdated operational concepts. They would cut manned aircraft, aircraft carriers, and armored vehicles, substituting smaller unmanned and distributed systems.

Strategists will therefore likely question NGAD, arguing that developing another expensive manned aircraft is looking toward the past and not the future.

> **Strategists will likely question NGAD, arguing that developing another expensive manned aircraft is looking toward the past and not the future.**

Perhaps for this reason, the Navy chief of naval operations has indicated some softness in support when discussing NGAD: "We're making tough decisions on where the next dollar goes. I can't be buying stuff just to buy it."[199]

---

196 Jeremiah Gertler, "Next Generation Air Dominance Program: An Introduction," Congressional Research Service, October 5, 2020, https://www.everycrsreport.com/reports/IF11659.html.

197 Valerie Insinna, "The U.S. Air Force Has Built and Flown a Mysterious Full-Scale Prototype of Its Future Fighter Jet," Defense News, September 15, 2020, https://www.defensenews.com/breaking-news/2020/09/15/the-us-air-force-has-built-and-flown-a-mysterious-full-scale-prototype-of-its-future-fighter-jet/.

198 Mark Cancian, *Military Forces in FY 2021: The Budget and Strategy Overview — Four Challenges and a Wild Card* (Washington, DC: CSIS, October 2020), https://www.csis.org/analysis/military-forces-fy-2021-budget-and-strategy-overview-four-challenges-and-wild-card.

199 Mallory Shelbourne, "CNO Gilday: Navy Must Move Faster on Next Generation Air Dominance Program," USNI News,

The Tanker Force: Still Struggling with the KC-46

The KC-46 will replace the Air Force's aging tanker force, the current KC-135 and KC-10 tankers having an average age of 58 and 35 years, respectively. The program was thought to be low risk since the airframe is a variant of Boeing's widely used 767.

However, the program has been troubled from the beginning, with first delivery not occurring until January 2019, three years late, and continues to experience technical problems and production delays.[200] Boeing, the contractor, continues to execute the fixed price contract that it greatly underbid and on which the company is taking large losses (over $4 billion so far).[201] That underbidding strategy appears to have paid off, however, as the Air Force has announced that it would not recompete the contract after the current buy but would procure more KC-46s.

The bottom line is that the KC-46 program is still not quite ready, and the current tanker fleet of KC-10s and KC-135s will be around for a lot longer.

Tactical Mobility

This large fleet consists mainly of C-130s, initially fielded in 1956 and now on the "J" model. ("Tactical mobility" also includes a few specialty aircraft, mainly small VIP passenger aircraft.) The C-130 production line is operating smoothly, and the "J" model, after some initial problems, has settled down. The inventory is large: about 310 C-130s for tactical mobility and another hundred or so aircraft in specialty roles.

The most recent mobility requirements study affirmed a fleet requirement of 300, about where the fleet is now.[202] The problem is that the Air Force is not buying enough new aircraft to maintain its large inventory. The FY 2021 budget buys only four aircraft, and those are specialty models for special operations. The Air Force posture statement says, "we are looking closely at the right mix between modernized and legacy tactical airlift platforms."[203] The intention is likely to retire many of the older C-130H models and reduce the size of the fleet, despite the recent requirements study.

The challenge in cutting the fleet is that large numbers of these aircraft reside in the reserve components, and members of Congress are loath to lose flying squadrons in their districts.

October 13, 2020, https://news.usni.org/2020/10/13/cno-gilday-navy-must-move-faster-on-next-generation-air-dominance-program.

200 Valerie Insinna, "The Air Force Is KC 46 Tanker Has Another Serious Technical Deficiency, and Boeing Is Stuck Paying for It," Defense News, March 30, 2020, https://www.defensenews.com/air/2020/03/31/the-air-forces-kc-46-tanker-has-another-serious-technical-deficiency-and-boeing-is-stuck-paying-for-it/.

201 Courtney Albon, "Lord: Boeing's Fixed Price KC – 46 Contract the Root Cause of Programs Deficiencies," Inside Defense, October 1, 2020, https://insidedefense.com/daily-news/lord-boeings-fixed-price-kc-46-contract-root-cause-programs-deficiencies.

202 "Mobility Capabilities and Requirements Study (MCRS) 2018," United States Transportation Command, February 2019, http://www.airforcemag.com/DocumentFile/Documents/2019/MobilityCapabilitiesRequirementsStudy2018.pdf.

203 Air Force, *Air Force Posture Statement for FY 2021*, 6.

Strategic Mobility

This fleet consists of C-17s, upgraded C-5s (which were originally built in the 1970s and 1980s), and KC-10s (also classed as refuelers because they have dual missions). No production lines are currently operating, the last C-17 having been delivered in 2013. However, the fleet is relatively healthy because of the large investments made in the 2000s.

The most recent strategic mobility study, *Mobility Capabilities and Requirements Study 2018*, completed in February 2019, found that the fleets were sized adequately.[204] A relatively young fleet that is properly sized would seemingly indicate a lot of stability.

However, the *National Defense Strategy*'s focus on great power conflict raised the possibility of wartime attrition being a consideration for sizing the strategic airlift and sealift fleets, something that previous studies had not considered. Russia and China can threaten sea and air lines of communication in a way that regional threats, such as Iran or North Korea, cannot. Many outside analyses had pointed to this new threat. That would drive inventory requirements higher.[205]

Congress directed that the Department of Defense (DOD) revise the *Mobility Capabilities and Requirements Study* to consider the new strategic environment. Delivery of the expanded study has been delayed until at least spring 2021. In the meantime, Air Force Air Mobility Command has identified survivability as an issue and is looking at various aircraft self-protection upgrades in response to the new challenge.[206]

---

204 "Mobility Capabilities and Requirements Study (MCRS) 2018," United States Transportation Command.

205 Sydney Freedberg, Jr., "U.S. Needs More Tankers, Transports Since Russia and China Can Shoot Them Down," Breaking Defense, September 21, 2017, https://breakingdefense.com/2017/09/more-tankers-transports-needed-since-russia-china-can-shoot-them-down-everhart.

206 Sydney Freedberg, "Tankers, Transports Need Real-Time Threat Data to Survive: AMC," Breaking Defense, September 14, 2020, https://breakingdefense.com/2020/09/tankers-transports-need-real-time-threat-data-to-survive-amc/.

Remotely Piloted Aircraft (RPA)

Chart 5: RPA versus Manned Aircraft, 2005, 2010, 2021

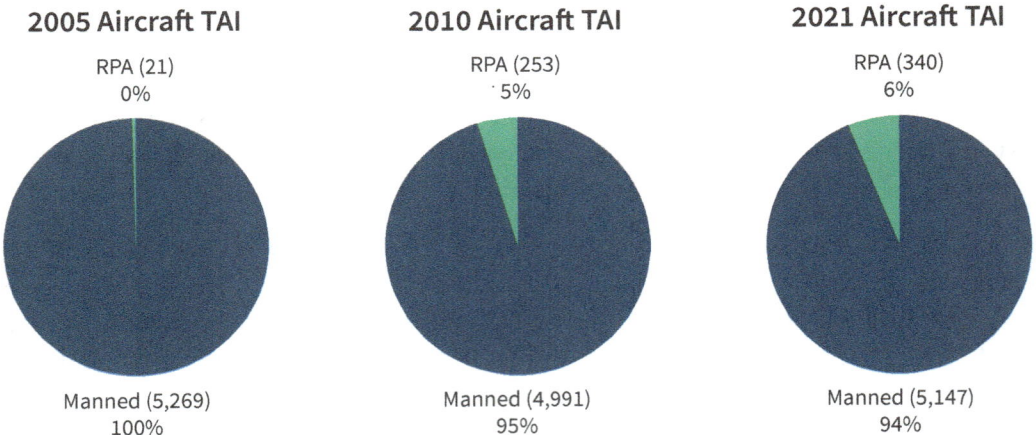

Source: Department of Defense, *United States Air Force Budget Overview Fiscal Year 2020*, 38; Air Force Association, "USAF Almanac 2011," *Air Force Magazine* 94, no. 5 (May 2011): 48, http://www.airforcemag.com/MagazineArchive/Magazine%20Documents/2011/May%20 2011/0511facts_figs.pdf; Air Force Association, "USAF Almanac 2006," *Air Force Magazine* 89, no. 6 (May 2006): 63, http://www.airforcemag. com/MagazineArchive/Magazine%20Documents/2011/May%202011/0511facts_figs.pdf; Air Force Almanac, Aircraft Total Active Inventory, 2019, 2010, 2005; 2020 numbers taken from the *Air Force FY2020 Budget Overview*, Appendix, Air Force Total Aircraft inventory.

For the Air Force, this revolution is over. Whereas the Navy's efforts to integrate unmanned systems into its aviation fleet are still controversial, slow, and limited, as described in this project's corresponding chapter on the Navy, the Air Force's incorporation of unmanned aircraft into its force structure—after strong resistance during the 1990s and early-2000s—has become routine.[207]

However, the Air Force has stalled in its effort to bring more remotely piloted aircraft (RPAs) into the force. The RPA proportion of the force has leveled off at 5 to 7 percent for 10 years, and current procurement plans show no change in the future. The FY 2020 budget procures no RPAs, and there are none in the five-year plan. The Air Force is moving to retire the RQ-4 Global Hawk fleet in favor of the manned E-11. By contrast, the FY 2021 budget procures 106 manned aircraft.[208]

> *The Air Force's incorporation of unmanned aircraft into its force structure . . . has become routine. However, the Air Force has stalled in its effort to bring more RPAs into the force.*

---

207 The Air Force is emphatic that these are aircraft and not "unmanned" but instead "remotely piloted." Hence, the Air Force uses the term "Remotely Piloted Aircraft." There are cultural reasons for this distinction, the Air Force being run by pilots. However, there is also a substantive argument in that, although there are no humans in the aircraft itself, there is a large ground-based support structure to launch, fly, and recover the aircraft.

208 Department of the Air Force, *Air Force Justification Book Volume 1 of 2, Aircraft Procurement* (Washington, DC: February 2020), x-xiii, https://www.saffm.hq.af.mil/Portals/84/documents/FY21/PROCUREMENT_/FY21%20Air%20Force%20Aircraft%20 Procurement%20Vol%20I_1.pdf?ver=2020-02-10-145310-973.

The Air Force is experimenting with "loyal wingman" RPAs under the umbrella of "Skyborg." The "Low-Cost Attritable Unmanned Aerial Vehicles" program explores low cost, autonomous, and attritable systems, thus allowing the Air Force to operate within an adversary's defensive zone. The program has produced the XQ-58A Valkyrie as a demonstrator aircraft. The Air Force is emphatic that these complement, rather than replace, manned aircraft. A study by the Air Force Association's Mitchell Institute reinforced this point: "[drones] are complementary, force multiplying capabilities, not replacements for fifth-generation stealth aircraft."[209]

These RPA initiatives might change the inventory balance in the future. However, none of these RPA programs are yet an official "program of record."

A major issue is whether to buy RPAs for permissive or non-permissive environments.[210] MQ-9 Reapers can only operate in permissive environments. That has been fine for the kinds of conflicts the United States has fought recently. However, in a conflict with a high-end adversary such as Russia or China, these aircraft would be vulnerable because of their slow speed, high visibility, and lack of defensive systems. The issue was illustrated dramatically in July 2019 when the Iranians shot down a Navy RQ-4.

The question, then, is twofold. First, are there concepts of operation that would enable current UAVs to contribute to a high-end warfighting campaign? Second, should the Air Force develop and procure stealthy and likely largely autonomous UAVs to operate inside these challenging air defense environments? One stealthy unmanned aircraft, the RQ-170 Sentinel, an Air Force/CIA collaboration, is known to exist because one was shot down over Iran in 2011 and exhibited to the public. A possible RQ-180, an unmanned long-range reconnaissance system, is also rumored to be flying and possibly operating.[211]

The Curse of Short Range

A recent concern is that the Air Force tactical aviation fleet is too short ranged for great power conflicts. Combat ranges of current aircraft run from about 550 to 750 miles. NGAD might have a range of up to 1,000 miles, but the program is mostly conceptual at this point.

The problem is that demands on the fleet have changed. During the Cold War, short range was not a problem because the forward fighter bases in NATO were close to the front line. It was not a problem after the Cold War because adversaries did not have strong antiair capabilities, and as a result, U.S. tactical aircraft could refuel as often as they needed.

However, in potential conflicts with China and Russia, operational range matters. The Pacific is vast. Although Kadena Air Force base on Okinawa is close enough to Taiwan (400 miles), it is 1,400 miles from the South China Sea, where such a conflict would likely take place. Anderson Air Force base on Guam is 1,400 miles from the South China Sea and 1,700 miles from Taiwan.

---

209 Mark Gunzinger and Lucas Autenreid, "Understanding the Promise of Skyborg and Low Cost Attritable Unmanned Aerial Vehicles," Mitchell Institute, October 1, 2020, https://www.mitchellaerospacepower.org/single-post/understanding-the-promise-of-skyborg-and-low-cost-attritable-unmanned-aerial-vehicles.

210 Mark Pomerleau, "Can the MQ-9 Reaper operate in contested environments?," C4ISRnet, October 4, 2016, http://www.c4isrnet.com/unmanned/uas/2016/10/04/can-the-mq-9-reaper-operate-in-contested-environments.

211 Guy Norris, "USAF Unit Moves Reveal Clues to RQ-180 Ops Debut," *Aviation Week and Space Technology*, October 24, 2019, https://www.defense-aerospace.com/articles-view/release/3/206919/-rq_180-stealthy-isr-drone-already-in-service%3A-report.html.

U.S. bases in Europe, even forward bases in Eastern Europe, are still far from potential battlefields. RAF Lakenheath, for example, is nearly 1,000 miles from the Baltic states, and Spangdahlem AFB in Germany is 850 miles. Further, airbases are again vulnerable, so U.S. aircraft may need to be based further away from their targets, and adversary air defenses may make aerial tanking risky.

As a result, many analyses recommend actions to increase standoff range and reduce vulnerability, including an emphasis on bombers because of their long range; the curtailment of F-35 procurements because of their short range; the dispersion of basing; and the development of long-range strike, especially unmanned systems. For example, in a congressionally-directed study, the Center for Strategic and Budgetary Assessments (CSBA) recommended, "the Air Force should rebalance its combat forces in favor of long-range, penetrating bombers." CSBA also recommended developing a new, long-range fighter/attack aircraft ("penetrating counter-air") to substitute for some F-35 inventory.[212] Similarly, in another congressionally-directed study, the MITRE Corporation recommended: "an increase in available long-range aircraft and bases [to] strengthen the conventional deterrence posture of U.S. forces."[213]

The Navy suffers from the same range limitation but has the advantage of being able to move its airfields (aircraft carriers) around, so this affects the Air Force more intensely.[214]

Nuclear Enterprise

After decades of stability and low visibility, the nuclear force is getting attention again as the cost of modernization programs makes them more visible, and controversial.

The ICBM force has leveled off at the New START limit of 400. The nuclear bomber force (B-2s and B-52s) holds steady at 96 (total active inventory, or TAI). DOD's *Nuclear Posture Review* (NPR), published in February 2018, laid out the direction of the nuclear enterprise. The NPR affirmed the need for the nuclear triad to deter nuclear and non-nuclear aggression and assure allies and partners.

After decades of stability and low visibility, the nuclear force is getting attention again as the cost of modernization programs makes them more visible, and controversial.

---

212 Gunzinger et al., *An Air Force for An Era of Great Power Competition* (Washington, DC: CSBA, March 2019), xi, https://csbaonline.org/research/publications/an-air-force-for-an-era-of-great-power-competition.

213 MITRE Corporation, *US Air Force Aircraft Inventory Study: Unclassified Report* (McLean, VA: 2019), http://www.airforcemag.com/DocumentFile/Documents/2019/MITRE-USAF-Aircraft-Inventory-Study.pdf; This is the unclassified version of a longer classified report on the Air Force aircraft force structure, directed by Congress; see also Rebecca Grant, "Air Force, Don't Cut a Single Bomber," Breaking Defense, April 30, 2020, https://breakingdefense.com/author/rebeccagrant/.

214 See Jerry Hendricks, *Retreat from Range: The Rise and Fall of Carrier Aviation* (Washington, DC: Center for a New American Security, October 2015), https://www.cnas.org/publications/reports/retreat-from-range-the-rise-and-fall-of-carrier-aviation.

Further, the NPR highlighted "the increasing need for this diversity and flexibility" as "one of the primary reasons why sustaining and replacing the nuclear triad and non-strategic nuclear capabilities, and modernizing NC3, is necessary now."[215]

However, after nearly three decades of low public visibility and relatively low cost, the nuclear enterprise is getting more attention because the systems acquired during the Reagan buildup of the 1980s are now reaching the end of their service lives and must be replaced. That brings opposition from arms-control advocates. Further, a Democratic administration will certainly revise nuclear weapons policy. It will want to reduce the number of nuclear weapons and the cost of modernization programs. For example, the Biden campaign website endorses arms-control and "the need to reduce the role of nuclear weapons."

Table 5 shows the most controversial nuclear modernization programs.

Table 5: Nuclear Modernization Programs ($ millions)

Program	FY 2020 enacted	FY 2021 proposed	Comment
Ground-Based Strategic Deterrent (GBSD)	414.4	570.4	GBSD has been controversial among arms-control advocates and some budget hawks who see it as unnecessary and would reduce the nuclear forces to a "dyad" or even a "monad."
Long-Range Standoff (LRSO) weapon	664.9	712.5	LRSO, a nuclear-armed cruise missile, has been controversial because bombers already have one nuclear munition, the B61 bomb.
B61 tail kit program	233.8	108.4	Designed to increase the accuracy of the B61 nuclear bomb, the program faces some opposition because of concerns that it makes nuclear warfighting more viable.

Note: The DOE NNSA budget provides funding for an Analysis of Alternatives to develop a low yield SLCM called for in the 2018 NPR.

Source: Office of the Under Secretary of Defense (Comptroller), *Program Acquisition Cost by Weapon System* (Washington, DC: Department of Defense, February 2020), https://comptroller.defense.gov/Portals/45/Documents/defbudget/fy2021/fy2021_Weapons.pdf.

These programs—with the B-21 bomber and the Columbia-class submarine—contribute to the nuclear modernization bow wave that the DOD faces in the 2020s and 2030s and which will require the DOD to either trim programs or increase the proportion of the budget allocated to nuclear forces.[216]

One piece of good news: in response to scandals several years back and several outside reviews, the Air Force (and the Navy) implemented a wide variety of actions to improve the standards and quality of their nuclear enterprise, both personnel and operations. The absence of any recent incidents indicates success. Here, no news is good news.

---

215 DOD, *Nuclear Posture Review* (Washington, DC: February 2018), https://media.defense.gov/2018/Feb/02/2001872886/-1/-1/1/2018-NUCLEAR-POSTURE-REVIEW-FINAL-REPORT.PDF.

216 Todd Harrison and Evan Montgomery, *The Cost of U.S. Nuclear Forces: From BCA to Bow Wave and Beyond* (Washington, DC: Center for Strategic and Budgetary Assessments, 2015), http://csbaonline.org/search/?x=0&y=0&q=harrison.

Creation of the Space Force

The Space Force is now a reality as the fifth DOD military service (the sixth U.S. military service, including the Coast Guard). Over the course of the year, the Air Force and DOD published a series of documents developing the organization and structure of the Space Force. About 6,000 personnel have been transferred to this new service, all from the Air Force. A later chapter on the Space Force will describe these actions in more detail.

So far, the split has been amicable. The Air Force has supported the establishment of the new service and facilitated its stand up. There has been none of the acrimony that is seen in most divorces. Nevertheless, major elements of the division of personnel, facilities, and organizations are still unresolved. Particularly sensitive will be the requirement that the creation of the Space Force entail no increase in the number of DOD personnel; every Space Force billet created will come out of the Air Force total.

Munitions as an Element of Strategy: Volume for a Long War

All the services are buying more munitions because many analyses show that U.S. forces would expend large amounts of munitions in a great power conflict. Thus, the Air Force budget procures a lot of munitions. This year the Air Force's strategy seems to have changed, maintaining production of long-range and air-to-air munitions but cutting air-to-ground munitions. This likely reflects the winding down of the air war in the Middle East and a judgment that great power conflict, particularly in the Western Pacific, would be less about ground operations and more about air and maritime operations.

Table 6: Major Munitions Procurement Quantities

	Program	FY 2020 Enacted	FY 2021 President's Budget
Short-range air-to-ground	JDAM	25,000	10,000
	Small Diameter Bombs (SDB-I and II)	8,253	3,600
	Hellfire Missile	3,859	2,497
Air-to-air and long-range air-to-ground	Joint Air-to-Surface Standoff Missile (JASSM)	390	400
	AIM-9X Sidewinder	355	331
	AIM120D Advanced Medium-Range Air-to-Air Missiles (AMRAAM).	220	414
	Long-Range Anti-Ship Missile (LRASM)	0	5

Source: John Pletcher, "Air Force FY 2021 Budget Briefing," (presentation, Air Force, Washington, DC, slide 13).

Procurement of munitions may not hold up if budgets decline. The downside of munitions acquisition is that they are sterile; once procured, they go on the shelf to be used in case of conflict. If no conflict requires their use, then the services must pay to dispose of the munitions at the end of their useful life. Because munitions are not visible, they may not contribute significantly to deterrence. For this reason, many U.S. allies and partners do not have large munitions stocks despite the wartime requirement.

By contrast, aircraft, ships, and vehicles get used every day; their visibility creates a perception of U.S. capability in potential adversaries and thus adds to deterrence. As a result, there is always pressure to buy platforms rather than munitions.

6

Space, SOF, Civilians, and Contractors

Beyond the traditional military services, military forces include the new Space Force as well as Special Operations Forces (SOF, which functions as a quasi-service), Department of Defense (DOD) civilians (which perform many functions that military personnel perform in other countries), and contractors (which form a permanent element of the national security establishment, not only in the United States proper but also on overseas battlefields).

KEY TAKEAWAYS
Space Force

- It exists!
- Major elements such as a headquarters, appropriations accounts, and capstone doctrine have been established.
- Major elements of structure are in place, but decisions are still pending about transfer of most personnel.
- Its small size will require heavy reliance on other services, particularly the Air Force, for support functions and a different approach to personnel management.

Special Operations Forces (SOF)

- SOF continues its gradual expansion and heavy dependence on Overseas Contingency Operations (OCO) funding.
- A broad set of actions to counter recent instances of ethical misconduct by its personnel seems to be having an effect.

DOD Civilians
- Despite administration skepticism about the federal bureaucracy, the number of DOD civilians stays at about the same level in FY 2021, retaining the growth of recent years.
- This strength reflects the civilian workforce's contribution to readiness and lethality.
- Former secretary of defense Mark Esper's review of the "fourth estate" cut defense-wide civilians by about 7,000, but increases in the Military Departments offset this decrease.

Contractors
- Contractors have become a permanent part of the federal workforce but remain controversial due to enduring questions about cost and what contractors should or should not do.
- Operational contractors continue to play a vital role in CENTCOM, holding a 2.8 to 1 ratio of contractors to military (up from 1.7 to 1 last year) as military forces exit Iraq, Syria, and Afghanistan while contractors stay behind.

Space Force

The Space Force, officially created on December 20, 2019, is taking shape. The split from the Air Force has been amicable so far, with about a third of the expected personnel having transferred to the new service. Next year will see the final organizational decisions and whether a Biden administration is fully on board with the new service. How the new service will operate long term remains an open question. It will need to create a new organizational culture, and its small size means that it will operate very differently from the other military services.

Table 1: Space Force Personnel

	Active-Duty Military	Civilians
FY 2020 Enacted	-	-
FY 2021 Request	6,434	3,545
Change	-	-

Source: Department of the Air Force, *Air Force FY 2021 Budget Overview* (Washington, DC: 2020), 8, https://www.saffm.hq.af.mil/Portals/84/documents/FY21/SUPPORT_/FY21%20Budget%20Overview_1.pdf?ver=2020-02-10-152806-743#:~:text=The%20U.S.%20Air%20Force%20FY,the%20FY%202020%20enacted%20funding. For FY 2021, these numbers are contained in the Air Force totals and are therefore not additive to the DOD total.

At the beginning of FY 2021, Space Force personnel are caught between their old identities in the Air Force and their new identities in the Space Force. Although the positions have been transferred, funding is still in Air Force military personnel accounts. This will likely change in FY 2022. Other appropriations—operations and maintenance; research, development, testing and evaluation (RDT&E); and procurement—will transfer in FY 2021.

BUILDING A NEW MILITARY SERVICE

The U.S. Space Force is a separate branch of the armed forces within the Department of the Air Force (motto "Semper supra," or "Always above"). It will be "organized, trained, and equipped to provide: freedom of operation in, from, into the space domain; and prompt and sustain space operations."[217]

Space Force will "remain mission focused by leveraging infrastructure of the U.S. Air Force except in performing those functions that are unique to space or central to the independence of the new armed force."[218] DOD's *Comprehensive Plan for the Organizational Structure of the U.S. Space Force* creates a group of career specialties referred to as the "space force core organic" to define those personnel who will be part of the Space Force.[219]

This guidance also means that the Space Force will rely on a lot of Air Force organizations, as the Marine Corps does with the Navy. However, because of its small size the Space Force will need to go much further in its reliance, so functions such as recruiting will likely come from Air Force institutions with embedded Space Force personnel. The comprehensive plan notes that Space Force will receive more than 80 percent of its critical support functions from the Air Force. This structure may have the advantage of focusing the Space Force on core activities rather than spreading attention across more bureaucratic activities.

Along with establishing the Space Force, the administration has implemented a wide variety of organizational changes as part of reorganizing and emphasizing the national security space enterprise:

- Established U.S. Space Command (SPACECOM). Although a combatant command and not a part of the Space Force, SPACECOM will be the operational expression for U.S. space activities and where many Space Force personnel will serve.
- Redesignated Air Force Space Command (AFSPC) as the first element of U.S. Space Force, and military members assigned to AFSPC were assigned to the U.S. Space Force.
- Appointed General John Raymond as the chief of space operations, the head of the Space Force, and Chief Master Sergeant Roger A. Towberman as the senior enlisted advisor of the U.S. Space Force.
- Created a Space Force service headquarters in the Pentagon. This has four major elements: a Human Capital Office, an Operations Office, a Strategy and Resources Office, and a Technology and Innovation Office.[220]
- Published plans for field commands: a Space Operations Command, a Space Training and Readiness Command, and a Space Systems Command. The systems command has received a lot of attention because many advocates want it to have authorities allowing more rapid acquisition and fielding of systems.

---

217 *The United States Space Force*, 10 USC 9081, https://www.law.cornell.edu/uscode/text/10/9081.

218 Mark Esper, "Memorandum: Establishment of the United States Space Force," Department of Defense, December 20, 2019, https://media.defense.gov/2019/Dec/20/2002228281/-1/-1/1/ESTABLISHMENT-OF-THE-UNITED-STATES-SPACE-FORCE.PDF.

219 Department of the Air Force, *Comprehensive Plan for the Organizational Structure of the U.S. Space Force* (Washington, DC: February 2020), https://www.airforcemag.com/app/uploads/2020/02/Comprehensive-Plan-for-the-Organizational-Struccture-of-the-USSF_Feb-2020.pdf.

220 John W. Raymond, *Chief of Space Operations Planning Guidance* (Washington, DC: U.S. Space Force, November 2020), https://media.defense.gov/2020/Nov/09/2002531998/-1/-1/0/CSO%20PLANNING%20GUIDANCE.PDF.

- Published a capstone doctrine manual, *Spacepower*, to give a broader context to military operations in space. (Note that "spacepower" is a single word, denoting a concept more than just power in space.)[221]
- Established a new assistant defense secretary for space policy position, a role that Congress required DOD to create in the FY 2020 National Defense Authorization Act (NDAA).
- Established (also per FY 2020 NDAA) assistant secretary for space acquisition and integration (ASAF/SP) within the Air Force who reports directly to the secretary of the Air Force.

The Space Force will *not* send astronauts into orbit. That is the exclusive purview of the National Aeronautics and Space Administration, a civilian agency. When the space age began, the United States intentionally made human spaceflight a civilian rather than a military function.

Neither will the Space Force control the satellites of the U.S. Intelligence Community. These fall under the National Reconnaissance Office (NRO). However, the Space Force and the NRO will exchange liaison cells.

STILL A WORK IN PROGRESS

About 2,400 military personnel will transfer to the Space Force during the fall of 2020; however, most space force personnel will still be Air Force personnel working in a Space Force organization. The transfer will come in FY 2021. The Space Force and Air Force are setting up a process by which individuals opt to leave the Air Force and join the Space Force.[222]

Transfers from other services will begin in FY 2022, although DOD has not yet laid out what that mechanism will be. In its FY 2021 budget, for example, the Army signaled plans to transfer 100 personnel. However, there will likely be some tensions about how to allocate space-qualified personnel since the other services are allowed to retain some space capabilities.

The *Comprehensive Plan for the Organizational Structure of the U.S. Space Force* notes that a wide variety of organic capabilities are "central to the independence of the new armed force," including doctrine, resources/matériel, personnel management, wargaming, test and evaluation, operational intelligence, and training. When these are established, many will be co-located with Air Force counterparts to leverage existing organizations. Still, the other military services devote thousands of personnel to these functions, numbers that the Space Force cannot match. Instead, it may use government civilians and contractors to a greater degree than the other services.

Early concepts included the eventual creation of a new military department for space, thus breaking the Space Force out from the Department of the Air Force. So far there has been no movement in that direction, and DOD's concept does not include it.[223]

---

221 U.S. Space Force, *Spacepower: Doctrine for Space Forces* (Washington, DC: June 2020), https://www.spaceforce.mil/Portals/1/Space%20Capstone%20Publication_10%20Aug%202020.pdf.

222 "Transferring to the U.S. Space Force FAQs," U.S. Space Force, https://www.spaceforce.mil/Transfer/#:~:text=A%3A%20Career%20fields%20that%20are,inherent%20to%20space%20operations%20only; and Lynn Kirby, "2.4 K Airmen to Transfer to Space Force Beginning September 1," Space Force News, US Space Force, September 1, 2020, https://www.spaceforce.mil/News/Article/2332258/24k-airmen-to-transfer-into-space-force-beginning-sept-1/.

223 Department of Defense, *United States Space Force* (Washington, DC: February 2019), https://media.defense.gov/2019/Mar/01/2002095012/-1/-1/1/UNITED-STATES-SPACE-FORCE-STRATEGIC-OVERVIEW.PDF.

Currently there is no reserve component to the Space Force, but there will certainly be one. A reserve component provides strategic depth for U.S. space operations and a mechanism to retain personnel with space-related skills. The politically powerful National Guard has argued for having a role, although the states have no authorities in space.[224] Several existing National Guard and reserve units do, however, perform space functions.

A DIFFERENT PERSONNEL STRUCTURE

Because the Space Force will be much smaller, even at full size, than the other services, its personnel structure will be unique. One effect may be cultural. To deal with a small number of personnel to cover so many tasks and organizations, General Raymond, the chief of space operations, has directed the use of mission command by the Space Force. This means that "subordinate echelons are expected to default to action except where a higher echelon has specifically reserved authority."[225]

Another aspect is the rank structure. Currently, the Space Force consists of 43 percent officers (2,742 officers out of a total strength of 6,434). That ratio might change a little as more personnel and other organizations are incorporated, but it is unlikely to change very much. Because so few Space Force officers will have the experience of leading troops, the culture will likely evolve to one of officers as highly skilled technicians rather than as leaders.

Table 2: Officer Percentage among the Services

Space Force	Army	Navy	Marine Corps	Air Force
42%	19%	16%	12%	19%

Source: Defense Manpower Data Center, *Military Personnel by Service by Rank/Grade* (Washington, DC: August 2020), https://www.dmdc.osd.mil/appj/dwp/dwp_reports.jsp.

For a service that will primarily operate satellites from home bases in the United States, the rank structure is not a problem. The challenge will arise when Space Force's technically focused officers enter the joint community. To prepare its officers for service in these organizations, Space Force will need to develop leadership opportunities and training.

The ability of the Space Force to produce the requisite number of senior leaders from such a small base will also be a challenge. Advocates expect that the Space Force will have two or three four-star officers: the chief of space operations, the vice chief of space operations, and probably the commander of SPACECOM.[226]

---

224 Sandra Irwin, "National Guard Leaders Press Case for Space National Guard," Space News, February 12, 2020, https://spacenews.com/national-guard-leaders-press-case-for-a-space-national-guard/.

225 Raymond, *Chief of Space Operations' Planning Guidance*, 5; The guidance also directs "clear verbal and written communication orienting to inform decisions and implement actions," which has this author's total support as an offset to the overly formal, indirect, and jargon-laden communications usually produced by the military services.

226 Currently, only the chief of space operations and the commander of SPACECOM are established in law as four-star positions. The vice chief, General Thompson, is currently a four-star officer, but the billet was transferred from the Air Force. Earlier versions of the Space Force legislation contained a vice chief at the four-star level, and all the other service vice chiefs are at the four-star level. It would undermine the purpose of creating a Space Force if its senior personnel were outranked by their equivalents in the other services. The secretary of the Air Force recommended the vice chair of the Space Force be a statutory four-star position. Department of the Air Force, *Comprehensive Plan for the Organizational Structure of the US Space Force* (Washington, DC: February 2020), 11, https://www.airforcemag.com/app/uploads/2020/02/Comprehensive-Plan-for-the-Organizational-Struccture-of-the-USSF_Feb-2020.pdf.

This challenge will ripple down through the organization as the Space Force needs to have officers at the same level as officers in other services in order to compete effectively in DOD's bureaucratic processes. A RAND study noted the problem, concluding, "being small could hurt the viability of the space force."[227]

WILL THE SPACE FORCE SURVIVE THE TRANSITION OF ADMINISTRATIONS?

Although space advocates had been pushing for a Space Force for many years, its creation had elements of a vanity project by a president who reveled in putting his personal stamp on organizations and events. It is unclear whether this association will taint the Space Force in the Biden administration.

Some progressives have recommended that Space Force be abolished as part of a broader effort to reduce defense spending. There is even a Twitter hashtag: #abolishspaceforce. Progressives particularly object to "militarization" of space and the cost of additional bureaucracy.[228]

However, neither the Biden campaign nor any of its surrogates have said anything against the Space Force. There has not even been a suggestion to re-study the question. Space Force looks permanent.

MEANWHILE, UP IN SPACE

The Space Force launched three major satellites and the X-37B space plane.

- A GPS Block III launched on June 30. GPS provides global positioning information, and Block III is the latest upgrade.
- An Advanced Extremely High Frequency (AEHF-6) satellite launched on March 26. AEHF replaces the Milstar constellation to provide highly protected communication for high-priority military assets and national leaders.
- A TDO-2 satellite launched on the same booster as AEHF-6. TDO-2 is a small satellite vehicle carrying multiple government payloads that will help provide space domain awareness for the Space Force through optical calibration and laser ranging.
- One of the two X-37B Space planes went up again in May for another extended classified mission.

Space Force maintains several major satellite constellations along with the ground stations, satellite relays, and space-launch facilities required to establish and sustain these constellations, including:

- Advanced Extremely High Frequency (AEHF)-MILSTAR, for secure communications;
- Wideband Global SATCOM System (WGS), for global communications;
- Global Positioning System (GPS), for global positioning;
- Defense Meteorological Satellite Program (DMSP), for weather;
- Space-Based Infrared System, for missile defense; and
- Geosynchronous Space Situational Awareness Program (GSSAP), for tracking and characterization of manmade orbiting objects.

---

227 Michael Spirtas et al., *A Separate Space: Creating a Military Service for Space* (Santa Monica, CA: RAND, 2020), https://www.rand.org/pubs/research_reports/RR4263.html.

228 For example, Center for International Policy, *Sustainable Defense: More Security, Less Spending* (Washington, DC: June 2019), 50, https://www.internationalpolicy.org/sustainable-defense-task-force.

LOOKING AHEAD

The Space Force has a massive RDT&E appropriation ($10.3 billion) for such a small service. Much of the effort is focused on maintaining and improving existing satellite constellations. The major development is Next-Generation Overhead Persistent Infrared (NexGen OPIR), a missile warning satellite system and follow-on to the Space Based Infrared System. The budget allocates $2.3 billion for the effort.

The largest element in the Space Force RDT&E account (35 percent, or $3.6 billion) is classified.

Several major challenges will shape the Space Force of the future:

- **The Final Composition of Space Force:** DOD owes Congress a plan for what personnel and organizations will be incorporated into Space Force. The plan will include elements from the other services as well as additional elements from the Air Force. The final plan will establish the size of Space Force. The larger it is, the easier it will be to staff support organizations and joint billets. However, the other services will want to hang onto some amount of space capability.

- **Relations with the NRO:** The U.S. Intelligence Community successfully fought to be excluded from Space Force. That means that about half of U.S. military launches and satellites do not fall under Space Force. The two organizations are actively working on the relationship, but there is lots of potential for friction.

- **The Role of Offensive Operations in Space:** Space weapons include space-to-space, ground-to-space, and space-to-ground. There are restrictions on nuclear weapons in space but not much else currently. Fears that space debris could render certain orbits unusable have engendered calls for restrictions on antisatellite weapons, but "continued tests of such systems appear to be normalizing the behavior."[229] There are also long-standing criticisms about the "militarization" of space, even though space has had a military function since the first human activity in that domain. (What critics actually mean is the "weaponization" of space.) Neither concern has yet produced binding agreements. The role of weapons in space may be a different matter.[230] Current U.S. space doctrine envisions some offensive use of space.

- **Reliance on Commercial Satellites versus Custom-Designed Military Satellites:** Military satellites offer a variety of protections, both physical and electronic, that commercial satellites cannot offer. However, commercial satellites are much less expensive. Further, when the government uses purchased services, it can adjust capacity as needed, buying more or less as the situation demands.

---

229 Kaitlyn Johnson, "A Balance of Instability: Effects of a Direct-Ascent Anti-Satellite Weapons Ban on Nuclear Stability," CSIS, October 21, 2020, 7, https://defense360.csis.org/a-balance-of-instability-effects-of-a-direct-ascent-anti-satellite-weapons-ban-on-nuclear-stability/.

230 Todd Harrison, *International Perspective on Space Weapons* (Washington, DC: CSIS Aerospace Security Project, May 2020), https://www.csis.org/analysis/international-perspectives-space-weapons.

Special Operations Forces (SOF)

Two themes continue—gradual force growth and dependence on OCO funding. Stress on the force has disappeared as a publicly stated concern, as is true of the rest of the department. Deployment-to-dwell numbers approach department goals. Ethical misconduct—a disturbing theme that arose in recent years—seems to have eased after extensive efforts to educate and discipline the force.

Table 3: Special Operations Forces – Military, Civilians, and Contractors

	FY 2020 Enacted	FY 2021 Request	Change
Military End Strength (active and reserve)	66,552	67,092	+540
Civilian FTEs	6,651	6,831	+180
Contractors	5,955	6,081	+126

Note: The Special Operations Command's (SOCOM) military and civilian personnel are reported in the respective service tables. These numbers are therefore not additional to what is shown in the service numbers.

Source: Department of Defense, *Fiscal Year (FY) 2021, Operation and Maintenance, Defense-Wide United States Special Operations Command* (Washington, DC: April 2020), II. Force Structure Summary, SOCOM-11, 16, https://comptroller.defense.gov/Portals/45/Documents/defbudget/fy2021/budget_justification/pdfs/01_Operation_and_Maintenance/O_M_VOL_1_PART_1/SOCOM_OP-5.pdf.

FORCE GROWTH
Chart 1: SOCOM Military Personnel, 1999 to 2021, Active and Reserve Component

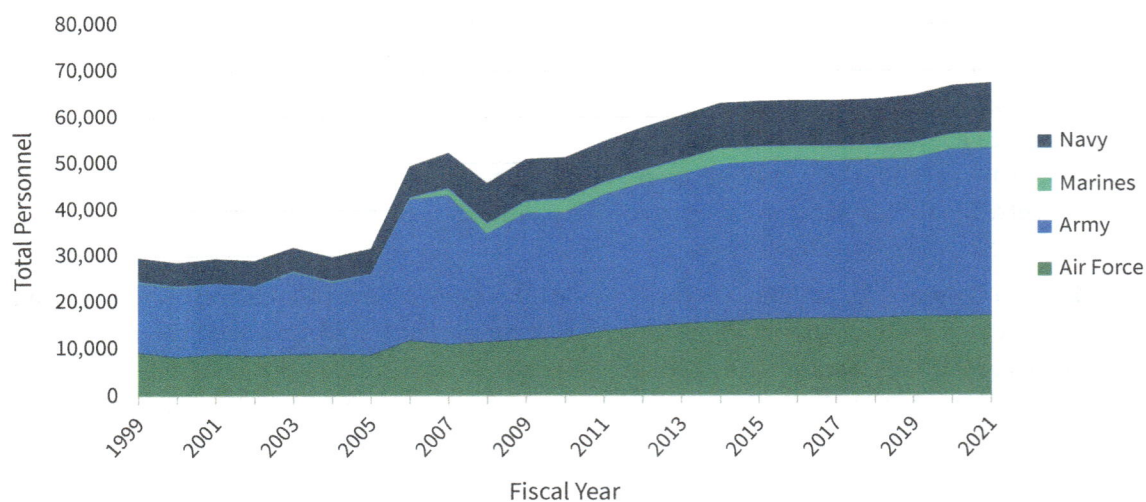

Source: Data for 2008 to 2021 comes from the Force Structure Summary tables in the yearly *President's Budget Operation and Maintenance, Defense-Wide United States Special Operations Command*; data for 2001 to 2007 comes from the Military Personnel sections of the respective Operation and Maintenance Overviews (Washington, DC: 2001–2007).

U.S. Special Operations Command (SOCOM) consists of service component commands from each of the four services—Army (Special Forces, Ranger Regiment, Special Operations Aviation, Delta Force), Navy (SEALs, explosive ordnance disposal), Air Force (special purpose aircraft and control teams), and Marine Corps (one "Raider" regiment). Joint Special Operations Command and seven Theater Special Operations Commands conduct operations. SOCOM develops joint doctrine and has the Joint Special

Operations University, while extensive service-specific school and doctrine activities reside within the service components.

Over the years, Congress has taken action to make special operations forces like a separate service. The commander of SOCOM has many more authorities than other combatant commanders, having influence over budgets, acquisition requirements, doctrine, promotions, and personnel assignments. The assistant secretary of defense (SO/LIC) has authorities like those of a service secretary for exercising administrative and policy control over designated forces. As a result, special operations forces have a great deal of independence.

SOCOM grew greatly in size during the wars, from 29,500 military personnel in 1999 to 67,092 today.[231] It is now approaching the size of the British Army Regular Forces (78,800 in 2020).[232] This large post-2001 increase was in response to DOD steadily increasing the number and type of missions SOCOM is expected to carry out. SOCOM has provided DOD's core direct action and counterterrorism capabilities, in addition to conducting other SOCOM missions such as foreign internal defense, irregular warfare, and civil affairs. Demand for all these missions has grown, not just in Central Command (CENTCOM) but globally as well. SOCOM became DOD's Coordinating Authority for Countering Violent Extremist Organizations, Countering Weapons of Mass Destruction, and transregional Military Information Support Operations. In effect, the additional responsibilities make SOCOM a "global COCOM."

SOCOM continues to grow, though slowly, as it accommodates its expanded mission set.[233] The challenge, as the Congressional Research Service observed, will be, "[h]ow much larger US SOCOM can grow before its selection and training standards will need to be modified to create and sustain a larger force."[234] The history of special forces in other countries has often been one of expansion, as the desirable traits of such forces are recognized, followed by the eventual attainment of a size where quality cannot be sustained. Then, a new elite group ("special" special forces) is created to regain the quality that has been lost through expansion. It is worth watching for such a phenomenon in SOCOM, although so far there is no indication of the emergence of such units.

RISKS: DEPENDENCE ON OCO FUNDING, ALIGNMENT WITH NEW STRATEGY, AND PERSONNEL STRESS

SOCOM is highly dependent on OCO funding. For FY 2021, it has requested $3.7 billion in OCO, 28 percent of its total funding and nearly three times the department's rate overall (10 percent). This heavy usage occurs due to SOCOM's extensive wartime operations because SOCOM is allowed to fund

---

231 Government Accountability Office (GAO), *Special Operations Forces: Opportunities Exist to Improve Transparency of Funding and Assess Potential to Lessen Some Deployments*, GAO-15-571 (Washington, DC: July 2015), http://www.gao.gov/products/GAO-15-571.

232 "UK Armed Forces Quarterly Service Personnel Statistics," Ministry of Defense, July 1, 2020, p. 4, https://assets.publishing.service.gov.uk/government/uploads/system/uploads/attachment_data/file/920074/1_July_2020_SPS.pdf.

233 Budget data for SOCOM is less available for FY 2021 than in past years, perhaps reflecting DOD's policy of not releasing data that could be useful to potential adversaries. There is, for example, no SOCOM posture statement for FY 2021.

234 Andrew Feickert, *U.S. Special Operations Forces: Background and Issues for Congress*, CRS Report No. RS21048 (Washington, DC: Congressional Research Service, April 13, 2018), 2, https://fas.org/sgp/crs/natsec/RS21048.pdf; see also, Andrew Feickert, *U.S. Special Operations Forces: Background and Issues for Congress*, CRS Report No. RS21048 (Washington, DC: Congressional Research Service, March 11, 2020), https://crsreports.congress.gov/product/pdf/RS/RS21048/62.

global (not just CENTCOM) counterterrorism operations in OCO, unlike the military services, and because many base budget elements such as personnel are funded in the service budgets.[235] Ninety percent of SOCOM's OCO funding is for enduring activities.[236] Fortunately for SOCOM, OCO appears to be relatively secure, with no immediate effort to eliminate it without compensating increases to the base budget.

The risk is that a Biden administration might make some changes, as elements of the Democratic Party's left-wing have proposed ending OCO without a full transfer to the base.[237] So far, this has not resounded with the broader Democratic national security community.

Dependence on OCO funding raises the broader question of SOCOM alignment with the new *National Defense Strategy* (NDS). SOCOM's current operations focus on terrorism and stability operations and demand all of its attention. There is little bandwidth available to think about or prepare for the kind of great power conflicts that the new strategy prioritizes. In the near term, this gap is not a major problem since there is strong support for SOCOM's current operations.

However, this misalignment could become a longer-term challenge if day-to-day operations decline. This might happen in the context of "ending forever wars" as the Democratic Party platform promises. Travis Sharp notes that "under the NDS [SOCOM's counterterrorism operations] should consume fewer resources and SOF's budget share should shrink accordingly."[238] Although SOCOM's capabilities are broadly useful, how their application would change from a stability operation/regional conflict to a great power conflict needs considerable thought.

High operational tempo (OPTEMPO) plagued SOCOM in the past, putting stress on personnel and their families, resulting in retention challenges and an increase in suicides. However, stress was not mentioned in the FY 2020 posture statement (the last available) and does not appear in official statements since then. It is unclear whether this reflects a reduction in operational demands, a gradual increase in the number of troops to meet the demand, or a change in policy regarding articulation of force stress.

ACQUISITION INNOVATION: LIGHT-ATTACK AIRCRAFT

In addition to acquiring modified versions of service aircraft (e.g., MH-47Gs and MH-60s) SOCOM has picked up the light-attack aircraft program that the Air Force dropped. Called "armed overwatch," the program would acquire propeller driven aircraft for attack and reconnaissance. The budget proposes to buy 5 aircraft in FY 2021 and 10 aircraft a year from FY 2022 to FY 2025.

---

235 "Funding Policy for Overseas Contingency Operations," Letter from Steven Kosiak, Associate Director of the Office of Management and Budget, to Robert Hale, Under Secretary of Defense (Comptroller), September 9, 2010, http://asafm.army.mil/Documents/OfficeDocuments/Budget/Guidances/omb-gd.pdf.

236 Raymond A. Thomas, "United States Special Operations Command and United States Cyber Command," Testimony before the Senate Armed Services Committee, February 14, 2019, https://www.armed-services.senate.gov/hearings/19-02-14-united-states-special-operations-command-and-united-states-cyber-command.

237 Mark Cancian, "Death to OCO: What Would Dem Sweep Mean for War Funding?," Breaking Defense, July 29, 2020, https://breakingdefense.com/2020/07/death-to-oco-what-would-dem-sweep-mean-for-war-funding/.

238 Travis Sharp, *Did Dollars Follow Strategy? Analysis of the 2020 Defense Budget Request* (Washington, DC: Center for Strategic and Budgetary Assessment, 2019), 21, https://csbaonline.org/research/publications/did-dollars-follow-strategy-a-review-of-the-fy-2020-defense-budget.

This aircraft would operate in relatively permissive environments where sophisticated jets are not needed. The advantage is that it would be much less expensive to acquire and operate. The budget allocates about $20 million per aircraft, with estimates of operating cost running about $500 per flying hour. By contrast, an F-35 costs about $100 million per aircraft and $30,000 per flight hour.[239] Thus, the program addresses the inconsistency of having hundred-million-dollar jet aircraft laden with sophisticated electronics and survivability features to drop bombs on insurgents armed with rifles.

If implemented, this would be a radical change in the way air support is provided. The historical trend has been toward multirole jet aircraft which can operate in both high-end and permissive environments, although at extremely high cost. It would also provide SOCOM with a new kind of capability and some independence from support provided by the Air Force. So far, however, Congress has expressed skepticism, questioning whether this new capability is needed, so the program may not survive.[240]

ETHICAL CHALLENGES

In the last few years, ethical misconduct emerged as a new and disturbing theme for SOF, raising broader questions about SOF personnel attitudes and marring the reputation of SOF, especially the SEALs. Special operations personnel were involved in a variety of crimes, including murders, and then covered up the crimes.[241] The risk with any special force is that personnel come to believe that they are not restricted by the rules that bind other servicemembers.

The incidents engendered a lot of soul-searching in the special operations community.[242] General Richard Clark, SOCOM commander, ordered an ethics review. The review concluded that the force did not have a "systemic ethics problem." However, it found that the emphasis on sustained deployments "impacted our culture in some troublesome ways." The review recommended a variety of actions to improve leadership, discipline, and accountability.[243]

There is always some question when an institution investigates itself and finds that there are no fundamental problems. Nevertheless, the lack of recent incidents indicates that new policies may be having an effect.

---

239 Overwatch procurement cost from SOCOM, *FY 2021 Defense Wide Procurement, Special Operations Command* (Washington, DC: April 2020), "Armed Overwatch/Targeting" P-1 line #55, volume 1-1, https://comptroller.defense.gov/Portals/45/Documents/defbudget/fy2021/budget_justification/pdfs/02_Procurement/SOCOM_PB2021.pdf.

240 Rachel Cohen, "Congress Questions Need for New Overwatch Airplanes for SOCOM," *Air Force Magazine*, July 1, 2020, https://www.airforcemag.com/congress-questions-need-for-new-armed-overwatch-planes-for-socom/.

241 For examples of SOF abuses: Todd South, "Army Green Beret major pleads not guilty to Afghan murder charge," *Army Times*, June 27, 2019, https://www.armytimes.com/news/your-army/2019/06/27/army-green-beret-major-pleads-not-guilty-to-afghan-murder-charge/; Elliot Ackerman, "Even a War Hero Is Not Above the Law," *New York Times*, December 17, 2018, https://www.nytimes.com/2018/12/17/opinion/mathew-golsteyn-trump.html; Meghann Myers, "Two Army Green Berets plead guilty in plot to smuggle 90 pounds of cocaine from Colombia," *Army Times*, January 4, 2019, armytimes.com/news/your-army/2019/01/04/two-army-green-berets-plead-guilty-in-plot-to-smuggle-90-pounds-of-cocaine-from-colombia/; and Meghann Myers, "7th Special Forces Group soldier arrested for raping two children," *Army Times*, April 20, 2018, https://www.armytimes.com/news/your-army/2018/04/20/7th-special-forces-group-soldier-arrested-for-raping-two-children/.

242 For example, Daniel Steward, "None of Us Is 'That Man' – All Must Aspire to Be," U.S. Naval Institute, *Proceedings* 146, no. 2, February 2020, 19–22, https://www.usni.org/magazines/proceedings/2020/february.

243 Special Operations Command, *Comprehensive Review of SOF Culture and Ethics* (Washington, DC: January 2020), https://sof.news/ussocom/ussocom-sof-culture-ethics-report-2020/.

DOD Civilians

After years of growth, the number of DOD civilians would decrease slightly in FY 2021. The deepest cuts are in DOD-wide activities, reflecting former secretary Esper's fourth estate review. The relative strength of DOD civilian numbers occurs because civilians help readiness, most being in maintenance and supply functions, not in headquarters (as is often believed).

Table 4: DOD Civilians

	DOD Civilians (U.S. Direct Hire)	Total DOD Civilians (Including Foreign Direct Hires)
FY 2020 Enacted	760,300	774,900
FY 2021 Request	759,200	773,600
Change	-900	-1,300

Note: Full-time equivalents. Total includes U.S. and foreign direct hires, excluding classified activities, OCO funded, and indirect hires.

Source: Office of the Undersecretary of Defense (Comptroller), *Defense Budget Overview: Fiscal Year 2021 Budget Request* (Washington, DC: April 2020), Figure 2.3, 2–8, 6–18, https://comptroller.defense.gov/Portals/45/Documents/defbudget/fy2021/fy2021_Budget_Request.pdf.

The United States is unusual in that it has many civilians working in its military establishment where other countries have military personnel. DOD's civilians perform a wide variety of support functions in intelligence, equipment maintenance, medical care, family support, base operating services, and force management. The department does this because civilians provide long-term expertise, whereas military personnel rotate frequently. Further, the civilian personnel system, for all of its limitations, is more flexible than the military system in that civilian personnel do not need to meet the strict standards for health, fitness, combat skills, and worldwide assignments that military personnel do.

Civilians are often viewed as "overhead" who staff Washington headquarters. In fact, most civilians (96 percent) are outside Washington. Only about 4 percent (31,000) work in management headquarters, and only 27,000 of these work in Washington. Most (73 percent) are in the Military Departments, not in defense-wide activities.

DOD argues that "[e]ffective and appropriate use of civilians allows the Department to focus its Soldiers, Sailors, Airmen, and Marines on the tasks and functions that are truly military essential—thereby enhancing the readiness and lethality of our warfighters."[244]

---

244 Under-Secretary of Defense (Comptroller), *Defense Budget Overview: United States Department of Defense Fiscal Year 2021 Budget Request* (Washington, DC: Department of Defense, February 2020), 2–8, https://comptroller.defense.gov/Portals/45/Documents/defbudget/fy2021/fy2021_Budget_Request_Overview_Book.pdf.

Chart 3: Total DOD Civilians, 1999–2021

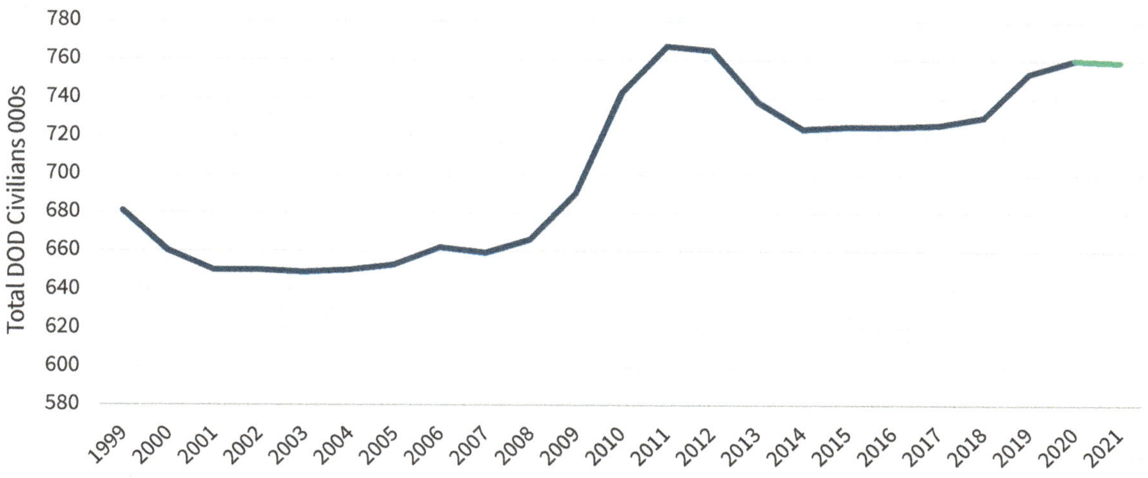

Source: Office of the Under Secretary of Defense (Comptroller), *National Defense Budget Estimates for FY 2021*, Table 7-5: Department of Defense Manpower, 260–262.

The large increase in civilian numbers since 2017 occurred for several reasons:

- A long-standing initiative to move functions from higher-cost, and difficult to recruit, military personnel to lower-cost civilian personnel; and
- Recent DOD efforts to remedy readiness shortfalls, for example, in maintenance and supply, which require more people.

CIVILIAN PAY RAISE

The second key metric on how civilians are faring, after employment numbers, is the annual pay raise. For many years, parity with military pay raises was the norm, but that practice broke down in 2010. In most years since, government civilians have received a smaller pay raise than military personnel.

For FY 2021, the administration proposed a 1.0 percent civilian pay raise (government-wide), whereas the military would get a 3.0 percent increase. This disparity would continue in the future, as the military is projected to receive pay raises of 2.6 percent in FY 2022 through FY 2025, whereas civilians would receive 2.1 percent.[245] Congress has frequently been more supportive of civilians but does not seem inclined to change the administration's proposal this year.

One piece of good news is that the FY 2021 budget implements the expansion of paid parental leave.

SECRETARY ESPER'S "DEFENSE-WIDE REVIEW"

As secretary of the army, Secretary Esper conducted a process called "night court," whereby he and other senior leaders, civilian and military, reviewed all of the Army's programs to identify savings that could

---

245 Under-Secretary of Defense (Comptroller), *National Defense Budget Estimates for FY 2021 (Green Book)* (Washington, DC: Department of Defense, April 2020), Table 5-12, https://comptroller.defense.gov/Portals/45/Documents/defbudget/fy2021/FY21_Green_Book.pdf.

then be transferred to higher priority programs.[246] Over the last year, he has done a similar review for defense-wide activities, mainly the defense agencies and field activities—otherwise known as the "fourth estate."[247] Since defense-wide activities are staffed mostly by civilians, reductions particularly affect the civilian workforce.

The review, appropriately enough called the Defense-Wide Review (DWR), examined all DOD organizations, programs, functions, and activities outside of the Military Departments to identify savings in FY 2021 and in future years. DOD claimed to have found "over $5.7 billion in FY 2021 savings for reinvestment in lethality and readiness, and an additional $2.1 billion in activities and functions to realign to the Military Departments."[248]

For this reason, the number of civilians in defense-wide activities would decline by 7,000 in FY 2021 (though the total number of civilians in DOD stays about the same because of increases in the Military Departments).

END OF THE CHIEF MANAGEMENT OFFICER?

The chief management officer (CMO) has a mission of "delivering optimized enterprise business operations to ensure the success of the national defense strategy."[249] The CMO also deals with all the government-wide reform initiatives, ideas for improved governance generated by outside commissions and task forces, and pet projects flowing out of OMB and the White House.

The CMO set up a department-wide reform council and participated in the DWR, eventually documenting real savings. The CMO seemed to be settling into a role of overseeing the fourth estate.[250]

Despite this apparent success, there has been one widespread dissatisfaction with the office. The position has often been vacant, reflecting a perceived lack of priority. Further, the task is arguably impossible. There is widespread dissatisfaction with DOD's management, and many observers want to see substantial savings for management reform. However, there is disagreement about the specifics of changes, with every savings proposal facing intense opposition by advocates.

The Defense Business Board recommended abolishing the position.[251] Both the House and Senate draft authorization acts would also eliminate the position. It may be doomed like several of its predecessors, for example, the Business Transformation Office.[252]

---

246 For a description of "night court," see Mark Cancian, "Mark Esper Is About to Put Every Pentagon Program Through The Ringer," Forbes, July 24, 2018, https://www.forbes.com/sites/markcancian/2019/07/24/theres-a-new-sheriff-in-the-pentagon/#40bf23f87e74.

247 Deputy Secretary of Defense, "Defense Wide Review," DOD, memo, August 2, 2019, https://admin.govexec.com/media/gbc/docs/pdfs_edit/norquistmemo.pdf.

248 Under-Secretary of Defense (Comptroller), *FY 2021 Defense Budget Overview*, 1–10.

249 "Chief Management Officer," DOD, https://cmo.defense.gov/Home/.

250 Department of Defense, *FY 2021 Annual Performance Plan* (Washington, DC: January 2020), https://cmo.defense.gov/Portals/47/Documents/Publications/Annual%20Performance%20Plan/FY%202021%20Annual%20Perf%20Plan%20&%20FY%202019%20Annual%20Perf%20Report.pdf.

251 Defense Business Board, *The Chief Management Officer of the Department of Defense: An Assessment* (Washington, DC: June 2020), https://insidedefense.com/sites/insidedefense.com/files/documents/2020/oct/10262020_cmo.pdf.

252 MacKenzie Eaglen, "The Top Five REALLY Important in DAA Policies," Breaking Defense, July 13, 2020, https://breakingdefense.com/2020/07/the-top-5-really-important-ndaa-policies/.

GOVERNMENT-WIDE CHANGE AND REORGANIZATION

In its waning days, the Trump administration has proposed creation of a new class of civilian positions called "Schedule F." This would cover "employees serving in confidential, policy determining, policymaking, or policy advocating positions that are not normally subject to change as a result of a presidential transition." In effect, this would make some civil service positions more like political appointments.[253]

The proposal was widely denounced as an administration effort to ensure loyalty and will likely be repealed by the Biden administration. It undermines the political neutrality of the civil service, which was a major achievement in the late-nineteenth century. Nevertheless, it gets to a frustration that every administration has, though much more pointedly in the Trump administration, that the bureaucracy is unresponsive to its initiatives.

Contractors

Contractors have become a permanent element of the federal workforce. Although service contractor numbers seem to be declining, poor data makes that conclusion uncertain. Operational or battlefield contractors now greatly outnumber military personnel in the CENTCOM region (15,000 to 43,800), and the ratio of contractors to military personnel has increased from 1 to 1 in 2008 to 2.8 to 1 today.

Nevertheless, both service and operational contractors remain controversial because of unresolved questions about cost and the appropriate delineation of functions. Although these concerns have been muted for several years, the issue may again arise in a Biden administration because Democrats are more protective of government employees and more skeptical of the private sector.

SERVICE CONTRACTORS

These contractors provide services to the government and are distinct from contractors who provide products.

---

253 "Executive Order on Creating Schedule F in the Federal Excepted Service," White House, October 21, 2020, https://www.whitehouse.gov/presidential-actions/executive-order-creating-schedule-f-excepted-service/.

Chart 4: DOD Service Contractor Full-Time Equivalents (FTEs)

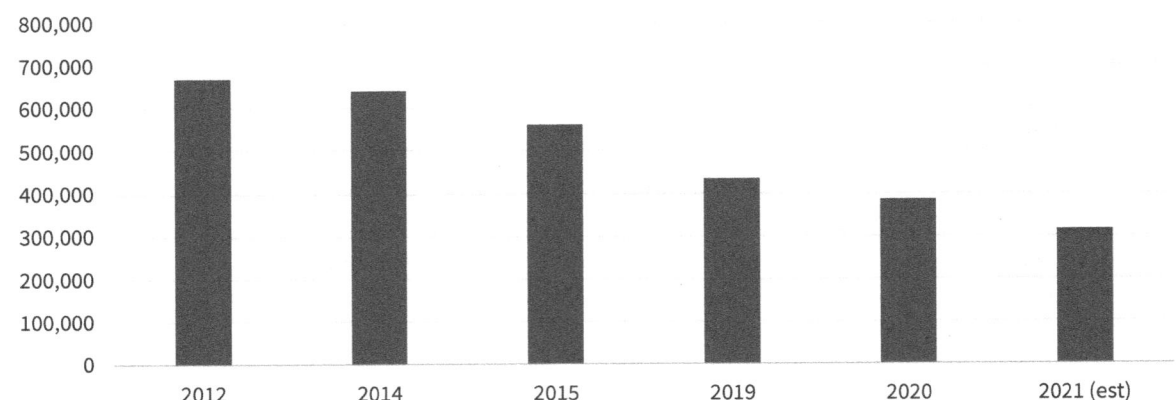

Note: Excludes MILCON, RDT&E, and Classified Activities; excludes operational contractors overseas.

Data for FY 2019, FY 2020, and FY 2021 from Office of the Under Secretary of Defense (Comptroller), *FY 2021 Operations and Maintenance Overview: Contract Services* (Washington, DC: February 2020), 156, https://comptroller.defense.gov/Portals/45/Documents/defbudget/fy2021/fy2021_OM_Overview.pdf; data for FY 2015, FY 2014, and FY 2012 from "Defense Manpower Requirements Reports," Office of the Under Secretary for Personnel and Readiness, https://prhome.defense.gov/M-RA/Inside-M-RA/TFM/Reports/

Chart 4 seems to indicate that the number of service contractors is declining. Many view that as a positive development, regarding contractors as "the invisible government" that lacks visibility and oversight.[254] Unfortunately, DOD's accounting for service contractors is such a mess that it is hard to be sure what is happening.

Numbers for FY 2019, FY 2020, and FY 2021 come from an FY 2021 budget exhibit. However, the numbers exclude service contractors in military construction, RDT&E, and Classified Activities. Although the reason for excluding classified activities is clear, the reason for excluding military construction and RDT&E is not. Numbers for previous fiscal years are inconsistent with numbers for later fiscal years. Numbers for FY 2012, FY 2014, and FY 2015 come from the Defense Manpower Requirements Reports for those respective years. However, they do not include classified organizations, and reporting stopped with FY 2015. These numbers appear to be inconsistent with the later numbers.

Service contractors are controversial because they raise questions about what the government should do and what the private sector should do. On the one hand, government regulations (OMB Circular A-76) state that only government employees should conduct "inherently governmental" activities. On the other hand, the same document states the government should not compete with its citizens and therefore should buy from the private sector whenever it can.[255]

---

254 Paul Light, *The True Size of Government* (Washington, DC: Brookings Institution Press, 1999).

255 "Performance of Commercial Activities," Office of Management and Budget, OMB circular no. A-76, August 4, 1983 (revised 1999), https://www.whitehouse.gov/sites/whitehouse.gov/files/omb/circulars/A76/a076.pdf.

Chart 5: Process for Converting Government Jobs to the Private Sector

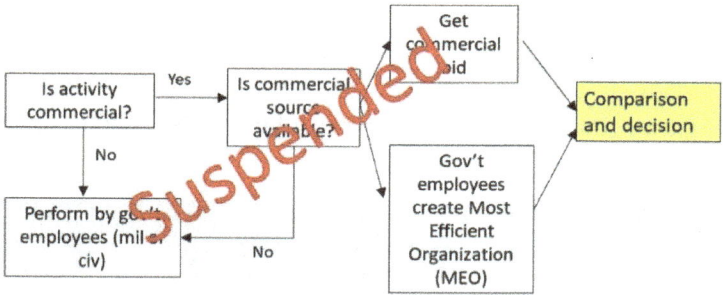

Source: "Performance of Commercial Activities," Office of Management and Budget, OMB circular no. A-76, August 4, 1983 (revised 1999), https://www.whitehouse.gov/sites/whitehouse.gov/files/omb/circulars/A76/a076.pdf.

Outsourcing had been an element of the Clinton and Bush administrations' "reinventing government" initiatives, but in 2008 to 2010 the Democratic-dominated Congress effectively shut this effort down, and then the Obama administration blocked conversions permanently. This shutdown occurred partly because of concerns about disruptions to the workforce, partly because of questions about the actual achievement of savings, and partly in response to complaints by unions anxious to protect their members' jobs. The Obama administration believed that it would save money by bringing activities in-house. However, these savings did not materialize when all of the costs of "insourcing" were considered, and the effort ended. Thus, the balance between contractors and the federal workforce has reached a position of equilibrium—there are restrictions against moving in either direction.

This equilibrium is driven in part by unresolved questions about relative costs between the two sectors. Some argue that government is inherently less expensive because it does not need to make a profit. Others argue that government is generally more expensive because it does not need to compete and to be efficient to remain in business. Where commentators come down depends strongly on their views about government and the private sector, with Republicans generally relying more on the private sector and Democrats more on government.

The analytic problem arises from indirect costs. Private-sector prices must include all these costs if an organization is to remain in business over the long term. In government, these costs are widely distributed, so their identification and allocation are difficult.[256] A valid comparison requires developing fully-burdened costs—that is, personnel costs with all benefits and support included. DOD and the broader community have made progress on theoretical constructs about what costs to include, but actual numbers do not exist.

There is broad agreement, however, that DOD and the government as a whole do not have a clear strategy for allocating activities among the different elements of its workforce: active-duty military, reserve military, government civilians, and contractors. Organizations as diverse as the Project on

---

[256] Jacque S. Gansler, William Lucyshyn, and John Rigilano, *Toward a Valid Comparison of Contractor and Government Costs* (College, Park, MD: University of Maryland, Center for Public Policy and Private Enterprise, February 2012), https://calhoun.nps.edu/bitstream/handle/10945/54492/UMD-CE-11-209.pdf?sequence=1&isAllowed=y.

Government Oversight, the Defense Business Board, and CSIS have made this point.[257] While there is extensive literature on the active/reserve mix, there is much less on government civilians and contractors, largely because of the lack of an assessment of the full costs of each workforce element.

OPERATIONAL CONTRACTORS

Table 5: Department of Defense Military and Contractor Personnel in USCENTCOM Area of Responsibility, October 2020

	Total Military	Total Contractors	U.S. Citizens	Third-Country Nationals	Local/Host-Country Nationals
Afghanistan Only	4,500	22,562	7,856	9,639	5,067
Iraq/Syria Only	3,000	4,826	2,558	1,632	636
Other Locations	8,100	16,421	6,610	9,718	93
AOR Total	15,000	43,809	17,024	20,987	5,796

Note: Data exclude forces afloat and classified data for Iraq, Iran, Kuwait, and Syria.

Source: Contractor data from Deputy Assistant Secretary of Defense (Program Support), *Contractor Support of U.S. Operations in the CENTCOM Area of Responsibility* (Washington, DC: Department of Defense, October 2020), https://www.acq.osd.mil/log/ps/.CENTCOM_reports.html/FY20_4Q_5A_Oct2020.pdf; Military personnel data from Robert Burns and Zeke Miller, "United States withdrawing thousands of troops from Iraq and Afghanistan," Associated Press, September 9, 2020, https://apnews.com/article/afghanistan-middle-east-islamic-state-group-donald-trump-iraq-a6d9550ea12d041436dda09f30873f55; and "Military and Civilian Personnel by Service/Agency and Country/Location," Defense Manpower Data Center, June 2020, https://www.dmdc.osd.mil/appj/dwp/dwp_reports.jsp.

Operational contractor support (OCS) "provides supplies and services to the joint force within a designated operational area." These are the contractors found on overseas battlefields and who do many things that military personnel did in the past.

OCS now forms a permanent element of U.S. forces overseas, along with active-duty personnel, reservists, and government civilians. These contractors exist worldwide, in all the combatant commands. However, attention focuses on contractors in CENTCOM because they have been the most numerous and about which the most data are available.

Contractor numbers in CENTCOM have tracked consistently with the level of operations since 2008, when reporting began. With operations in Afghanistan and Iraq/Syria at a relatively low level and stronger controls and oversight in place, contracting scandals have virtually ceased, and the use of battlefield contractors has receded into the background as a political issue.

Although the widespread and routine use of operational contractors remains controversial in some quarters—Rachael Maddow, the MSNBC commentator, criticized "[reliance] on a pop-up army . . . of greasy, lawless contractors"—use for logistics and administrative functions has become routine

---

257 Defense Business Board, *Focusing a Transition: Challenges Facing The New Administration* (Washington, DC: DOD, 2016), http://dbb.defense.gov/Portals/35/Documents/Reports/2016/DBB%20Transition%20Report%202016%20-%2020160920.pdf; Mark Cancian, "Reforming the Civilian Workforce: Two Carrots and Two Sticks," Defense360, January 11, 2017, https://defense360.csis.org/reforming-the-civilian-workforce-two-carrots-and-two-sticks; and Scott Amey, "Pentagon Misses The Target When It Comes To Its Workforce," Defense One, April 17, 2017, http://www.defenseone.com/ideas/2017/04/pentagon-misses-target-when-it-comes-its-workforce/137074.

in contemporary operations because of the limited numbers of military personnel.[258] As a result, some analysts have suggested expanding the use of contractors as military manpower becomes increasingly stretched.[259]

DOD may have no choice, since force structure increases are modest, as described earlier, and are focused on combat units. This limited force expansion may be strategically sound but drives a greater need for contractor support. Further, administrations routinely put caps on the number of military personnel that can be in theater, but these caps do not include contractors. Thus, contractors can expand the range of military activities without breaking administration policy.

As Table 5 shows, contractors in CENTCOM outnumber military personnel overall, in Afghanistan and now in Iraq. This is a recent change in Iraq, as last year military personnel outnumbered contractors. Thirty-nine percent of operational contractors are U.S. citizens. The rest are third-country nationals and locals.

Other contractors in Iraq/Syria work for organizations outside the DOD—the Department of State, U.S. Agency for International Development (USAID), and U.S. Intelligence Community—but numbers for these are no longer published.

Chart 6: Contractors in CENTCOM, FY 2010–FY 2020 (by quarter)

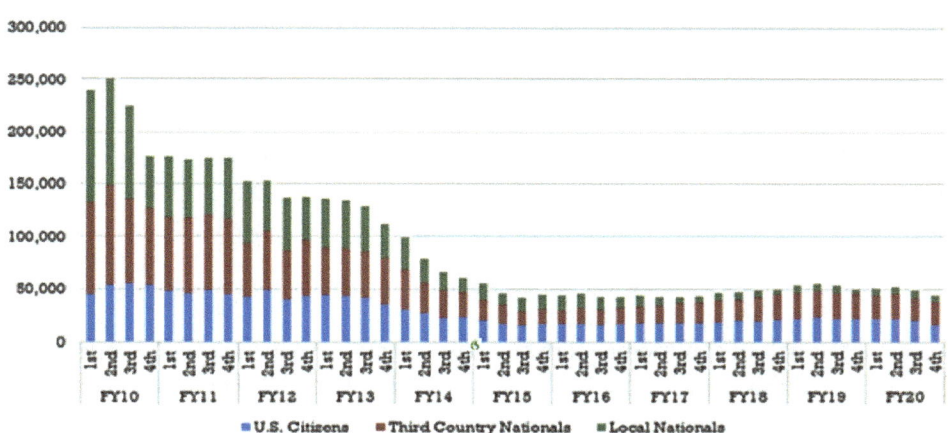

Source: "Contractor Support of U.S. Operations in the USCENTCOM Area of Responsibility," DOD, October 2020, https://www.acq.osd.mil/log/ps/.CENTCOM_reports.html/FY20_4Q_5A_Oct2020.pdf.

Total contractor numbers are down from a peak of 255,000 in 2008/2009. The ratio of military to contractors has also changed. Whereas in the past the ratio was close to 1 to 1, the ratio for Afghanistan, Iraq, and Syria today has soared to 1 military to 3.7 contractors (1 to 2.8 for CENTCOM overall).[260] This is up from 1 to 1.7 last year.

---

258 Rachael Maddow, *Drift: The Unmooring of American Power* (New York, NY: Crown Publishing, 2012), 186-187; and Mark Cancian, "Contractors: The New Element of Military Force Structure," Parameters 38, no. 3 (Autumn 2008), 61-77, https://ssi.armywarcollege.edu/pubs/Parameters/articles/08autumn/cancian.pdf.

259 Richard E. Wagner, *Optimizing Defense Use of Contract Services to Mitigate the Threat of a Hollow Force* (Carlisle, PA: U.S. Army War College Press, 2016).

260 Commission on Wartime Contracting, *Transforming Wartime Contracting: Controlling Costs, Reducing Risks*, (Washington, DC:

This higher proportion of contractors reflects three changes.

- First, the large recent decrease in the number of deployed military personnel. Contractor numbers typically lag since the contractors stay on to close up bases and ship out equipment.
- Second, troop caps. Because the president has restricted the number of military personnel but not the number of contractors, contractors are likely picking up some tasks formerly done by the military.
- Third, the nature of the mission. The more stability-related and less combat-focused, the more the ratio tilts toward contractors, who do support and logistics functions.

Table 6: Contractor Numbers in Iraq/Syria and Afghanistan by Function, October 2020

Category	Iraq and Syria	Afghanistan Only	Total
Base	1,033	2,963	3,996
Construction	367	1,517	1,884
IT/Communications Support	263	698	961
Logistics/Maintenance	1,815	7,543	9,358
Management/Administrative	256	1,429	1,685
Medical/Dental/Social Services	10	77	87
Other	39	275	314
Security	96	4,164	4,260
Training	5	1,093	1,098
Translator/Interpreter	550	1,228	1,778
Transportation	419	1,575	1,994
Total	4,826	22,562	27,388

Source: "Contractor Support of U.S. Operations in the USCENTCOM Area of Responsibility," DOD.

As Table 6 shows, about half of contractors perform logistics/maintenance functions and most of the rest do base operations and administrative tasks. Only a small number of contractors do combat-related tasks.

Of the 27,388 contractors in Iraq, Syria, and Afghanistan, 4,260 are in security functions, and of these, 1,813 are in Personnel Security Detachments (PSDs), all in Afghanistan. This latter function is highly sensitive because these contractors carry weapons, interact with the civilian population routinely, and have committed highly publicized abuses in the past. In general, their function is to protect high-value individuals.

DOD requires all contractors to conform with either U.S. or international standards for training, recruiting, and conduct. The industry is participating through its professional organizations—the Professional Services Council, the International Stability Operations Association, and the International Code of Conduct for private security providers Association, among others. The fact that no incidents have arisen recently indicates that the oversight and controls instituted in the last decade have been effective.[261]

August 2011), 200, 205, http://www.acq.osd.mil/dpap/pacc/cc/cowc.html.
261 Whitney Grespin, "Well Behaved Defense Contractors Seldom Make History," War on the Rocks, April 21, 2016, http://

DOD recognizes that operational contractors are a permanent element of its force structure. As a result, DOD has standardized and institutionalized the contracting process that supports not just conflicts but also peacetime needs, such as natural disasters and humanitarian assistance. Some actions DOD has taken are to conduct operational contracting exercises, to incorporate operational contract support into combatant command plans, and to gather lessons-learned systematically.

---

warontherocks.com/2016/04/well-behaved-defense-contractors-seldom-make-history.

About the Author

Mark F. Cancian (Colonel, USMCR, ret.) is a senior adviser with the CSIS International Security Program. He joined CSIS in April 2015 from the Office of Management and Budget, where he spent more than seven years as chief of the Force Structure and Investment Division, working on issues such as Department of Defense budget strategy, war funding, and procurement programs, as well as nuclear weapons development and nonproliferation activities in the Department of Energy. Previously, he worked on force structure and acquisition issues in the Office of the Secretary of Defense and ran research and executive programs at Harvard University's Kennedy School of Government. In the military, Colonel Cancian spent over three decades in the U.S. Marine Corps, active and reserve, serving as an infantry, artillery, and civil affairs officer and on overseas tours in Vietnam, Desert Storm, and Iraq (twice). Since 2000, he has been an adjunct faculty member at the Johns Hopkins School of Advanced International Studies, where he teaches a course on the connection between policy and analysis. A prolific author, he has published over 40 articles on military operations, acquisition, budgets, and strategy and received numerous writing awards. He graduated with high honors (magna cum laude) from Harvard College and with highest honors (Baker scholar) from Harvard Business School.